HISTORIC HOMES OF NEW ALBANY INDIANA

HISTORIC HOMES OF NEW ALBANY INDIANA

David C. Barksdale &
Gregory A. Sekula, AICP

The History Press

Published by The History Press
Charleston, SC
www.historypress.net

First published 2015

Manufactured in the United States

ISBN 978.1.46711.773.9

Library of Congress Control Number: 2015948831

This book is dedicated to those countless individuals who have worked through the years to preserve New Albany's rich and diverse residential architectural heritage. Their stewardship of these historic homes has given the city its unique character and sense of place and is a gift to future generations of New Albanians.

Contents

Acknowledgements

The authors wish to express their gratitude to our families for their support during the writing of this book, particularly our wives, Debbie Barksdale and Robyn Davis Sekula. We are also grateful to the staff of the Stuart Barth Wrege Indiana History Room of the New Albany–Floyd County Public Library who assisted with historic photographs and resources from the collections. Gratitude is also extended to the following individuals who provided support and guidance for various aspects of the publication: Laura Renwick and Suzanne Stanis of Indiana Landmarks; Jessica Stavros, Culbertson Mansion State Historic Site; Steve Wiser, Louisville Historical League; Caitlin Pollock, Indiana University–Purdue University Indianapolis Library; and to the many homeowners who graciously opened their homes and shared information on the history of these unique spaces.

Introduction

River towns are often known for their interesting history and rich architectural patrimony. New Albany, Indiana, is no exception. Situated strategically below the only natural obstruction along the Ohio River's 981-mile trek from Pittsburgh, Pennsylvania, to Cairo, Illinois, New Albany quickly became an important settlement in the newly formed Indiana Territory. Founded in 1813 by New York natives and brothers Joel, Abner and Nathaniel Scribner, the new town was named in honor of the New York state capital city and established three years prior to Indiana achieving statehood.

With its river access and nearby abundance of natural resources like timber, New Albany quickly developed in the early decades of the nineteenth century, building an economy based on shipbuilding and related industries, such as lumber production, iron work and glass manufacturing. Incorporated as a city in 1839, New Albany became Indiana's largest city by 1850, attracting a diverse population of immigrants of German, Irish and African American descent, among others. Northerners from Ohio, Pennsylvania, New York and New England settled in this Ohio River Valley community, along with southerners from Kentucky, Virginia and the Carolinas. This blending of North and South has been a cultural mainstay of New Albany from its earliest days.

New Albany boasted one of the state's earliest rail lines with the completion of the New Albany and Salem Railroad in 1851. By the 1880s, the Kentucky and Indiana Bridge expanded rail traffic over the Ohio River at New Albany, opening up southern markets. Rail lines, along with a growing network of roads that radiated from the city from its earliest days, allowed for the distribution of goods to distant markets.[1]

Prosperity revealed itself in the architecture of the community. While civic, institutional, religious and commercial buildings reflected the growth of New Albany and its optimism for the future, the residential development that occurred more intimately chronicled the diverse socioeconomic makeup of its residents and the building traditions that they brought with them. Elegant, yet diminutively scaled frame and brick town houses, built in the tradition of East Coast cities, gave way to large estates with fashionable Italianate- and Second Empire–style mansions that spoke of incredible wealth in the dawning of the industrial era. Steamboat and rail transport made possible the shipment of stylish lighting, ironwork, stained glass, silver hardware and marble mantels to outfit the homes of some of Indiana's leading citizens of the day who called New Albany home. For some, architect-designed homes were a means to show status; for others, pattern books provided ideas for house designs, and rail transport made it possible to acquire building parts from distant markets. For the majority of New Albany's residents, local builders and carpenters provided basic shelter, utilizing vernacular house forms of no identifiable architectural style, but embellishing those structures with a decorative element here or there to achieve some level of individuality and conveying a statement of the occupant's socioeconomic standing in the community.

Collectively, these historic residential buildings that remain along New Albany's streets tell the story of the community in a unique way. Grand or modest, large or small, the historic homes of New Albany are the physical embodiment of the lives that shaped the community in the first 125 years of its existence. Preservation of these buildings allows that story to continue to the present day as residents work to restore and maintain this architectural legacy for future generations.

1

Downtown New Albany

New Albany's central business district historically was the civic, mercantile, residential and religious heart of the community in its earliest days. Plat 93, also referred to as the Original Town Plat, laid out a series of streets and lots that extended from the Ohio River north, east and west, establishing numbered streets running perpendicular to the river on either side of State Street, which became the centerline for street addressing, dividing upper and lower numbered street designations. Named streets, including Water, High, Market, Spring, Elm and Oak, were laid out running parallel to and upland from the river.[2]

As the town developed in the first half of the nineteenth century, mercantile activities were concentrated mainly at the river's edge along Water Street and farther upland on Main and Market Streets, as well as State Street. Residential development hugged these commercial arteries. As commerce increased, commercial establishments began to supplant residential development, particularly along the blocks immediately adjacent to State Street to the east and west. Main Street (originally High Street), Market Street, Pearl Street (originally Upper First Street), Bank Street (originally Upper Second Street) and Spring Street became the heart of downtown New Albany by the late nineteenth and early twentieth centuries. Two-, three- and four-story brick- and stone-clad Greek Revival and Italianate commercial blocks rose along these streets. Greek Temple form structures—such as the Indiana State Bank, the Second Presbyterian Church and the Floyd County Courthouse—spoke of the confidence of community leaders to establish a permanent architecture reflective of the optimism of continued future prosperity.

This rich legacy of building has been largely preserved by generations of New Albany residents. Retention of many of these historic structures led to the establishment of a downtown historic district that was placed in the National Register of Historic Places in 1999. Several buildings along Main Street were also included in an earlier Mansion Row National Register Historic District listed in 1983. For purposes of this book, geographic boundaries for downtown New Albany consist of the Ohio River on the south, Oak Street on the north, West Fifth Street on the west and East Fifth Street on the east. The following residential properties are located within these boundaries and are rare survivors.

JOEL SCRIBNER HOUSE

106 East Main Street

For New Albany residents, the Joel Scribner House is hallowed ground. The oldest surviving documented residence in the city, the two-and-a-half-story frame dwelling was completed in 1814 for one of three brothers who had founded the town of New Albany the previous year. An early community leader, Joel Scribner was New Albany's first postmaster and later first appointed clerk of the court in the newly established Floyd County. He remained clerk for more than four years, serving until his death in 1823.[3] He is buried in New Albany's Fairview Cemetery.

Remarkably, the Joel Scribner House remained in continuous ownership by New Albany's founding family until its purchase from Joel's granddaughter, Harriet Rowland Scribner, in 1917 by the New Albany Piankeshaw Chapter Daughters of the American Revolution (DAR). The acquisition was one of the earliest preservation efforts in Indiana at a time when acquisition of buildings and sites associated with important persons or events in history was the focus of historic preservation activities across the nation.

It is now set in a small park-like setting and overshadowed by a three-story Italianate commercial block to the east and the 2008 Floyd County Branch of the YMCA to the west. The Joel Scribner House, in its day, was a remarkable accomplishment for a frontier town that had great aspirations for its future. Most residential dwellings until that time had been crude log

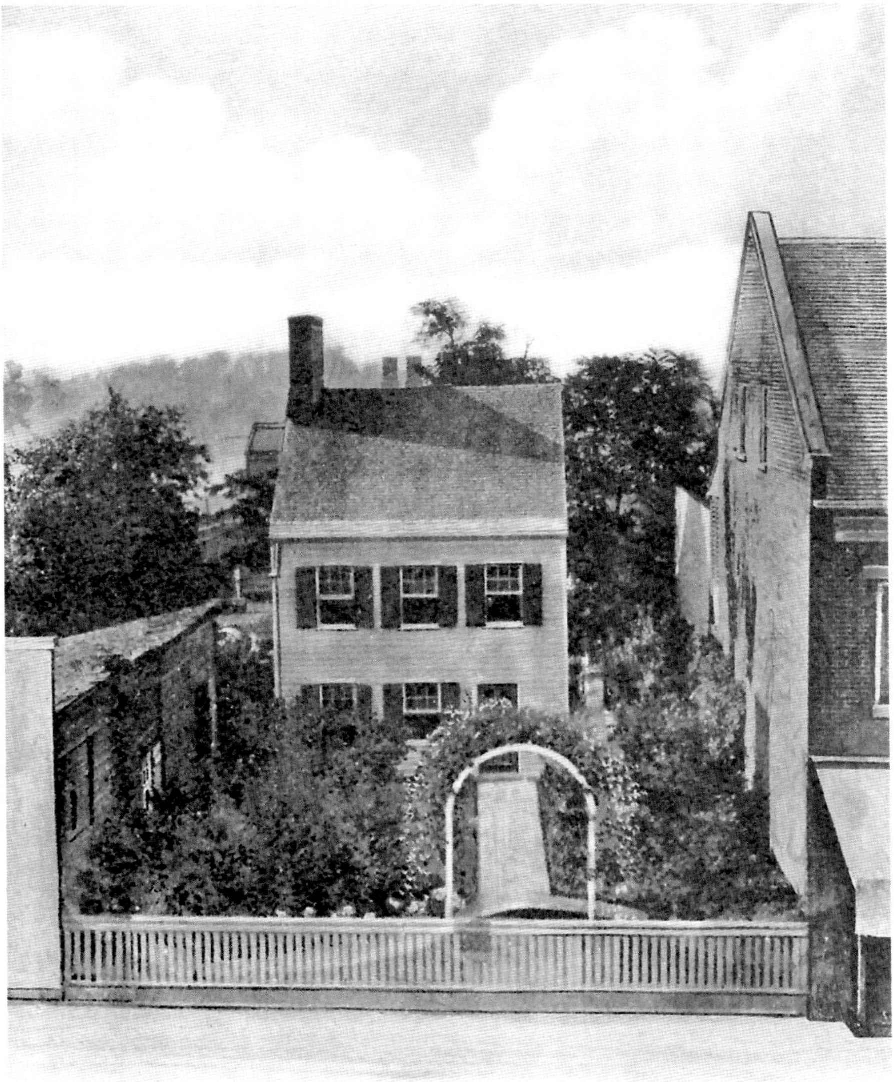

A 1913 Centennial Celebration postcard depicting the Joel Scribner House in 1850. *Barksdale collection.*

structures made from available timbers that covered the shores of the Ohio River in the new Indiana Territory. The Joel Scribner House represented a shift to a more permanent domestic architecture. Its form—the town house—suggested the builder's knowledge of the more urban eastern seaboard communities of New York, Philadelphia and Boston, where the building form, with its side hall plan, was ideal for compact, narrow lots.

Crude log house construction gave way to a heavy timber frame skeleton at the sill plate, corners and between floors whose framing members were connected with mortise-and-tenon joinery. For insulation and fireproofing, brick nogging was infilled between the framing members. The house's frame, in turn, was sheathed in weatherboard siding to protect it from the elements.

In the case of the Joel Scribner House, a simple bracketed cornice, six-over-six divided light windows and a doorway entrance with heavily molded architrave and modillion blocks provided an air of elegance and refinement to the street façade. Double-tiered rear porches—supported by chamfered square posts and a simply molded handrail with narrow pickets, or balusters—provided the occupants with access to river breezes to the south. A small, one-story, gable roof structure, built around 1850, is situated at the rear of the sloping lot. This building has served a variety of functions, including a summer kitchen and a medical office for the second Scribner family member to own the house—Dr. William A. Scribner. After the DAR acquired the property, the building also served as the caretaker's cottage.

The interior of the Joel Scribner House retains its original layout, open staircase with handsomely turned newel post and slender balusters and modest woodwork. Surviving fireplaces on the first and second stories, adapted during the late nineteenth century for coal, are adorned with simple wooden mantels with shallow ogee arches and chamfered pilasters. A larger brick fireplace with wooden mantelshelf is situated in the basement level where the original kitchen was located. Many original Scribner furnishings remain with the house, which is operated by the DAR as a house museum. Restoration of the exterior and interior is an ongoing effort with recent grant awards in 2014 and 2015 to repair damaged sill plates and other framing members on the west and north sides of the house. Siding work was also undertaken at that time. Window restoration was the focus of the work in 2015.

The Joel Scribner House was listed individually in the National Register of Historic Places in 1977.

William Young House—Padgett Museum

509 West Market Street

Presently the home of the Floyd County Historical Society, the William Young House was constructed in 1837 and was likely built by Nathaniel

Webb, who purchased lot 3 of out lots A and B of the Original Town Plat in 1836 from real estate speculator Mason Fitch for the sum of $800. Webb sold the property in April 1838 to William and Amelia Young for $3,200, thus suggesting that the lot had been improved with a dwelling.

William Young made his early living as a steamboat captain navigating the New Albany–built *Western Belle*, which traveled the Ohio and Mississippi Rivers from Cincinnati, Ohio, to New Orleans, Louisiana. By the late 1840s, he had become a partner with B.F. Stewart in a shoe and boot emporium and manufacturing enterprise located on East Main Street between Pearl and Bank Streets. The business imported boots, shoes and slippers from eastern cities and also produced its own shoes for sale. Tragedy struck the Young family in 1848 when his wife, Amelia, passed away. Later that year, Captain Young married Mary Eliza Dwyer, and she tragically died only three years later. The couple also had lost an infant son the previous year.

By 1853, Young had lost his home, and it was purchased at a sheriff's sale by Jonathan Knepfly for $1,600, a substantial reduction in value. Within five years, the house was sold to Jonathan Woodward. It remained in the Woodward family until 1891.[4] The house was subsequently owned by the McPherson, Hilt and Rosenbarger families. In 2004, the house was donated to the Arts Council of Southern Indiana and was later sold by the group in

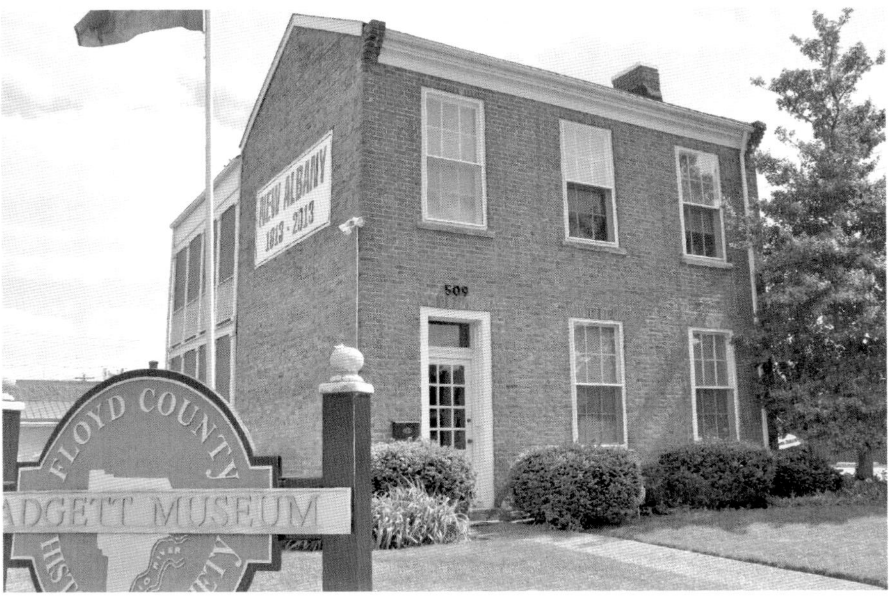

The 1837 William Young House serves as New Albany's local history museum. *Gregory Sekula.*

2006 when a larger house—the Crawford-Moosmiller House at 820 East Market Street—was made available to the organization. The William Young House was then purchased by James and Beverly Padgett, who graciously made the property available to the Floyd County Historical Society.

Like the Joel Scribner House, the William Young House embraces the town house form and plan that exemplifies New Albany's earliest surviving residential dwellings. In a restrained Federal style, the house features a Flemish bond brick façade consisting of contrasting header and stretcher courses of brick. Splayed brick lintels and original multi-light, divided sash windows define the façade. A simple wood entablature cornice is located below the roofline. A double-tiered side porch on the house's rear ell is now enclosed.

The interior of the house reflects a transition between Federal and Greek Revival architectural taste. While the original hallway staircase was removed at some point and relocated to the enclosed rear porch area of the house, the William Young House does retain its essential floor plan and exhibits a sophisticated degree of architectural integrity with its finishes. Bold, flat woodwork with fluted surrounds and corner blocks with roundels define door and window openings. Large, double-leaf, ten-paneled doors separate the principal first-floor rooms. Both first-floor rooms feature mantels with disengaged Doric columns and compound moldings framing a panel above, suggesting the influence of popular pattern books of the day, including Asher Benjamin's *The American Builder's Companion; or, A System of Architecture, Particularly Adapted to the Present Style of Building in the United States of America.*[5] The second floor contains two principal bedrooms, repeating the first-floor plan. Columned mantels are found in each room, with the front room mantel containing floral scrollwork in the paneled area below the mantelshelf. Built-in closets with flat panel doors flank the fireplace in the rear bedroom, with only one closet to the left of the fireplace in the front bedroom.

The William Young House was listed individually in the National Register of Historic Places in December 2010.

CHARLES AND SARAH MILLER HOUSE

314 West Market Street

Charles and Sarah Miller purchased this property in October 1906 for $1,600 and built this one-story, frame, Queen Anne–style cottage, replacing

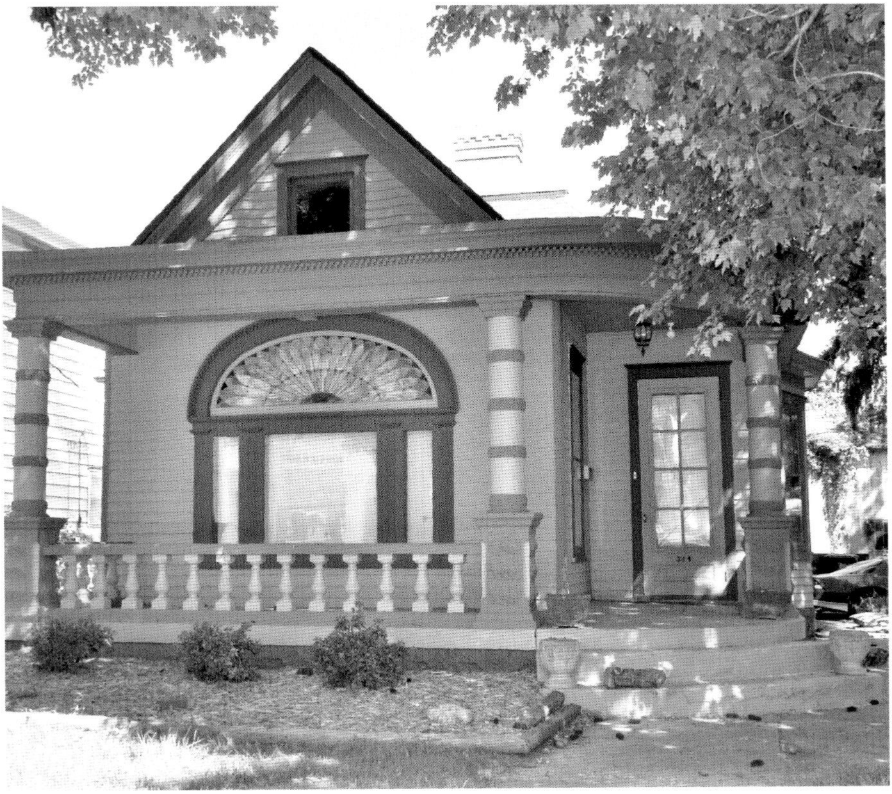

Probably completed in late 1907, the Charles and Sarah Miller House is an excellent example of a Queen Anne–style cottage. *Gregory Sekula.*

an earlier two-story brick structure that had stood on the property. Charles Miller was listed in the *New Albany City Directories* of 1909–12 as being involved in the concrete business. Between 1913 and 1916, he is listed as a contractor. Thus, it is probable that he was responsible for the construction of this dwelling.

By the late 1910s, Charles Miller was the manager of the numerous New Albany theaters that were owned by the Switow family of Louisville, Kentucky. Theaters under his management included the Grand, Kerrigan and Elba Theaters, the latter named for the Millers' daughter, Elba. The Elba was later renamed the Indiana Theater.

Miller took an active role in Republican politics, especially in the western part of the city, and was also a delegate to the Republican state conventions on numerous occasions. In his later years, he was treasurer of the New Albany wholesale grocery concern of P.N. Curl Grocery Company. Sarah Miller passed away in March 1923 and Charles Miller in September 1934. After his death, Elba married Frank Haller in 1936, and the couple made their home here until their deaths: Frank in September 1963 and Elba in March 1979.

The Charles and Sarah Miller House features a large wraparound porch supported by segmental cast-concrete columns with a concrete railing with heavy turned balusters. The house's most distinguishing exterior feature is a three-part window under the sheltered porch with a broad arched fanlight above ornamented with stained glass. Behind the house stands a large frame Board and Batten–sheathed carriage house, which is one of the largest remaining structures of its kind in the city.

FRANK AND GEORGE DEVOL DOUBLE HOUSE

219–221 Lafayette Street

Now facing the embankment wall of Interstate 64, this rare transitional Greek Revival/Italianate–style double house originally was part of a fashionable residential enclave that fronted New Albany's first planned public open space—Scribner Park. At that time, this street was known as Lower Third Street. The gable-front frame structure was built for the Frank S. and George H. Devol families by their father, Horatio, who lived next door at 225 Lafayette Street. Brothers Frank and George were both involved in their father's business—the H.N. Devol Company—which supplied stocks of articles necessary for housekeepers, hotels, steamboats, tinners, country merchants and the public generally. George remained with the company until his retirement in 1915, while Frank became a bookkeeper for the City Gaslight & Coke Company. In 1884, Frank became a director of that company. Both men dabbled in politics, with George being elected city councilman and Frank as city treasurer. George was also a member of the New Albany Board of Police Commissioners.

Frank remained in his half of the house (219) until his death in 1906, at which time his son, Robert, a druggist, continued occupancy of the structure until his death in 1948. George and his wife sold their half of the house (221) in May 1889. The John Newhouse family, who then lived next door at 225 Lafayette Street, purchased 221 in March 1894 and apparently used it for rental property. In 1948, Stella Newhouse, John's daughter, and her brother's widow, Josephine Newhouse, moved into 221 and remained there until their deaths in January 1966 and June 1986, respectively. Later subdivided into four units, the house has recently been returned to its original duplex use.

Surviving exterior features of note include the decorative shallow-arched window trim work with original six-over-six window sashes, some of which retain their original convex glass. An arched louver gable vent is found in the attic level, and a Queen Anne–style side porch with turned posts and spindle work frieze survives on the north side of the house associated with the 221 address. Paired bracketing originally was found along the eaves but was sadly removed in recent years. The interior retains much of its original woodwork and simple post-and-lintel Greek Revival–style mantels. Rare surviving plaster ceiling medallions are found in the front rooms of each unit and in the dining room of 221.

HORATIO N. DEVOL HOUSE

225 Lafayette Street

Horatio N. Devol purchased this lot, on what was originally Lower Third Street, in 1833 and had a house built here shortly thereafter. By 1858, the house had been enlarged to its present Greek Revival–style appearance to accommodate the needs of his wife, Margaret, and their four children. Devol began his career as a cabin boy on the great steamboats that traversed the Ohio River. He quickly became a steamboat engineer and remained in this line of business until 1852. Toward the final years of his steamboating career, Horatio and business partner, Peyton Key, purchased their own steamboat named the *Belle Key*. In 1852, Devol purchased the stock and fixtures of a stove and tin ware business, located on the south side of East Main Street between State and Pearl Streets, along with a copper, sheet iron and jobbing shop located on the west side of State Street between West Main and Water Streets. The H.N. Devol Company supplied stocks of articles necessary for housekeepers, hotels, steamboats, tinners and country merchants.[6] This business would support the Devol families for the next sixty-three years. Horatio had the double house built next door at 219–21 for his sons, George H. and Frank S. in 1865. Horatio Devol died in 1886

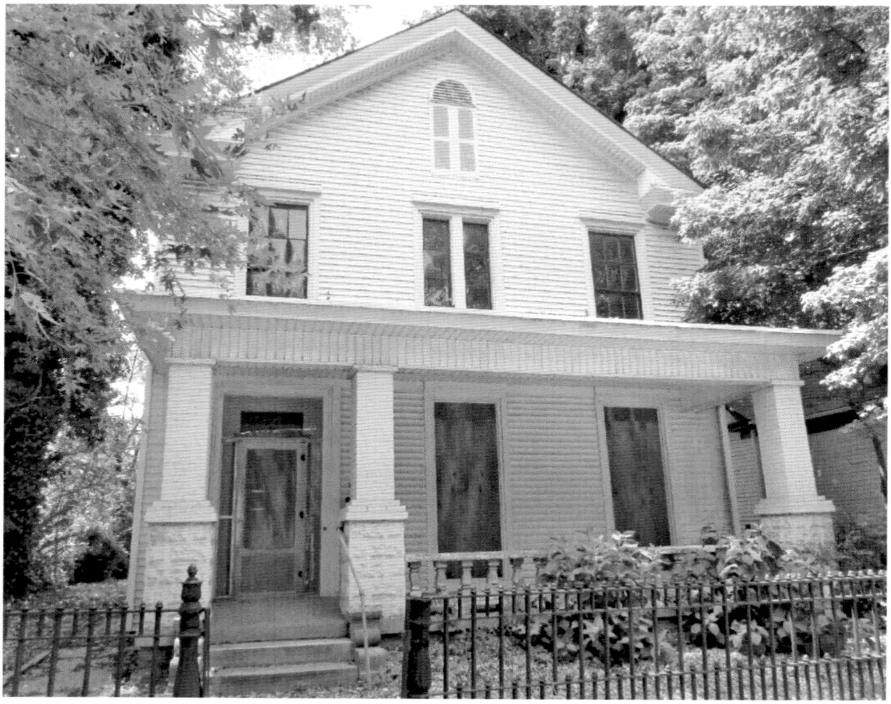

The Horatio N. Devol House once faced the city's now lost public promenade Scribner Park. *Gregory Sekula.*

and his widow, Margaret, lived in the home until February 1890, at which time the John Newhouse family purchased the home.

John Newhouse was a grocer. Successive generations of the Newhouse family remained in the house until May 1948. In February 1952, the Bruce Jacobi family became the owners of the property, and it remained in the Jacobi family for over a half-century.

The two-and-a-half-story house retains many outstanding architectural features. The exterior is notable for its original divided-light window sash with distinctive molded glass and arched louvered vent in the front façade gable. The present full-width front porch dates from the 1930s and replaced an earlier cast-iron porch for which an early photograph survives. A heavy ornamental iron fence graces the front yard.

The interior speaks to the elegance for which this once-fashionable address was known. The Horatio N. Devol House's entrance hall retains its original curved Italianate-style staircase with chestnut newel post, cherry handrail and maple balusters. The spacious front parlor features wide board pine flooring with a cherry finish and a fireplace with a slate mantel. The centerpiece is an original gasolier light with bronze finish featuring a globe-and-book theme. The fixture has been converted to electricity and retains antique colored-glass shades with a ruffled edge. The fixture hangs below a central cast plaster ceiling medallion with an acanthus leaf design. A library and second sitting room are located behind the front parlor. The library retains its plaster ceiling medallion and converted gasolier light fixture with an Oriental theme boasting elephant heads. Later reverse painted–glass shades are found on this fixture. The room also contains a fireplace with a turn-of-the-twentieth-century quartersawn oak mantel with fluted Doric columns and a white tiled hearth. The adjoining room also has a fireplace with a slate mantelpiece. This nicely sized room also boasts a plaster ceiling medallion and an 1890s Victorian light fixture with a wreath-and-swag design. A large dining room features a built-in china cabinet. The second floor features seven rooms and a large bathroom with a claw-foot tub. Two of the bedrooms contain fireplaces with Federal-style mantelpieces and woodwork that are believed to have been a part of the original Horatio N. Devol House that stood on this site.

JACOB AND SARAH ANTHONY HOUSE

210 West Main Street

Jacob and Sarah Anthony purchased the west twenty feet of lot 20 in New Albany's Original Town Plat in April 1832 and had this two-story brick town house constructed. Mr. Anthony originally was the proprietor of the High Street House at the southeast corner of Lower First and Main Streets. He later ran a livery stable on State Street between Market and Spring Streets and still later became the surveyor of customs for New Albany.

After his death in the late 1870s, Sarah remained in the house, and even after her death in the 1890s, the house remained in the Anthony family through 1924. The house had numerous owners from that time on and, by 1980, had fallen into disrepair and was threatened with demolition. Local businessman Larry Ricke and his business partner at the time, James Hartfield, purchased the condemned building and embarked on an ambitious rehabilitation, adapting the structure for office use. Double galley porches on the east side of the house were replaced with a new brick addition to expand the footprint of the original building.

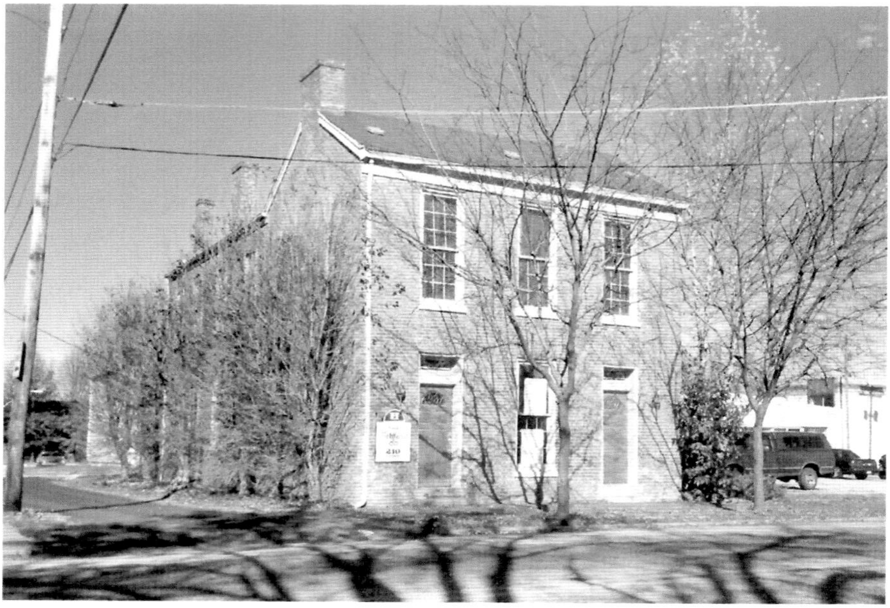

The Jacob and Sarah Anthony House is one of downtown New Albany's earliest surviving brick town houses. *Barksdale collection.*

The simple exterior design of the Jacob and Sarah Anthony House reflects the Federal style that first blossomed in New Albany as a more permanent architecture, replacing crude temporary log structures that were prevalent in the frontier. Flemish bond brick with its alternating header and stretcher courses is the hallmark of many of the city's earliest brick structures and is reflected in the Anthony House. Splayed brick lintels and an unadorned wooden frieze board at the house's cornice line are its only ornaments. Two entry doors with narrow transom windows above define the façade, along with large narrow window openings that originally had multi-light divided window sashes, since replaced.

The interior of the house retains its beautifully restrained cherry staircase with paneled wall, molded handrail, slender balusters and attenuated turned newel post. Six-paneled, triple leaf folding doors survive between the two front rooms of the house. An Italianate cast-iron mantel in the front parlor is a later Victorian update to this rare survivor of New Albany's formative years.

Wolfe Investment Houses

218–224 East Main Street and 43 East Third Street

This charming trio of brick town houses, along with a similarly designed house executed in frame around the corner on East Third Street, was constructed between 1878 and 1882 as investment properties for Simeon K. Wolfe, a prominent New Albany lawyer. The houses replaced an earlier brick 1820s building and have had a variety of owners and tenants over the years. Remarkably, they have maintained their architectural integrity on both the exterior and interior.

Steeply pitched side gable roofs and façades with arched windows highlighted by segmented-stone arched lintels add to the charm of these narrow town house dwellings. A simple iron fence is found along the front yard at the sidewalk. Entrances for three of the four houses are positioned at the sides of the dwellings, two of which are sheltered by wooden porches with simple Italianate details. The house at 43 East Third Street is further embellished with decorative bargeboard trim at the eaves and gable ends—a feature either lost or never added to the brick houses. The town house at 224 East Main Street takes advantage of its corner lot with a more elaborate entrance with double leaf arched doors leading to a small vestibule. The interiors of the houses have retained their simple woodwork, some doorways with transom windows above and cast-iron arched fireplace mantels in the principal rooms despite some modifications to their floor plans to accommodate office uses.

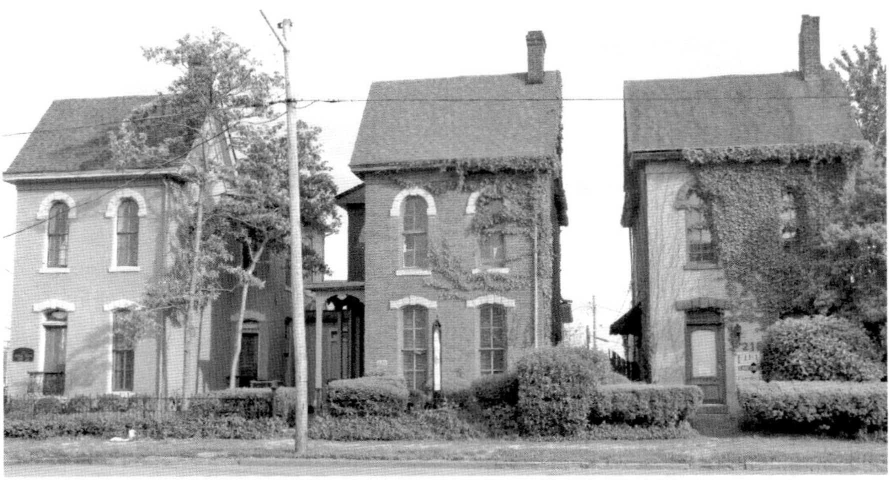

Simeon K. Wolfe constructed these three brick houses and a frame house on East Third Street for investment purposes. *Gregory Sekula.*

CONNER-CLOKEY HOUSE

412 East Main Street

This classic brick town house was built around 1848 and was the home of James Wesley Conner, a steamboat captain who helped pilot New Albany's most famous steamboat—the *Robt. E. Lee*.[7] The fabled steamboat is revered to this day for a famous race held in the summer of 1870 when it beat a competing steamboat—the *Natchez*—in a trip on the Mississippi River from New Orleans, Louisiana, to St. Louis, Missouri. Traveling a distance of 1,154 miles, the *Robt. E. Lee* reached its destination in three days, eighteen hours and fourteen minutes—nearly four hours ahead of the *Natchez*, whose journey had been plagued by fog delays.[8]

A second resident of note connected with this house is Joseph Clokey Jr., who was born here in 1890 and became a nationally known organist and composer of sacred and secular music. The son of Joseph Clokey, Presbyterian minister at New Albany's Second Presbyterian Church, Joseph Clokey Jr. was educated at Miami University in Oxford, Ohio. He later became a professor of organ music and dean of the School of Fine Arts from 1939 to 1946. His prolific body of work included religious choral hymns, organ works, operas, orchestral suites and even two symphonies, one known as the *Dorian Symphony*.[9]

Now adapted as a law office, the Conner-Clokey House exhibits a transition Federal/Greek Revival style with its restrained exterior detailing with its brick work accentuated with simple rectangular stone lintels at each window opening and at its entrance door, which is flanked by narrow sidelight windows and transom above. The interior retains its original mahogany staircase with turned newel post and paneled wall below. Woodwork is in the Greek Revival taste with fluted surrounds and large roundel-decorated corner blocks in the principal rooms.

ROYCE-FRIEND HOUSE

229 West Spring Street

This two-story brick house was spared from the destruction of Interstate 64, which claimed numerous residences that were once a

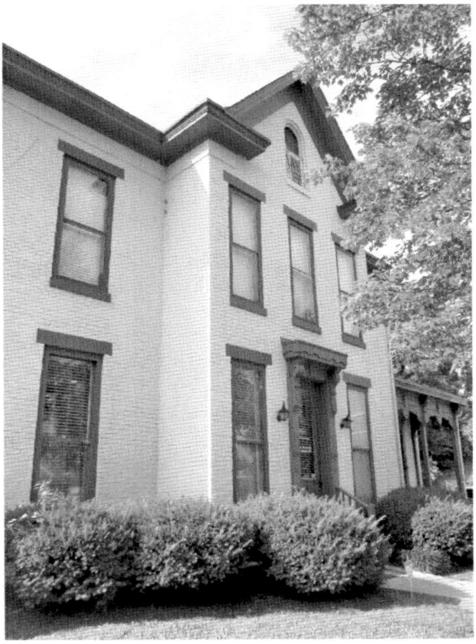

The Royse-Friend House is a remnant of the once fashionable Scribner Park neighborhood, lost to the construction of Interstate 64. *Gregory Sekula.*

part of a fashionable residential enclave built around New Albany's original public open space—Scribner Park. Between 1851 and 1855, Henry Royce, a dealer in iron, stoves and tinware, built this house. It remained in the Royce family until December 1874, when it was purchased by Isaac B. Friend. Friend was the proprietor of the New Albany Planing Mill and a local builder who was responsible for the construction of many fine New Albany residences and downtown buildings. During his ownership, numerous improvements were made to the house, including the addition of the south bay window in the 1890s, the bracketed entry door hood and the Italianate-style side porches with their post and spandrel bracketing. On the interior, a monumental Eastlake-style newel post with incised carving was incorporated into the stairway and originally included a gasolier light on top, now lost.

The house remained in the Friend family until it was sold on January 17, 1935, to Harold L. and Mary McIntosh. Mr. McIntosh was a superintendent at E.V. Knight's New Albany Veneering Company. Mrs. McIntosh continued living in the home even after the death of Harold in the late 1940s. By the 1970s, the house had begun to be used as commercial office space, with an insurance company maintaining an office there for nearly thirty years. In 2006, Louisville resident David Brown purchased the house and undertook an extensive rehabilitation for continued office use, which preserved many of the house's remaining original features, including much original woodwork and numerous cast-iron fireplace mantels. In 2014, attorney Marc Sedwick purchased the house for his law office.

LEMON-FUNK HOME AND OFFICE

315 East Spring Street

Built in 1886, this unusual frame structure with Italianate- and Queen Anne–style features was historically a mixed-use property containing a doctor's office and a residence. First owned by Dr. John Lemon, the building, by the early 1890s, was occupied by Dr. Edwin A. Severinghaus. In 1912, it became the home and office of physician Dr. Chester Funk, and it remained in the Funk family for several decades. The building was rehabilitated in 2013 as a residence for local real estate agent Paul Kiger, who maintained a home office on the first floor.

The two-story frame structure retains its distinctive bracketed door hood, Eastlake-style entry door and second-floor projecting oriel window. A three-part window with molded and bracketed hood decoration graces the first-

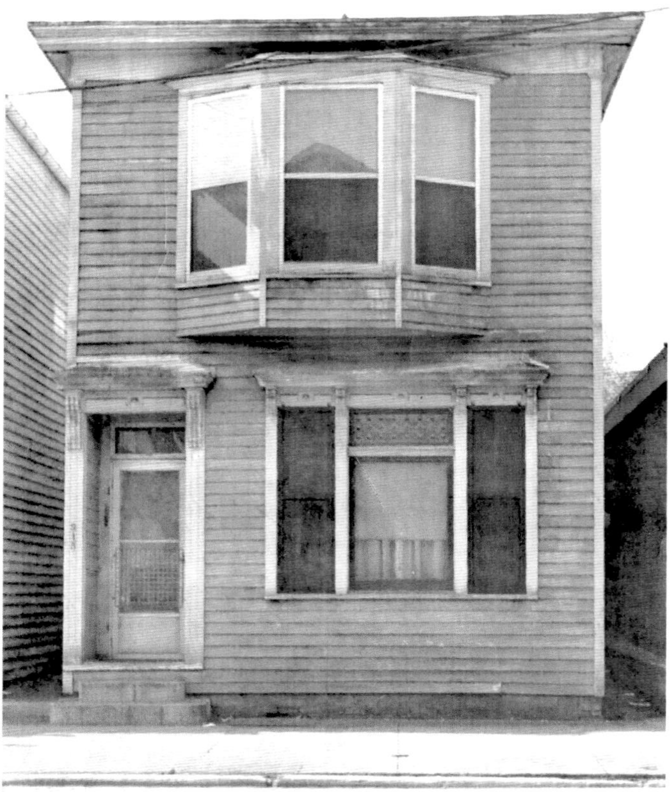

The 1886 Lemon-Funk Home and Office, shown here in this circa-1965 photo, is an early example of a mixed-use property. *New Albany–Floyd County Public Library.*

floor front façade. A small stained-glass transom window with jeweled and beveled-glass insets highlights the central window. The building's façade is sheathed in clapboard siding that was previously obscured by aluminum siding prior to Paul Kiger's renovation work.

The interior retains most of its original simple wood trim and paneled doors. Pocket doors with their original faux grain painting divide the front room from the second room, which was originally used for patient examinations. Three additional rooms, including the kitchen, are located beyond the enclosed staircase leading to the second floor. The second floor, largely untouched since the 1940s when the 2013 rehabilitation occurred, contains three to four bedrooms and a full bath with vintage fixtures. Early twentieth-century lighting fixtures have survived in several of the second-floor rooms.

Josephine Graf House

414 East Spring Street

Widow Josephine Graf erected this brick bungalow in the summer of 1927 on a lot where an earlier frame Victorian house once stood where she and her late husband, Henry, had resided. The Grafs purchased the property in April 1914. Mr. Graf was president of the New Albany Wall Plaster Company located at 134 East Market Street in downtown New Albany. He died in October 1925, and his widow remained in the home for two years before replacing the structure with a "modern bungalow," as reported in the *New Albany Ledger*, dated May 6, 1927.

Josephine Graf was a member of a well-known pioneer family named Newhouse. She was also a charter member of the official board of the Culbertson Widows' Home. She remained in the new house until her death in February 1946. Following her passing, her son Chester, a dealer in explosives, and his wife, Alice, took up residence in the house and remained there through August 1955. It was subsequently sold to Dr. Harold Exline, who opened his dental practice in the house. He retained ownership of the property through the mid-1970s.

A blend of Arts and Crafts and Classical Revival styles, the Josephine Graf House features a wire-cut brick veneer exterior with a side-gabled roof with exposed ornamental rafter ends at the eaves. Large brick piers with concrete caps support a large front porch with exposed rafter eaves

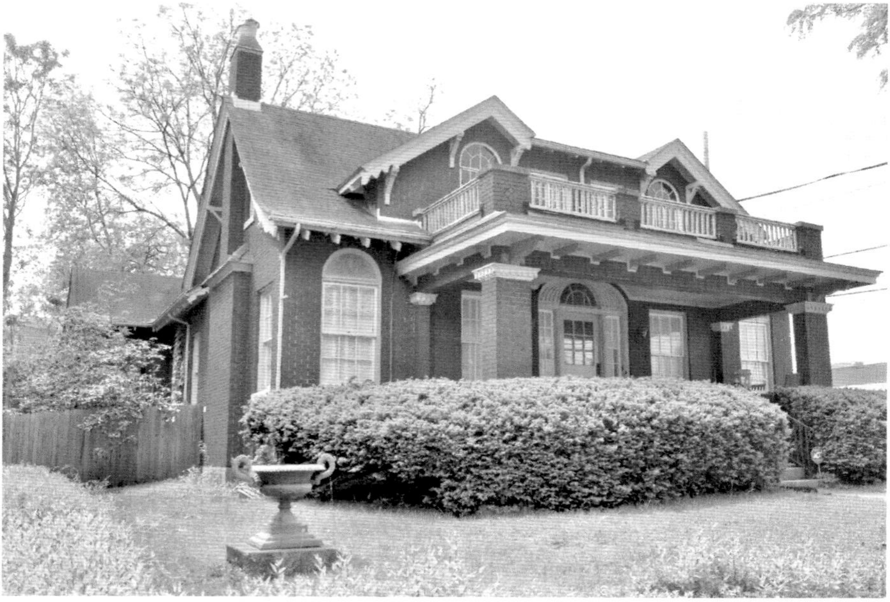

The 1927 Josephine Graf House blends Arts and Crafts and Classical Revival architectural styles. *Gregory Sekula.*

centered on the façade. A wooden balustrade with brick piers adorns the porch rooftop. Paired gabled dormers with triangular knee braces and arched windows are bridged by a shallow pitched "hyphen" containing two sets of paired casement windows. The house's front entrance door is embellished with multi-light sidelights, unusual braided columned pilasters and an arched transom window reinforcing the classical vocabulary of this prominent downtown "modern" residence. Simple trim, a plaster cornice in the entry foyer, strip oak hardwood floors, French doors, cast-iron radiators and a tiled fireplace with wooden mantelshelf in the front parlor are original features that remain with this well-preserved home.

O'Neill-Brown House

210 Bank Street

This modest frame dwelling incorporates a brick structure to the rear that once was the bank cashier's living quarters for the Indiana State Bank located directly to the south of the house. The property was purchased from the First National Bank in May 1902 by Elizabeth Meyer for $337.50. She owned the lot only briefly, selling it in February 1903 to Andrew and Lucinda O'Neill for $375.00. The O'Neills appear to have had the Queen Anne cottage built immediately adjoining the original brick structure. Andrew O'Neill was a carrier for the U.S. Post Office.

By the mid-1910s, Harry K. Smith, a foreman with the *New Albany Ledger*, was occupying the house but did not purchase it until the early 1920s. In April 1924, Alta Veit bought the home, and it remained in her possession until shortly before her death in February 1937. She was the widow of William and mother to twin sons, William Charles and Charles William, who also lived in the home.

The Veits lost their house to a sheriff's sale in August 1936, and the structure then saw numerous occupants until Elbert and Sylvia Brown took up residency in the home around 1950. Although the Browns did not purchase the property until January 1959, they remained in the house until the death of Mrs. Brown in March 2012. Elbert Brown—or "Brownie," as he was known—was employed at the New Albany Box & Basket Factory located on East Eighteenth Street in the east end of New Albany. Following

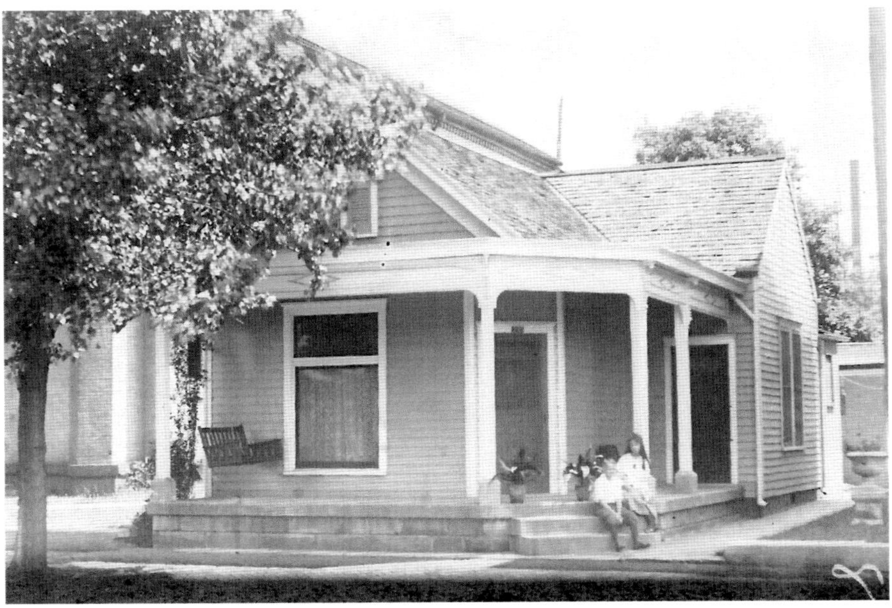

Brother and sister Eugene and Mary Louise Smith pose for this circa-1915 real photo postcard that was sent to family members. *Baumgartle Collection.*

rehabilitation by local investors in 2013, the house was purchased for use as an insurance office.

The vernacular Queen Anne–style cottage features a clapboard exterior in the front with a gabled roof decorated with a hooded vent. A wraparound porch with sawn-work bracketed posts is ornamented with applied wooden frieze board panels and shelters the house's two original entry doors. Original interior trim, a large paneled pocket door dividing the front room from the bedroom and dining areas and wide board wooden floors were retained in the conversion to office use.

Peter Vernia Double House

407–409 Bank Street

Peter Vernia was a carpenter with prolific New Albany master builders and architects William and James Banes. The Banes brothers were responsible for several notable residential commissions, including the William S. Culbertson Mansion at 914 East Main Street and the Culbertson Widows' Home at 704 East Main Street. Vernia purchased this lot in 1872, and it is highly likely that he, along with the Banes brothers, constructed this building. Peter Vernia used the double house for investment purposes, since his own residence was located on the south side of East Oak Street above Vincennes Street. There were also at least two other documented houses built by the Banes brothers on this block of Bank Street. A newspaper account from the *New Albany Daily Ledger*, dated May 31, 1882, reported, "Mr. John Hieb is erecting two handsome modern style two story residences at the corner of Bank and Elm streets…William and James Banes are the architects and contractors."

In 1883, Peter Vernia passed away, and his heirs sold the property to Mary Knirihm. It remained in the Knirihm family until 1948. The house passed through numerous owners until being sold to attorney Robert Kelso in 1973. Kelso renovated the building as his law office at a time when many businesses where leaving downtown New Albany. The building continues today as a law office, owned by attorney Rick Fox.

The two-story, side-gabled roof, brick structure features shallow arched windows with stone arched lintels. Two doors, one at each end of the house's front elevation, mark the entrance to each of the dwelling units. Few attached dwellings survive in New Albany, suggesting that the housing type never gained widespread popularity in this river town. The interior of the building reflects the 1970s renovation with exposed brick walls, wood-burning fireplaces and two-story spaces with some exposed structural framing. A spiral staircase to the second floor has been incorporated into the building and originally led to attorney Kelso's law library.

Farrell-Kepley House

425 Bank Street

This well-preserved Greek Revival–style brick town house was built around 1845 for Andrew Farrell, who was employed in the steamboat industry. A native of Eastport, Maine, Farrell moved to New Albany in his youth. As the *New Albany Daily Ledger* reported on October 23, 1872, in his obituary, "During the period of his active manhood he followed the river for a livelihood, and for many years was recognized as one of the most competent 'mates' who managed the palatial steamers of the valleys of the Ohio and Mississippi."

In 1865, Noah and Elizabeth Cobb purchased the home from Andrew Farrell for $3,600. The Cobbs had resided at 514 Main Street before purchasing this property. Noah Cobb had owned a wholesale grocery business in downtown New Albany before becoming involved in the woodworking company of Noah H. Cobb & Son, proprietors of the Park Furniture Factory.

After the Cobb family sold the home in the mid-1870s, the house saw numerous owners until it was purchased in July 1904 by Charles Kepley, who was employed in a livery business established by his father on State Street. The house remained in the possession of the Kepley family until 1988, when Larry Ricke purchased it. He sensitively rehabilitated the house for his financial services firm. Ricke, an ardent supporter of downtown New Albany, had previously rescued the Jacob and Sarah Anthony House at 210 West Main Street from destruction, too. He was also one of the original founders of Develop New Albany, the city's nonprofit main street organization, which is still active in revitalization efforts in downtown New Albany today. Larry Ricke's sister, Barbara Ricke, owner of Barbara Ricke Interiors of Lexington, Kentucky, provided the sensitive and tasteful interior design work for the office conversion.

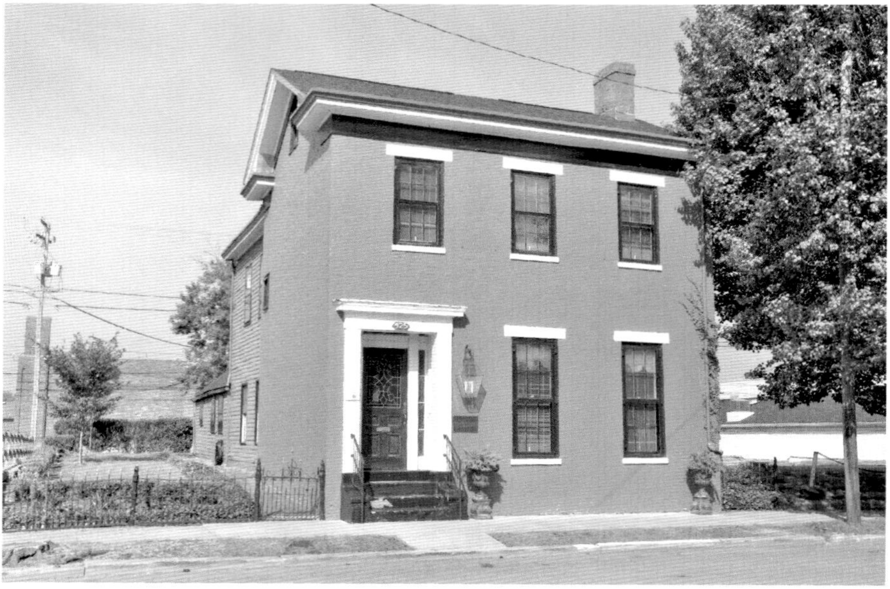

The circa-1845 Farrell-Kepley House is one of the few remaining residential dwellings that survive on Bank Street. *Gregory Sekula.*

The two-and-a-half-story brick house features the classic side hall entrance plan, with its recessed front door embellished with a simple surround with paneled pilasters and hooded entablature. Narrow leaded-glass sidelights and a three-part transom window frame the paneled wooden entry door with leaded glass. Simple stone lintels and sills define the window openings, which retain their original six-over-six wooden window sashes. The interior maintains its original staircase and much of its original woodwork and flooring. The front parlor fireplace mantel with a beveled mirror and columns is a Victorian update.

DANFORTH-BRIGGS-CODY HOUSE

330 East Third Street

Thomas Danforth, a partner in Day & Danforth insurance agents, purchased the lot on which this brick town house stands in June 1853. By January 1854, Danforth is listed in the *New Albany City Directory* as living here.

Three years later, in June 1857, New Albany entrepreneur John Briggs had purchased the property for $5,000. Briggs had been engaged in numerous business ventures beginning in 1838 when he arrived in New Albany. Born in England, Briggs had started in business as a journeyman tailor. He later purchased a grocery and general store and operated these businesses in Orange and Washington Counties in Indiana. In 1850, he returned to New Albany and became engaged in the wholesale grocery and liquor trade, a business that was very successful. Briggs then pursued a career in the iron and hardware trade, where he established John Briggs & Sons, which also proved profitable. He remained in that business until retirement. He was also an original stockholder and director of the New Albany National Bank. The Briggs family remained owners of the house through the mid-1920s. Mary Spence, daughter of John and Mary Briggs, was the last family occupant.

Between 1935 and 1936, the Girl Scout council occupied the house. In 1937, the American Red Cross acquired the dwelling at "Sycamore Corner"—as it was referred to in a November 10, 1937 article of the *New Albany Tribune*—for its local chapter house. In 1941, New Albany historians

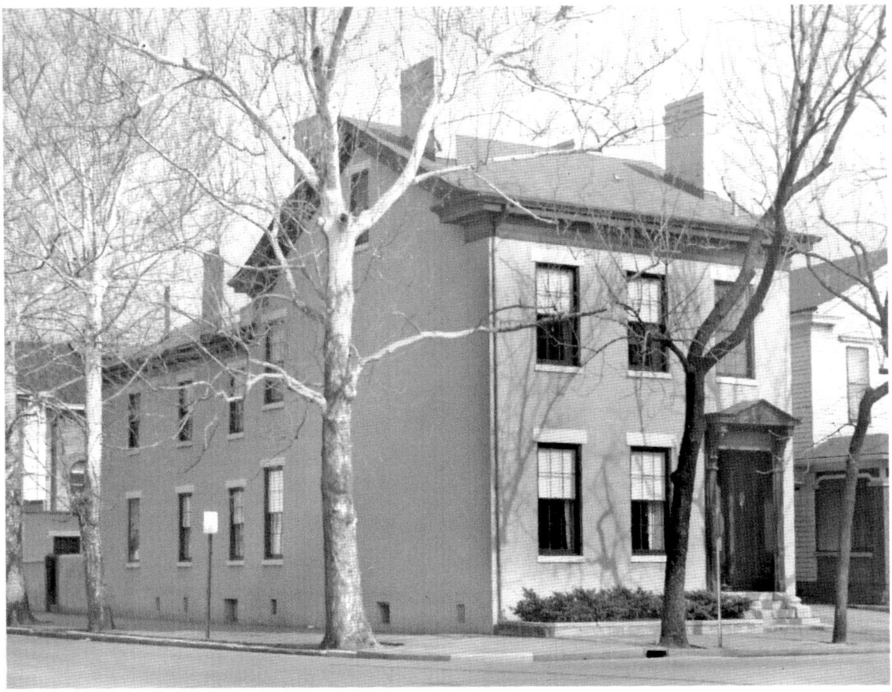

A circa-1960 photo of the Danforth-Briggs-Cody House shows several of the remaining sycamore trees along East Spring Street's "Sycamore Corner." *Cody Collection.*

John A. and Elizabeth "Bebe" Cody Jr. purchased the home and began a residency here that lasted over sixty years and ended with the death of Bebe Cody in 2004. John Cody had passed away in 1998. The Codys were founding members of the Floyd County Historical Society and were early pioneers in building awareness of New Albany's local history and the importance of its early architecture.

The Danforth-Briggs-Cody House is a classic New Albany town house with its side hall plan and two-and-a-half-story side-gabled roof with two-story rear service ell. Its most prominent exterior feature is an elaborate Victorian-period bracketed and pediment door hood that shelters a recessed entry door with beveled-and leaded-glass. The interior of the house has been beautifully preserved, retaining its open hardwood staircase, Greek Revival woodwork and simple post-and-lintel wooden mantels. The house remains in the Cody family.

2

Mansion Row

New Albany's Mansion Row was the city's first designated historic district, having been listed in the National Register of Historic Places in 1983. The historic district is primarily concentrated along East Main Street, originally called Upper High Street, and extends generally from State Street on the west to East Fifteenth Street on the east. Portions of East Market Street are included in the Mansion Row Historic District boundaries but, for the purposes of this publication, are organized separately in the East Market Street chapter that follows. This chapter also includes two houses that are located in the city's Dewey Heights section located to the east of Mansion Row in an area that was originally platted by Epaphras Jones as a separate town called Providence. Envisioned by Jones as a rival to neighboring New Albany, the development proved to be short-lived and was quickly absorbed into New Albany.

The Mansion Row Historic District contains the city's finest concentration of historic residential properties. The street chronicles, through its architecture, the rise in prominence of a river town that began as a pioneer settlement in the early decades of the nineteenth century and ultimately reached its zenith by the middle decades of the Victorian era when some of Indiana's most powerful and influential citizens made East Main Street their home. Access to distant markets made possible by river commerce and a burgeoning railroad network—coupled with an abundant supply of natural resources that fueled the production of lumber, glass and iron, among others—led to the development of a sophisticated domestic architecture that is revealed along this most esteemed of streets in New Albany.

ISAAC P. SMITH HOUSE

513 East Main Street

This stately brick home was the personal residence of architect and master builder Isaac P. Smith. Smith arrived in New Albany from Newark, New Jersey, around 1837 and was listed in city directories of the period as a mechanic, master builder and architect. As New Albany asserted its position as Indiana's most influential and populous town in the 1840s and 1850s, Smith became a leading designer and builder and was responsible for such public buildings as the city hall (demolished), the sheriff's residence and jail (demolished) and the Second Presbyterian Church (now the Second Baptist Church, 300 East Main Street), among others. He also was responsible for several notable residential commissions, several of which are featured in this book.

Constructed between 1848 and 1853, the two-and-a-half-story Isaac P. Smith House exhibits many of the characteristics that defined Smith's residential work in New Albany for the city's mid-nineteenth-century mercantile elite. Smith's residential designs favored a rectangular building mass with an emphasis on symmetry and the use of classical detailing. In his own residence, one finds a beautifully proportioned façade with paired windows evenly spaced to achieve balance and symmetry. First-floor windows are elongated to the floor level, and all window openings are defined by simple stone lintels and sills. Like the Smith-designed Montgomery-Cannon House at 518 East Main Street, the Isaac P. Smith House entrance is embellished with a heavy bracketed entablature supported by broad wooden pilasters. A slightly recessed door with narrow sidelights and transom window above provides natural light into the front hallway. An iron fence at the public sidewalk helps to demarcate public and private spaces. Double galleried porches are located behind the center hall and overlook a brick courtyard that was developed in the 1980s by owners Don Smith and Sid Spear.

The interior of the Isaac P. Smith House contains a central hall with an open staircase with simply turned hardwood newel post and balusters. Two back-to-back principal rooms flank the center hall. On the east side of the hall are double parlors, while a sitting room and dining room are situated on the west side. Family sleeping chambers are located on the second floor. A secondary rear ell is located behind the main rectangular building block and houses additional bedrooms, storage and kitchen and food preparation areas. Greek Revival wood trim with shouldered architraves and simple

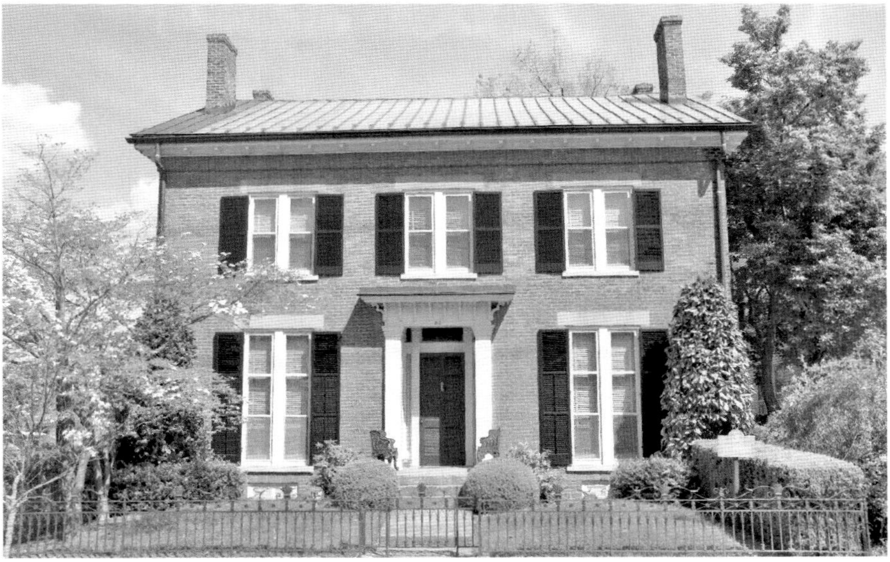

Mansion Row contains many homes designed and built by master builder Isaac P. Smith, including his own Greek Revival–style residence. *Gregory Sekula.*

post-and-lintel mantels with shallow ogee arches and chamfered pilasters are found in the principal rooms. Large paneled double leaf doors divide the double parlors on the east side of the house. Of note in the dining room is the scenic Zuber wallpaper depicting a Parisian scene—an elegant addition by owner Don Smith who professionally worked as an interior designer.

The Isaac P. Smith House has been documented in the Historic American Buildings Survey with measured drawings housed at the Library of Congress in Washington, D.C. The property is also protected with an architectural façade and conservation easement held by Indiana Landmarks, a statewide, nonprofit historic preservation organization.

McCartney-Cobb-Danforth House

514 East Main Street

In June 1847, Alexander and Eliza Jane McCartney purchased this lot and are believed to have built this brick Federal-style town house, completing it likely in 1848. The couple sold the home to John Conner in February

1850 for $2,800. Conner died in May 1852, and his estate was divided into six equal parts, each going to his relatives, including one share to his son Benjamin. In June 1852, Benjamin Conner purchased the other five shares of this property and made his home here with his wife, Isabella. He was listed in the 1848 *New Albany City Directory* as being a steamboat captain and in the 1850 census as a ferryman. Conner passed away in March 1853, and his wife inherited the house. Isabella Conner remarried just ten months later to Louisville resident John R. Knott, and the couple made their home in Louisville but continued to own this East Main Street house.

After almost losing the property to a city tax sale in 1855, John Knott advertised the sale of the house in 1857, and by July of that year, the property was sold to neighbor Captain Samuel Montgomery for $3,000. Captain Montgomery, in turn, sold the home to Captain Noah Cobb and his wife, Eliza, in November of that same year for $3,200. Not only was Noah Cobb extensively engaged in the merchandising of groceries and produce, he was a steamboat captain, being the owner and commander of several steamboats. Cobb also served the Third Ward on the city council in 1848. It

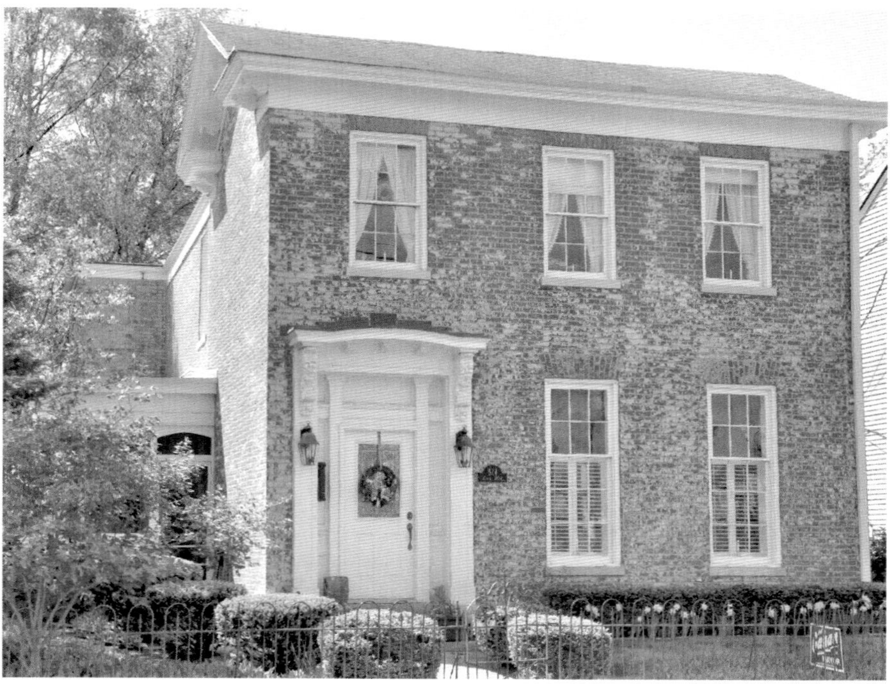

The circa-1848 McCartney-Cobb-Danforth House was enlarged around 1865 in the transitional Greek Revival/Italianate architectural styles. *Gregory Sekula.*

appears that Captain and Mrs. Cobb lost their property in 1862. The Cobbs would eventually purchase the Farrell-Kepley House at 415 Bank Street in September 1865.

Thomas and Adaline Danforth bought the home in April 1864 for $2,500. Thomas Danforth was one of the earliest dry goods merchants in the city. After retiring from merchandising, he was elected secretary of the New Albany Insurance Company, the first legitimate banking institution in New Albany. He also served on the city council in 1848, representing the Fourth Ward. Thomas Danforth died suddenly in February 1878 at age seventy-two.

In July 1882, Dr. Elijah Newland and his wife, Margaret, purchased the property from Adaline Danforth for $2,400, and one month later, the Newlands presented the home to St. Paul's Episcopal Church for use as its parsonage. At the time, St. Paul's Church was located across the street in the 600 block of East Main Street. The McCartney-Cobb-Danforth House remained the parsonage for St. Paul's until the early 1940s, when it became a boardinghouse run by Hazel A. Davis.

Physical evidence suggests that the original 1848 house was enlarged with the addition of a two-story section to the front of the house, containing the front rooms on each floor, along with an extension of the front hall on the first floor and a small nursery or possibly trunk room off the second-floor front bedroom. The house's elaborate shallow arched bracketed door hood is similar in design to the Culbertson Widows' Home at 704 East Main Street and the James Marshel House at 1209 East Main Street. This suggests that this addition may have been added in the 1860s or 1870s by the Danforth family and possibly executed by architects and builders James and William Banes, who are known to have designed the Culbertson Widows' Home. The house's elongated front first-floor windows also reveal that this feature was an update to the original design of the addition as evidenced by seams in the house's brick and interior woodwork.

Whoever was responsible for construction of the addition, meticulous care was taken to replicate the house's original, two-part Greek Revival interior trim and post-and-lintel mantels. Other notable features of the interior include a handsome open staircase with cherry handrail and newel post and slender, attenuated balusters set above a flat paneled wall. A large plaster ceiling medallion with acanthus leaf decoration is found in the front hall at the foot of the staircase.

Joshua Bragdon House

517 East Main Street

This stately frame house survives as one of architect and master builder Isaac P. Smith's most elaborate residential commissions. It is similar in design to the now lost Abbey C. Butler House, a frame Isaac P. Smith–designed residence built in 1854 that once stood at 1612 Dewey Street. That dwelling was demolished in 1960 to make way for the Riverview Manor Apartments. The Joshua Bragdon House was constructed in 1856 for Joshua Bragdon, who was originally associated with the steamboat business and piloted the famed New Albany–built *Eclipse* steamboat, which had navigated California's Sacramento River.[10] Bragdon later became the owner of the New Albany Rolling Mill, which fabricated rails for the growing network of rail lines connecting Indiana's most populous town with markets near and distant.

The Joshua Bragdon House offers a sophisticated application of Greek Revival detailing with hints of the Italianate style that was gaining favor by midcentury. Isaac Smith favored a boxy, rectangular building form with a double-pile floor plan featuring a center hall flanked by two principal rooms back to back. In the case of the Joshua Bragdon House, a shallow truncated hipped roof with wide overhanging eaves covers the main rectangular building block and was originally punctuated by four towering brick chimneys—one for each of the four principal rooms. A wide entablature or frieze board wraps the house and is embellished with simply detailed wooden brackets—a nod to the emerging Italianate taste. Wide corner boards have the effect of picture-framing the house's façade, which features symmetrically placed paired windows with heavy molded hoods. On the ground level, a center entrance door is framed by sidelights and transoms with opaque blue slag glass, which likely replaced clear glass. A hipped roof porch with classical entablature cornice with dentil molding, triglyphs and metope ornamented with laurel wreath appliques spans the façade and is supported by fluted Doric columns; the inner columns are arranged in pairs. On the east side of the porch, two dressed limestone steps from the demolished New Albany home of eleventh Indiana governor Ashbel P. Willard are of particular note. They were added to the house around the first decade of the twentieth century by dry goods merchant Charles Hassenmiller, who, along with his wife, Elizabeth, purchased the Bragdon home in 1906. In the mid-twentieth century, the home was the residence of prominent local judge Paul Tegart and his family.

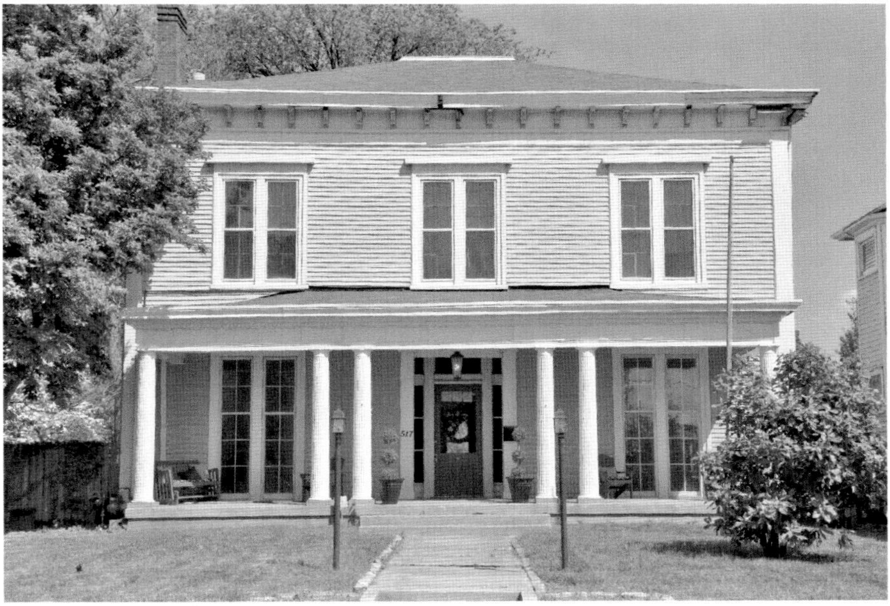

Steamboat pilot Joshua Bragdon had this frame Greek Revival–style house built in 1854 by famed master builder Isaac P. Smith. *Gregory Sekula.*

On the interior, the house features a wide center hall that spans the full depth of the house with a second entry door with sidelights and transom leading to a back porch at the far end. A plaster ceiling medallion with acanthus leaf and modified Greek key decoration is the focal point of the hall ceiling. A molded plaster cornice frames the ceiling hall. An open staircase to the second floor—typically the centerpiece of the main hall—is tucked away in a separate room between the two principal rooms on the west side of the house. The stair features a tapered mahogany newel post with unusual heart-shaped exposed joinery embellishment at the top. Turned balusters and a simple molded handrail complete the elegant ensemble. Each of the principal rooms on the first floor features a center fireplace with simple wooden mantels in the Greek Revival taste. Shouldered architraves frame doors and windows. The richness of the double parlors on the east side of the first floor is achieved by the presence of heavily molded plaster cornices and ceiling medallions with an acanthus leaf design. A triple-arch opening supported by fluted Ionic columns separates the two rooms to monumental effect. This is truly one of New Albany's grand residential rooms of the 1850s.

On the second floor, Smith deviated from the typical center hall layout, creating a central core square hall with a bedroom or sleeping chamber at each corner. In one bedroom, a simple post-and-lintel mantelpiece adorns a fireplace. Wood stoves likely heated the three remaining rooms given the lack of mantels and the narrower dimension of the chimneys. Two smaller rooms bookend what typically would have been the center hall. These rooms originally may have functioned as a nursery and trunk room.

MONTGOMERY-CANNON HOUSE

518 East Main Street

With its ornate cast-iron porch and bracketed cornice, the Montgomery-Cannon House is one of East Main Street's most imposing dwellings. Constructed in 1850 for riverboat pilot Samuel Montgomery, the house was later purchased by Greenbury C. Cannon, a wholesaler in fancy goods and notions. Following the deaths of the Cannons, the property was sold at public auction in December 1914 and purchased by Frank Sisloff, who converted the house into a duplex. The house's two front doors have been thoughtfully incorporated into the original entrance frame with its over-scaled bracketed hood supported by broad wooden pilasters.

The work of architect and master builder Isaac P. Smith, the Montgomery-Cannon House, as originally conceived, adhered to the double-pile plan so favored by the designer and evidenced in several neighboring houses also attributed to him. On the exterior, the rectangular block of the house features symmetrical fenestration with elongated divided-light window sashes. The delicate ironwork found in the porch supports and railing—a rare survivor in New Albany—dominates but does not overwhelm the façade. A wide bracketed cornice at the second-floor eaves helps ground the house to its site but also achieves a level of monumentality for which Smith's work is associated. Originally, crenelated metal decoration was incorporated at the roof level of both the house and front porch and masked the low-pitched hip of both, as evidenced by a surviving historic photograph. A simple hairpin iron fence enclosing the front yard contributes to the grandeur of the house on its corner lot.

While the house's first-floor center hall was sacrificed for the duplex conversion and additional adjustments to the floor plan on both floors were made to accommodate the house's conversion into apartment units, the adjoining principal first-floor rooms have retained their original dimensions

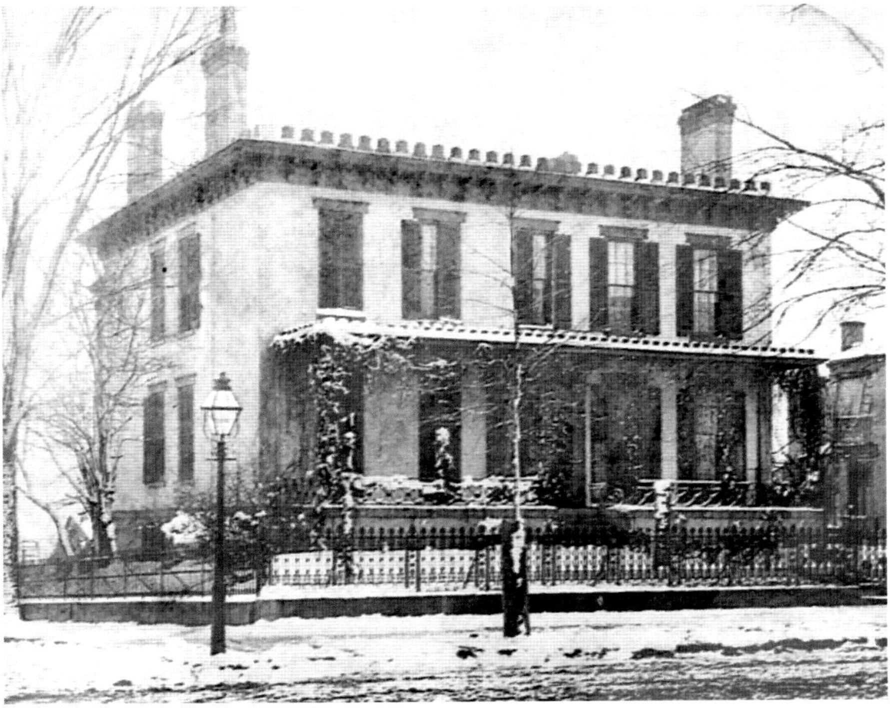

This circa-1875 stereo view of the Montgomery-Cannon House showing its now lost crenelated metal rooftop ornamentation. *Cannon Collection.*

and grandeur with wide Greek Revival–style moldings, twelve-foot-tall ceilings, paneled doors and a few surviving marble mantels. Second-floor woodwork has also largely remained intact. In 2014, the house sold to John and Leza Eldorado, who are working to restore it back to single-family use.

SLOAN-BICKNELL-PARIS HOUSE

600 East Main Street

With its octagonal cupola, large-scaled bracketed cornice and unusual convex glass window panes, the Sloan-Bicknell-Paris House remains one of Mansion Row's most striking residences. One of a cluster of houses designed by noted architect and master builder Isaac P. Smith, the two-and-a-half-story brick house displays Smith's characteristic boxy building form and emphasis on a

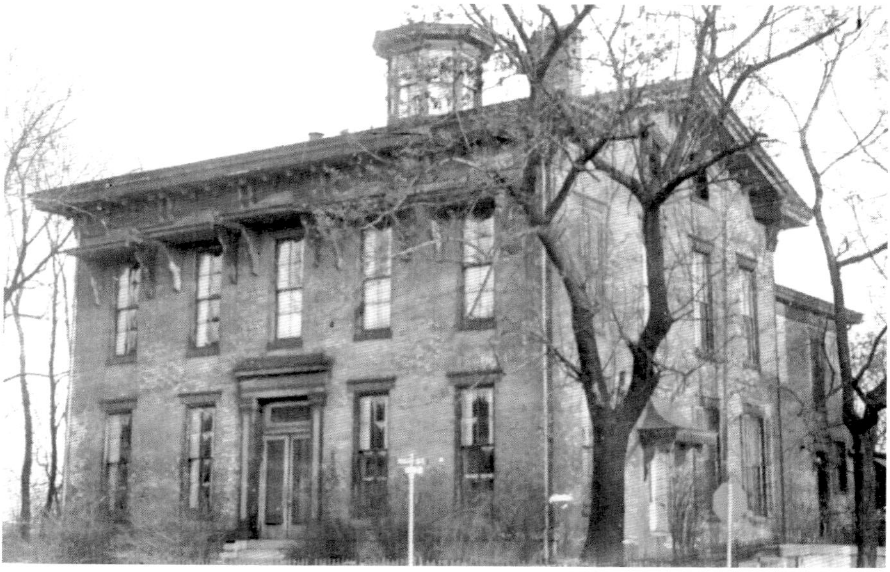

The 1854 Sloan-Bicknell-Paris House, shown in this 1945 photo, is known for its octagonal cupola, bracketed cornice and convex windowpanes. *New Albany–Floyd County Public Library.*

symmetrical façade. While many of Smith's residential commissions displayed a merging of Greek Revival and Italianate details, the Sloan-Bicknell-Paris House presents an almost dual personality with its staid classical entrance with simple entablature and first-floor windows with unadorned lintels contrasting with the robust bracketed second-floor window hoods sheltered by alternating large and small paired brackets at the roofline. A hooded side entrance door on the East Sixth Street side of the house, believed to be original, marks the entrance to the office of physician John Sloan, who was the first owner of the house. The *New Albany Daily Tribune* announced the construction of the house in January 1854 when it reported:

> *Speaking of fine dwelling houses reminds us that we neglected to notice the draft of a splendid mansion, laid upon our table a few days since by I.P. Smith, Esq., architect, &c. We mean the draft was laid upon our table, not the mansion. The house is to be built early in the season for Dr. Sloan, on the corner of Main and Upper Sixth Street, and if the design of the architect is followed out it will combine beauty with comfort and convenience to an extent not surpassed by any other dwelling in that, the Court end of the city.*

Following the death of Dr. John Sloan, his daughter, Ann, and her husband, Rear Admiral George A. Bicknell, occupied the house until their deaths. A graduate of the United States Naval Academy in 1866, Bicknell served honorably with the U.S. Asiatic Fleet between 1868 and 1870 and commanded the USS *Niagara* during the Spanish-American War. In 1907, he was promoted to rear admiral and retired the following year. He died in 1925 and was buried in New Albany's Fairview Cemetery.[11] By 1937, Judge John Paris and his family resided in the house. The Paris family retained ownership until 1996. Lucille Paris, dean of girls at New Albany High School, passed away in December 1997. Following the house's sale at auction, the Scharlow family rehabilitated it. A subsequent owner transformed the house into an elegant bed-and-breakfast.

The interior of the Sloan-Bicknell-Paris House retains its original woodwork, interior wooden shutters and winding mahogany staircase with cherry balustrade that is illuminated by the house's cupola. Of special note in the residence are the matching French pier mirrors in the front parlor and dining room and a rare surviving intercom system throughout the house that was installed by Rear Admiral Bicknell.

George and Eliza Devol House

601 East Main Street

One of New Albany's more idiosyncratic examples of the Queen Anne style, this two-and-a-half-story frame dwelling was built in 1889 for George H. and Eliza L. Devol. Mr. Devol was a dealer in stoves, tin, copper, sheet iron, plumbing and gas fittings. The *New Albany Daily Ledger* reported on December 19, 1889, on the completion of the Devol residence with the following description:

> *One of the most elegant residences erected in the city this season has just been completed on east Main street, near St. Paul's Episcopal church, for Mr. Geo. H. Devol. In architecture and exterior and interior finish Mr. Devol has secured a family mansion as beautiful as it is commodious and comfortable. It is essentially modern in all its appointments, being heated by hot water throughout, fully equipped with gas and water, including luxurious bath rooms and every modern convenience…*
>
> *The exterior appearance of this elegant residence is very attractive,*

including charming decorations and spacious verandahs. But the interior is "a thing of beauty," quite as complete in artistic finish and fine workmanship as any residence in the city...

This splendid residence is the handiwork of Mr. James Johnson, the well known carpenter and building contractor, who had the contract for its erection and gave personal attention to every detail of the work... The plastering was by Mr. Jack Phillips, the painting and graining by Thomas Mullineaux.

For many years, the Devols' daughter, Harriett, conducted music lessons from the residence. The Devols were owners of the property for almost forty years.

With its hipped roof with metal finials, towering corbelled brick chimneys, wide front porch with turned posts and projecting two-story façade bay with engaged conical roof, the George and Eliza Devol House evokes the Queen Anne style through its asymmetrical massing and use of varying wall textures. Paneled wood sections in the front bay and on the porch combined

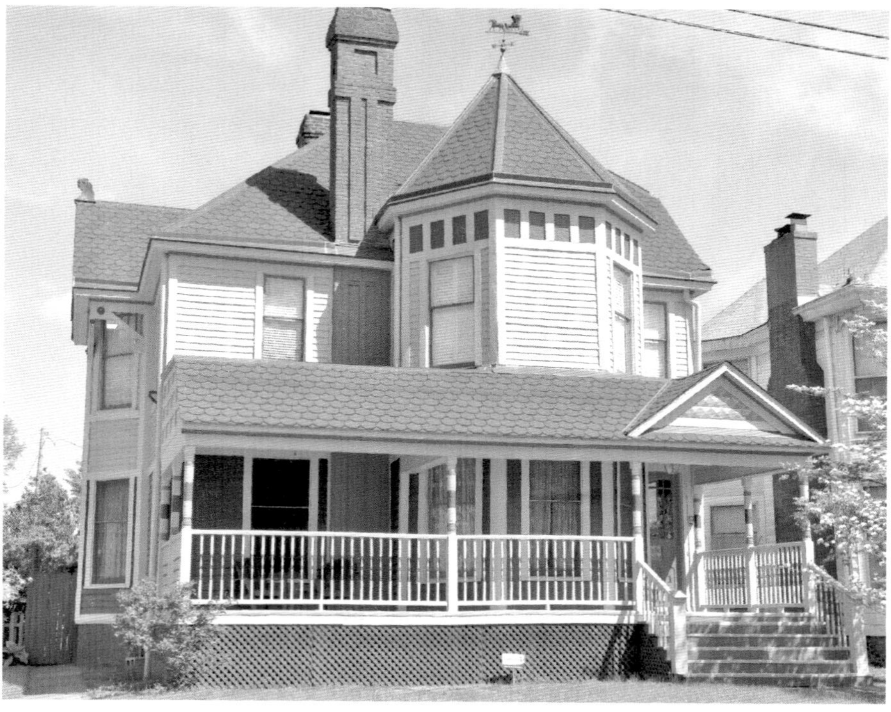

Queen Anne in architectural style, the George and Eliza Devol House is one of East Main Street's most elaborate Victorian residences. *Gregory Sekula.*

with horizontal banding between sections of clapboard siding give the house visual richness, made all the more effective by the use of a multicolored paint scheme chosen by the present owners.

The interior of the house features an elaborate Eastlake-style staircase with chamfered oak newel posts and paneled apron below. Original cast-iron fireplaces survive in a first-floor sitting room off the house's dining room and in the upstairs front bedroom, the latter of which is embellished with decorative tiles featuring pre-Raphaelite–style figures on the shelf brackets. Original woodwork with heavily molded corner blocks, decorative cast-iron radiators and strip oak flooring are found throughout the principal rooms of the residence. A curious feature is the presence of an earlier Greek Revival–style mantel in the first-floor stair hall that predates the house and may have come from the Horatio N. Devol House at 225 Lafayette Street, the home of George Devol's parents.

The George and Eliza Devol House may be the work of architect Milton C. Pritchett, who maintained practices in New Albany and Bedford, Indiana, and Louisville, Kentucky, throughout his career. Pritchett is known to have designed another house on this block, now no longer extant. Pritchett favored the Queen Anne style in his residential practice in the 1890s, and the George and Eliza Devol House shares some similarities with other known or probable works of his. Further research is needed to verify Pritchett as the architect of this unique New Albany home and to establish any connections between Pritchett and the builder, James Johnson.

THE BEEHIVE

612 East Main Street

Known affectionately by locals as the Beehive, this imposing Second Empire–style dwelling with mansard roof was originally constructed without this hallmark feature around 1845 by Asa Mann, who had acquired the property four years earlier in 1841. In 1863, the property became the home of Mary Ann Silliman-Ayres-Lindsay-Richardson-Lapsley. Mary Ann had eight children, none of whom reached maturity. She also outlived four husbands, all of whom collectively left her with considerable wealth and business acumen. Elias Ayers, her first husband, was a successful dry goods merchant who donated $15,000 in 1847 for the establishment of the New

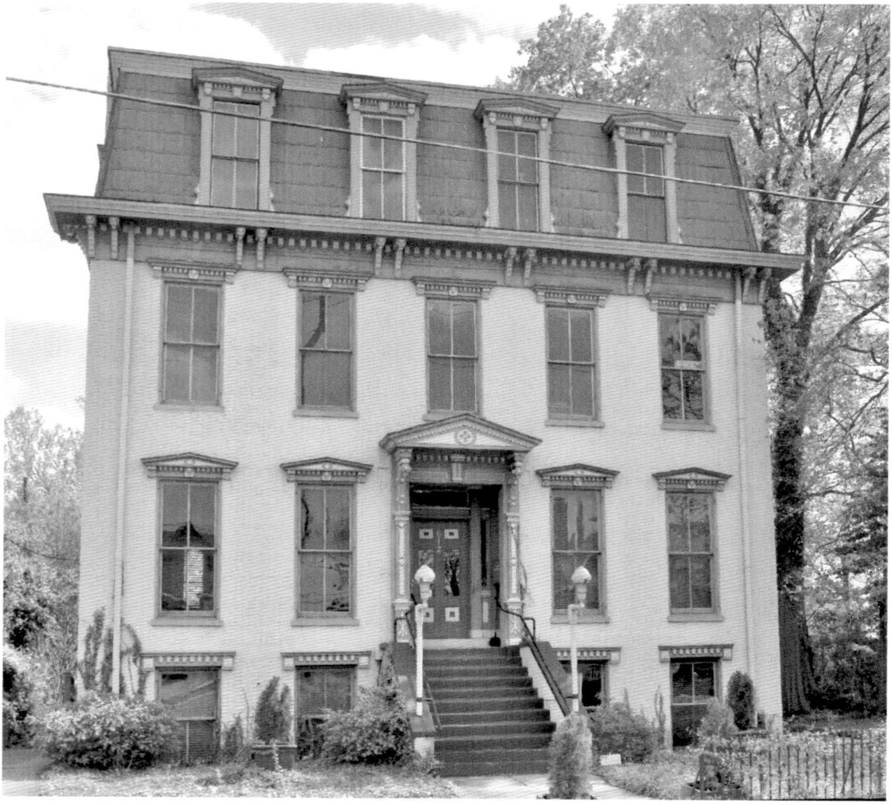

The Beehive was built circa 1845 and updated in 1885 with a mansard roof and bracketed embellishments. *Gregory Sekula.*

Albany Theological Seminary located on East Elm Street. The seminary eventually was reestablished in Chicago as the McCormick Theological Seminary, which is an active Presbyterian seminary still in existence today.

In 1885, the dormered mansard roof, bracketed cornice and decorative bracketed gabled entry door were added to the house's exterior to update its appearance, creating one of the city's most imposing Victorian residences. The house's elevated first floor is reached by a set of central steps leading to a paneled-glass entry door flanked by sidelights. The interior of the house follows a center hall plan and has an open hardwood staircase that rises three stories. Wide flared woodwork with heavy architraves in the Greek taste embellishes window and door openings throughout the house. Elaborate marbleized cast-iron mantels, several with Eastlake detailing, are likely from the 1880s remodeling and remain in several locations. The house has been tastefully converted into efficiency apartments without significantly compromising the original interior floor plan.

McCulloch-Newburger Houses

616 and 620 East Main Street

This pair of frame houses was constructed in 1900 as investment properties for John F. McCulloch, president of the New Albany National Bank. The first tenant of 620 East Main Street was Samuel W. Newburger and his wife, Leah. The house at 616 East Main Street was occupied by their son, William S. Newburger. Samuel Newburger was a prominent Jewish merchant who founded the prestigious S.W. Newburger Company's White House Department Store in downtown New Albany. His son, William, also worked in the store. The institution was a Pearl Street anchor for ninety-seven years. The senior Mr. Newburger died suddenly at his store

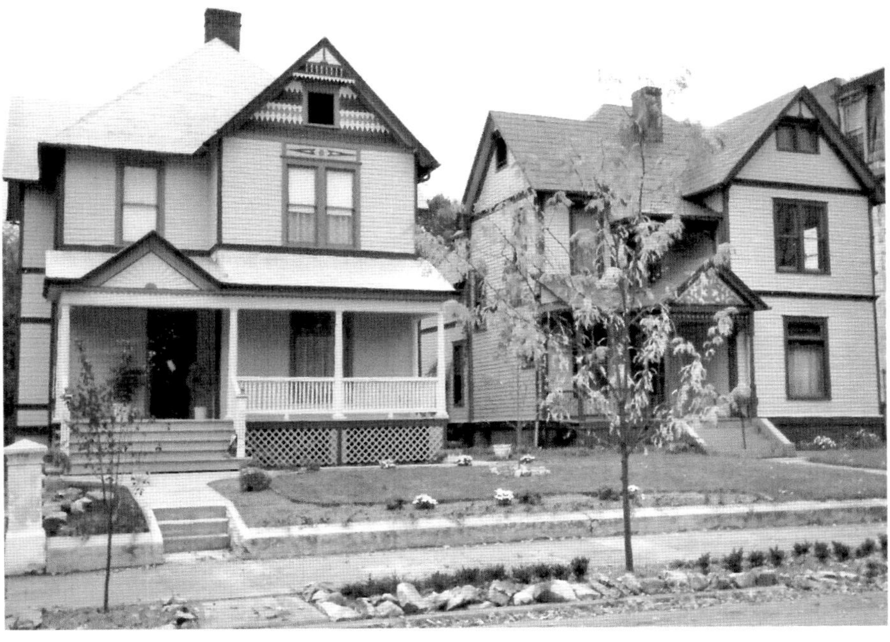

The McCulloch-Newburger Houses were built in 1900 as investment properties for John McCulloch, president of the New Albany National Bank. *Barksdale collection.*

in March 1908. His widow remained in her house until 1915, when she relocated to Salt Lake City, Utah, to live with her daughter. The house at 620 East Main Street remained a rental property until 1921, when the Collins family purchased it. The house at 616 East Main Street remained a rental house until purchased by Frank Lind in 1985.

These vernacular Queen Anne–style dwellings exhibit complex rooflines with steeply pitched hipped roofs with lower cross gables. Decorative sawnwork shingles are found in the gable ends. The 620 East Main Street house has a full-width front porch supported by Tuscan-style columns. A sunburst design ornaments the porch gable, and a panel with applied moldings adds visual interest to the paired second-floor windows above the front porch. A partial porch embellishes the house at 616 East Main and is supported with turned posts and spindle work spandrels in between. Lattice-patterned scrollwork ornaments the porch gable.

CULBERTSON WIDOWS' HOME

704 East Main Street

The construction of this brick mansion for New Albany widows was made possible because of the philanthropy of one of New Albany's most preeminent citizens—William S. Culbertson—who, in 1873, contracted with architects and master builders William and James Banes to erect a residence befitting of the mansions of New Albany's East Main Street. Moved by the plight of women left widowed by the Civil War and himself recently married to a woman who had been in that situation, Culbertson donated $25,000 for the construction of the facility, as well as an endowment of $150,000 for its operations. The widows' home was designed to accommodate thirty to forty women at a time; the only qualifications for admission were a good moral character, lack of a home and an inability to support oneself.

The *New Albany Ledger-Standard* described the Culbertson Widows' Home on the occasion of its opening in November 19, 1873:

> *Very few people in our city occupy dwellings near so luxurious as our friends here. The visitor goes over this Home, feeling really this is a home, indeed. Nothing stingy, nothing mean, because it would be cheap, can be detected in any part of the workmanship, but every part is grand, massive, just the*

thing for ages.

The widows' home operated until 1971, when the board of trustees closed the facility and sold the furnishings at public auction. The home itself was sold two years later to Charles and Roberta Mitchell, who used it as their residence. Mrs. Mitchell was widowed herself in the mid-1980s and lived alone in the house until her death in March 2000. Steve Goodman and Carl Holliday then purchased the house to use it as their residence and a bed-and-breakfast. Today, they operate it as an apartment house.

William and James Banes designed the structure to resemble not an institutional building but a large single-family dwelling in keeping with other mansions of New Albany's civic and business elite. The house is a gable-and-wing form with Italianate-style detailing that was favored by the Banes brothers and appears in several residential commissions, including the Judge Alexander Dowling House on East Spring Street and the Herman and Johanna Rockenbach House on Ekin Avenue. In the Culbertson Widows' Home, we see a steeply pitched front gable with an arched window in the attic level and paired window sashes on the first and second floors. Paired brackets embellish a simple brick corbelled frieze at the eaves, and

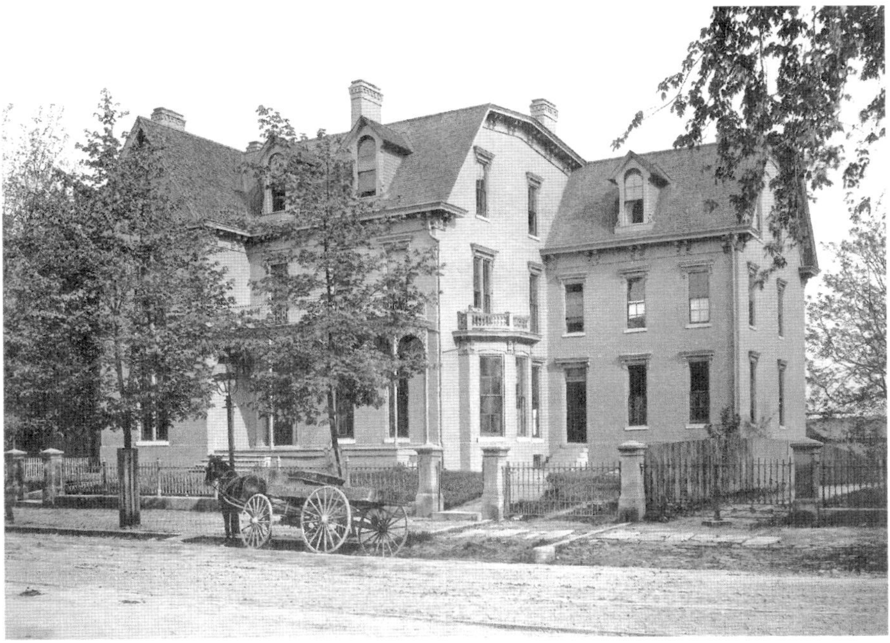

William S. Culbertson donated $25,000 for the construction of the Widows' Home, built in 1873 and pictured here in 1893. *From* Art Work of New Albany, 1893.

an ornate cast-iron porch spans the side wing of the house on the front façade, sheltering the front paneled entrance door with its shallow arched hood supported on the sides by oversized acanthus leaf brackets anchored on paneled pilasters. Bracketed and molded metal hoods adorn the house's windows and the entry door. A one-story bay window is prominently sited on the house's west elevation. A large two-and-a-half-story wing with a modified gambrel roof sits back from the main building block of the house on the west side, significantly enlarging the structure's building footprint. The roofline is punctuated by gabled dormers with arched windows. An original wrought-iron fence with a limestone base and pillars defines the front of the property.

The interior of the Culbertson Widows' Home retains most of its original two-part woodwork throughout. Ten original cast-iron fireplace mantels remain, several of which retain their original faux-painted marbleized finishes. The front hall features its original open mahogany staircase with a second open stair of similar style in the west wing of the mansion. Pocket doors divide the principal first-floor rooms on the house's east side, and a large plaster arch frames the bay window on the west side of the house.

Nunemacher-Hangary House

709 East Main Street

Constructed in 1853 and attributed to architects and builders William and James Banes, this one-and-a-half-story brick house, with raised first floor, was first occupied by John R. Nunemacher, owner of the City Bookstore on East Main Street in downtown New Albany. The second owner was Jacob Hangary, one of the founders of the Merchants National Bank.

With its cast-iron and steel front porch supported by Corinthian style columns, cast-iron carriage entrance porch on the east side of the residence and steeply pitched cross-gabled roof, the Nunemacher-Hangary House reflects both Gothic Revival and Italianate architectural influences. Elongated windows on the first floor and an entrance door with an arched window, narrow sidelights and a three-part transom above reinforce the verticality of the residence and give it a regal presence along East Main Street.

The interior of the Nunemacher-Hangary House features a floor plan more in keeping with southern building traditions than is typical of midwestern domestic layouts. The house's lower level originally housed the

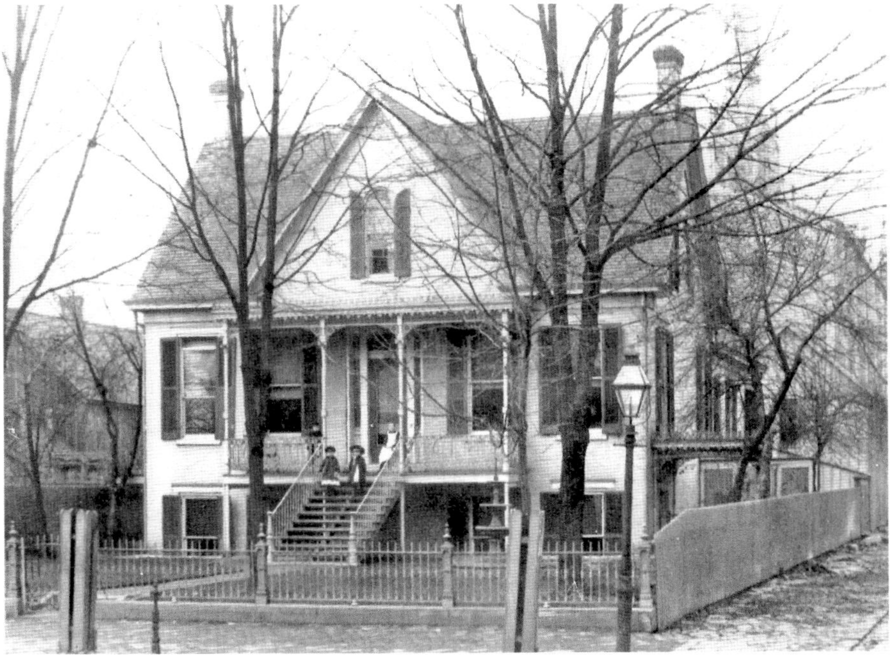

An 1887 image of the Nunemacher-Hangary House showing its elaborate cast-iron and steel porches and fencing. *New Albany–Floyd County Public Library.*

kitchen, dining room, storage room and servant's bedroom. The elevated main floor contained a central hallway flanked by a formal parlor and music room. A bedroom originally was located in the rear wing, and additional bedrooms were located on the second floor, reached by an enclosed steep staircase. There is some evidence that the house's gabled upper story may have been constructed later. Changes in woodwork and door hardware, along with evidence of framing modifications suggest that originally the house may have had a shallow hipped or even a flat roof when constructed in the early 1850s.

Most of the house's original woodwork remains intact, including wood wainscoting in the lower level spaces. Fireplace mantels on the elevated main floor likely date to the 1890s and are of quartersawn oak. The west music room mantel is embellished with turned column supports, a beveled-glass mirror and carved panels with foliated vines and griffins. The east room fireplace features a simpler quartersawn oak mantel with an arched top with an arched beveled mirror. Antique lighting survives in these rooms with 1880s converted brass and cloisonné gasoliers in an

Aesthetic Movement/Eastlake design. A simpler square brass and glass hanging light, also in the Eastlake style, is found in the front hallway.

Remnants of the house's original cast-iron fence remains along East Main Street. A cast-iron fountain originally graced the front yard and will soon be erected on the grounds of the William S. Culbertson Mansion. A Board and Batten–clad carriage house, constructed in the early 1990s, is located in the backyard and mimics the roofline of the house.

WASHINGTON C. DEPAUW MANSION

714 East Main Street

One of Mansion Row's grandest residences, this rambling Italianate-style frame house was built in 1870 as the winter home of one of New Albany and Indiana's leading citizens. Washington C. DePauw was born in Salem, Indiana, in 1822, the son of pioneer lawyer and judge, John DePauw, who had participated in the Indiana Constitutional Convention and had been elected four times to the Indiana legislature. John DePauw died in 1838, and his son, who was only sixteen years old, was forced to go out on his own. Washington C. DePauw became a successful businessman, having a diversified portfolio of business interests ranging from wholesale grain to farm equipment and, later, during the Civil War, government supplies. He arrived in New Albany around 1854. By 1864, with investments in banks, railroads, iron factories, a woolen mill and even a chemical plant, he was reputed to have had an annual income over $300,000, making him one of the wealthiest men in the state. In 1872, DePauw took over his cousin's New Albany glass company along the Ohio River and eventually expanded it, creating a business empire known as the American Plate Glass Works, which at one time was one of the nation's leading glass manufacturers.[12]

A devout Methodist, DePauw made provisions in 1881 to establish a Methodist university after his death to be named after him. Upon learning of these provisions, the trustees of Indiana Asbury University, located in Greencastle, Indiana, approached DePauw and asked him to consider directing his bequest to Indiana Asbury University. DePauw agreed, and DePauw University became the name for this venerable Hoosier institution of higher education.[13]

Designed by architect and master builder George B.F. Cooper, the

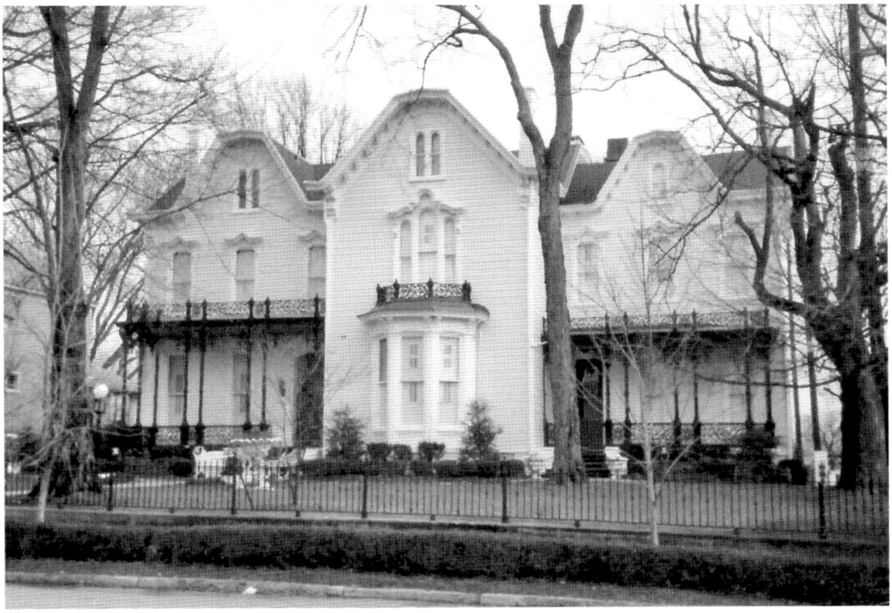

Designed by architect George B.F. Cooper, the 1870 Washington C. DePauw Mansion is one of New Albany's finest expressions of the Italianate style. *Barksdale collection.*

Washington C. DePauw Mansion is one of New Albany's finest expressions of the Italianate style. Sheathed in specialty siding meant to resemble blocks of stone, the house stretches linearly across multiple building lots for dramatic effect. A bracketed cornice; pediment window hoods; a central, projecting first-floor bay window with ornamental iron balustrade above; and elaborate cast-iron porches create a veritable feast for the eyes. A cast-iron fence with stone piers and retaining wall along with New Albany–manufactured Charles Hegewald Company planters and mature landscaping add to the ambiance of this historic property—one of the grand dames of Mansion Row.

CONNER-HEGEWALD HOUSE

716 East Main Street

This two-and-a-half-story frame house executed in a vernacular Queen Anne style was originally home to William C. Conner, proprietor of William C. Conner Wallpaper Company, located downtown on East Market Street.

Built in 1906, the house occupies land once owned by Washington C. DePauw, whose mansion stands next door to the west. In May 1918, the property was sold to Edwin C. Hegewald, secretary and treasurer of the Charles Hegewald Company, which was located on Water Street between State and West First Streets. The diversified company made a host of products, ranging from stationary to steamboat boilers, brass and iron castings to sheet metal and mill supplies. One coveted product was a decorative cast-iron yard planter whose scalloped planter bowl is supported by elaborate grotesque leg supports. These planters are still found in yards around New Albany, including next door at the Washington C. DePauw Mansion.

By 1939, Edward and Aldora Cummings had purchased the house. Cummings was associated with the E.M. Cummings & Son Veneer Company, still located on East Fourth and Oak Streets. In July 1942, the house was purchased by the Edward Flocken family, which continued to occupy the residence for the next thirty-two years.

The exterior of the Conner-Hegewald House features a hipped roof of standing seam metal with lower cross gables. In form, the house resembles other Queen Anne– or Free Classic–style dwellings popular during the last decade of the nineteenth and first decade of the twentieth centuries. Other examples include the Conner-Laub House at 321 East Ninth Street and the Henrietta (Borgerding) Slovensky House at 719 East Market Street, among others. Classical Roman Doric columns support a full-width front porch. An oriel window on the house's west side illuminates the interior stairwell.

DAY-KENNEY HOUSE

800 East Main Street

This Queen Anne–style dwelling, designed by New Albany architect Arthur R. Smith, is a near match to its neighbor at 716 East Main Street. Anthony T. Day, president of the Day Leather Company located at East Fourth and Oak Streets, purchased this lot in August 1908 from Newton DePauw at the cost of $1,500. DePauw, son of the late industrialist and philanthropist Washington C. DePauw, owned all of the property from 714 East Main Street to East Ninth Street. The month after purchasing the lot, Day hired local contractor Walter Weissinger to build this two-and-a-half-story residence, for $3,353, which was completed the following year. Anthony Day and his wife, Elizabeth, are first listed as living at this address in the 1909–10 *New Albany City Directory*.

In 1910, the Days' daughter, Nell, married New Albany native C. Elbert "Blue Bert" Kenney in the home. Kenney was a vaudeville and minstrel star who delighted thousands of theatergoers throughout the nation. After retiring from acting, he entered the radio industry and became a regular fixture on local WHAS radio in Louisville, Kentucky. The couple had a daughter, Juel Day Kenney. Sadly, the marriage ended in divorce in 1919.

Anthony Day died in June 1922 at the age of seventy-five, and Elizabeth remained in the home until she passed away less than one year later. Nell Kenney had come to live in the house with her parents after her divorce from Bert. She lived the remainder of her life here, passing away in March 1974. Nell's daughter, Juel, had married New Albany native and Hollywood writer Ray Allen in the early 1940s. Allen not only wrote for such Hollywood greats as Bob Hope, Bing Crosby, Dean Martin and Jerry Lewis but also worked in New York with early TV personalities Jackie Gleason, Jan Murray and Red Buttons. He also wrote the first *Tonight Show* for Jerry Lester.[14] Ray and Juel's marriage ended in 1962, and she moved back to New Albany and into her mother's home. Juel died at age seventy-four in June 1986, ending over

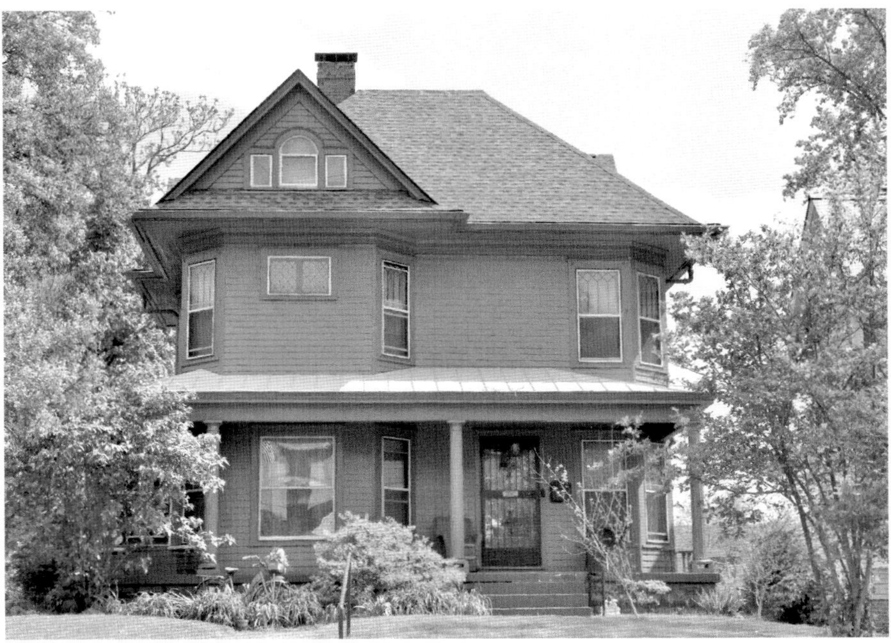

The Queen Anne–style Day-Kenney House is the work of New Albany architect Arthur R. Smith. *Gregory Sekula.*

seventy-five years of residency by the Day-Kenney-Allen family.

The most prominent feature of this vernacular Queen Anne–style house is its partial wraparound front porch with fluted Roman Doric columns. A two-story front bay, angled corner windows with decorative sashes with diamond-shaped muntins, a Palladian-style window in the front attic gable and a leaded-glass front entry door provide further visual interest to the house's front façade. A second bay window is found on the house's east elevation. The interior features original wood trim and an open staircase with paneled newel posts and turned balusters. Other interior features of note include stained-glass windows in the stair hall and dining room and a front parlor mantel with scrolled pilaster supports, a beveled-glass mirror and original tile work. The house's butler's pantry contains its original built-in cabinetry.

MOORE-DREYER-SCHROEDER HOUSE

815 East Main Street

This house, built in 1848, was a gift to Scott Moore and his wife, Mary Ann Conner, from Mary's father, John Conner. Moore was associated with the dry goods establishment of Conner & Company, located on East Main Street near Pearl Street. He would eventually own his own dry goods concern. In April 1869, the Moores lost their home as a result of foreclosure. The house subsequently saw a succession of owners, including the Blackistons, Trinlers and the Tablers. In June 1924, music professor Henry Dreyer purchased the property for rental purposes. It appears that a separate living quarter had been constructed in the upper floor of the house at that time. Professor Dryer had moved his concert band from neighboring Clark County, Indiana, into the Adelaide Packard Piano Forte School next door at 819 East Main Street in 1912. The school and band continued there until the 1940s. Edythe Dreyer, Henry's widow, moved into the apartment unit in this house in the late 1940s and lived here until her death in March 1961.

The Robert Schroeder family purchased the house in June 1962, and it remained in the Schroeder family for nearly fifty years. Mr. Schroeder was a parts manager for the old Craig Ford dealership located in downtown New Albany and, later, at the Jim O'Neal Ford dealership located in Sellersburg, Indiana. He also was an accomplished musician and woodcrafter. In June

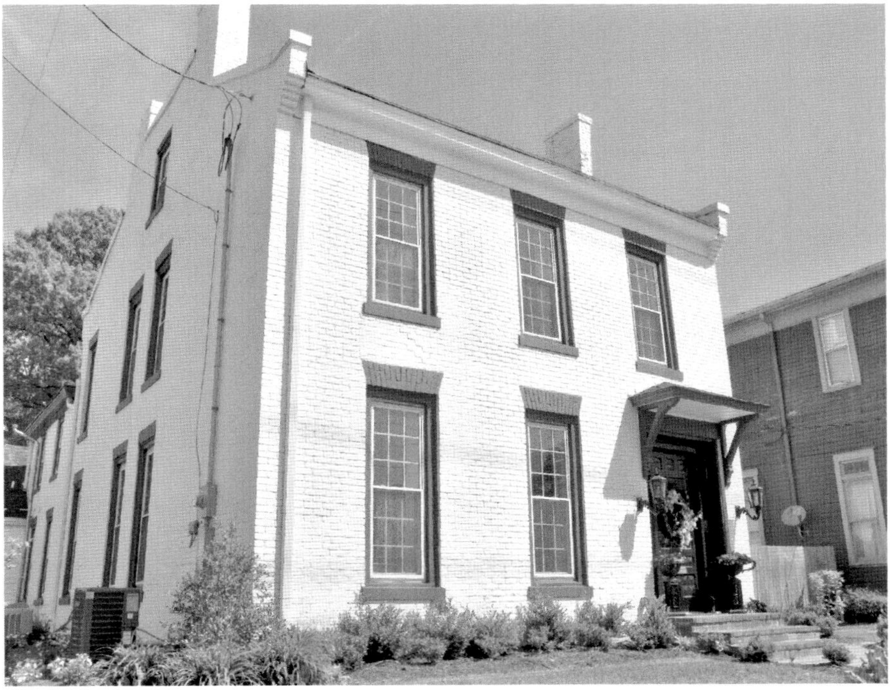

The Moore-Dreyer-Schroeder House was built in 1848 in a transitional Federal/Greek Revival architectural style. *Gregory Sekula.*

2012, Steve Thomas and Bob Jones purchased the two-and-a-half-story brick house and began an extensive rehabilitation.

The Moore-Dreyer-Schroeder House is a transitional Federal/Greek Revival–style town house. An unusual feature of the house is the presence of brick parapet walls at the side gable rooflines that span between the house's towering brick chimneys. Splayed brick lintels define the window openings on the front façade. A later Victorian multi-panel and glass entrance door is sheltered by a broad hipped roof hood supported by chamfered knee braces. A smaller scale door hood is located on the house's east side and shelters a pair of French doors leading to the entrance hall. The interior features its original cherry staircase and simple post-and-lintel wooden mantels in the parlor, dining room and second-floor bedrooms. Original compound Greek Revival–style moldings survive in numerous locations throughout the house. Newer built-in display cabinetry in the front parlor and the dining room complement the house's original architecture.

Culbertson West (Samuel A. Culbertson Mansion)

904 East Main Street

Standing just west of the William S. Culbertson Mansion and occupying half of the city block is the imposing brick mansion Culbertson had built for his son Samuel A. Culbertson and daughter-in-law, Louise Craig, of Pewee Valley, Kentucky, as a wedding gift in 1886. The couple was wed in April and moved into the house later that year after honeymooning in Europe. They would eventually have three children, one of whom would die in infancy.

Samuel Culbertson was born on August 15, 1862, the youngest of eight children born to William S. Culbertson's first wife, Eliza Vance Culbertson, who died of typhoid pneumonia in 1865. Astute in finance, Sam was elected cashier of New Albany's First National Bank in 1884 and remained in that position until 1892, when he became the bank's president. He also became president of the Fair Association. In 1894, he was elected director of the Union Trust Company in Indianapolis. Of interesting note, Samuel Culbertson had an apparent interest in theater and performed at the New Albany Opera House in the role of Lord Pish Tush in Gilbert & Sullivan's opera *The Mikado* to good reviews.[15]

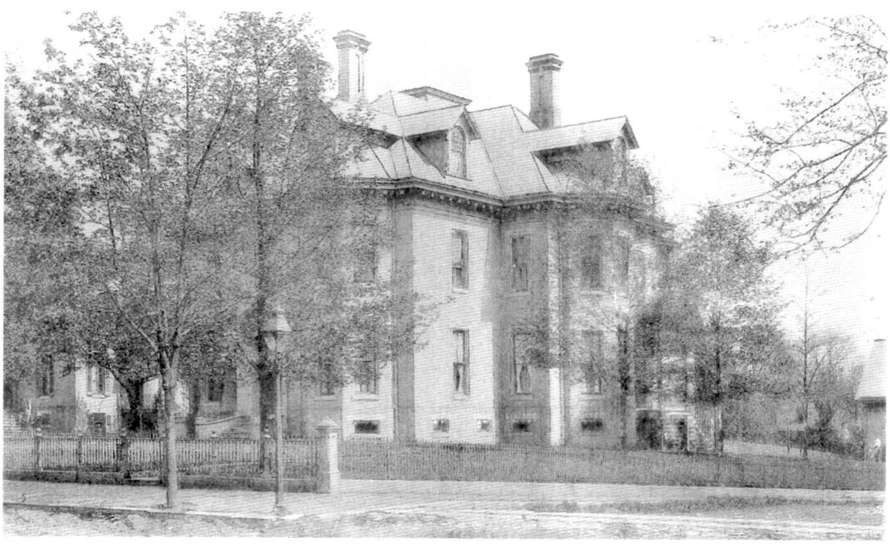

Samuel A. Culbertson's mansion, pictured here in 1893, was a wedding gift from his father, William S. Culbertson, in 1886. *From* Art Work of New Albany, 1893.

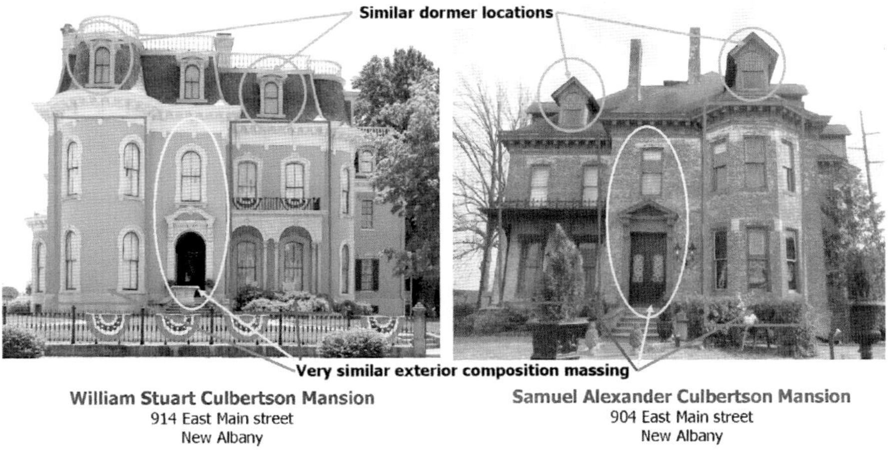

A comparison study of the Samuel A. Culbertson and the William S. Culbertson mansions. *Steve Wiser collection.*

In 1896, Culbertson purchased a lot on Third Avenue (now Street) in Louisville, Kentucky, and made plans to erect a new mansion on that site. In December 1896, the New Albany house was sold to Dr. John Hazlewood, and the Culbertsons, with their two sons, moved into their new Louisville mansion. Culbertson would go on to become president of the famed racetrack Churchill Downs in 1928 following his service on the board of directors of the Kentucky Jockey Club beginning in 1919. He remained president of Churchill Downs until 1937. It is Culbertson who is credited with conceiving the idea of the Garland of Roses that festoons the Kentucky Derby winner. The first Garland of Roses was placed on Kentucky Derby winner Burgoo King in 1932. Samuel Culbertson died of a heart attack in December 1948 at the age of eighty-six.[16]

In September 1939, the house was purchased by the Manzanita Tribe No. 276 Improved Order of Red Men, a men's fraternal organization, who used the house as its meeting facility and, in 1950, erected a large cinderblock Quonset hut-shaped structure at the back of the house for use as a recreation center. In 2004, the house was sold to Steve Goodman and Carl Holliday, who renovated the building as an events venue called Culbertson West, which continues to this day.

The work of architects and builders William and James Banes, the Samuel A. Culbertson Mansion is an architectural hybrid, blending both Queen Anne and Italianate architectural styles. With its complex hipped roof, gabled dormers, towering corbelled brick chimneys and multiple bay windows, the house, at first glance, embraces the Queen Anne style. However, below the roofline, the presence of a bracketed cornice, angular bay windows and incised-decorated window lintels harkens back to the Italianate style more popular in the 1860s and 1870s. Interestingly, a further study of the house shows a building mass nearly identical to the William S. Culbertson Mansion in the placement of the entrance, porches and bay windows. It is as if the house is a bookend to its neighbor to the east.

The interior of the Samuel A. Culberston Mansion retains a remarkable amount of original fabric despite its nearly seventy-year stint as a fraternal club. Most of the house's original woodwork with bull's-eye corner block detailing survives. At its far end, the mansion's central hall features a handsome open staircase with Eastlake-style newel post, originally topped by a light, and heavy turned balusters. The stair is illuminated by a large rectangular stained-glass window with multiple jeweled and faceted components in an arabesque style reflective of the Aesthetic Movement that was in vogue in the 1880s. A cased arched opening with sunburst motif at the archway corners frames paneled pocket doors that lead into the mansion's double parlors, which are highlighted by a central bay window and walnut fireplace with original hearth tiles and scrolled supports flanking hand-carved cranes in a marsh setting. An over-mantel with beveled-glass mirror, fretwork decoration and panels with a wooden basket-weave design provides further visual drama to the fireplace. The lower mantel is identical to one found in the 1892 Bruno Knoefel Residence and Drugstore located at 1417–19 East Spring Street. Both mantels may be the work of New Albany architect and wood carver Milton C. Pritchett, who trained in Cincinnati and whose skill is documented in a pulpit and communion table found in New Albany's St. John United Presbyterian Church. Other features of note in the interior include original paneled wooden window shutters, walnut mantels with over-mantels in the second-floor bedrooms, an entry vestibule with encaustic tile flooring and a third floor—virtually untouched since the date of the house's construction—with its original gas light sconces and built-in cabinetry. A large cast-iron Bridgeford & Company (Louisville, Kentucky) cookstove remains in the house's original kitchen.

Of note in the yard is an antique iron fence along the sidewalk, not original to the property, and a large cast-iron sculpture of a stag that originally stood in the front yard of the William S. Culbertson Mansion.

William S. Culbertson Mansion

914 East Main Street

In our era of supersized "McMansions," New Albany's most famous Victorian residence still provides the awe factor befitting the titan of business that called this edifice his home nearly 150 years ago. Designed by architects and master builders William and James Banes, the three-story brick mansion was begun in 1867 and completed in 1869 at a cost of $120,000. The mansion boasts twenty-five rooms with nearly twenty thousand square feet of living space. On Jully 11, 1869, the *New Albany Daily Commercial* provided a detailed exterior and interior room-by-room description of the mansion shortly after its completion:

> *The house is three full stories and a basement in height, the front elevation being 38 feet in height to the cornice, and 48½ feet to the top of the Mansard roof, and the rear 62 feet in height from the balustrades of the roof to the pavement. The house is composed of a centre building and two wings—one on the east and one on the west side. The style of architecture is a combination of the Anglo-French and modern Italian, and is very beautiful. The building is covered by a Mansard roof, the slates being of a dark brown color, and in fine contrast with the drab colored walls, and the stone coping, caps, &c. The roof is nearly flat on top, and is surrounded with iron balustrades, in fine harmony with the balance of the upper finish, and adding greatly to the general appearance of the edifice. Approaching the city by the river from either direction, this building is the central object of attraction, arresting the attention of the traveler at once by its beautiful location and commanding appearance. In these particulars it is more than an ordinary object of interest—for it is as much a master-piece of mechanical skill as it is a monument of modern architecture.*

A high-style example of the Second Empire architectural style, the William S. Culbertson Mansion is a tour-de-force of Victorian opulence, with its distinctive French-inspired mansard roof with slate shingles and rooftop balustrade, painted brick exterior, multiple bow and bay windows, stone-trimmed arched windows and bracketed and modillion block cornice. Unusual cast-iron arched spandrels with paired fluted columns and balustrade above embellish the mansion's front porch, while a double-tiered rear porch with chamfered wooden posts and turned baluster railing takes advantage of

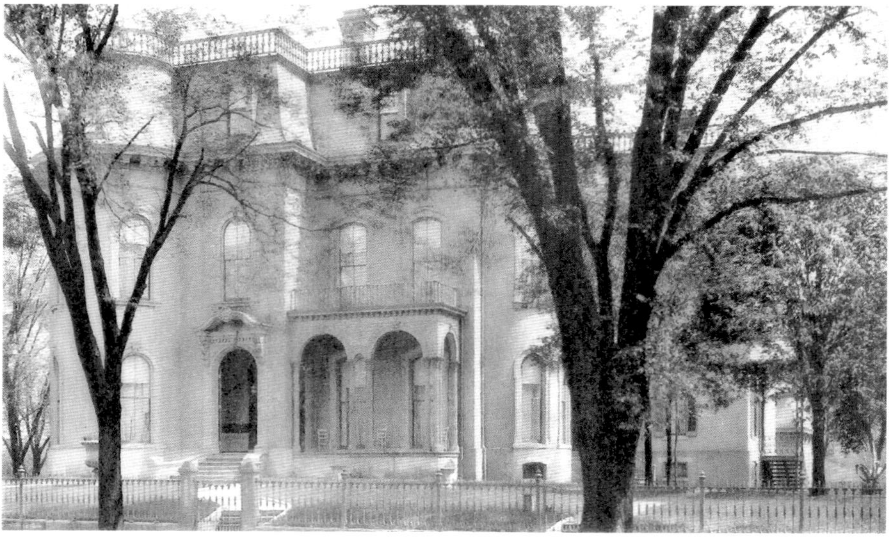

New Albany's most famous and imposing Victorian residence, the William S. Culbertson Mansion was completed in 1869 at a cost of $120,000. *From* Art Work of New Albany, 1893.

Ohio River breezes. A two-story mansard roof carriage house stands behind the mansion. An iron fence surrounds the house at the public sidewalk, and a large limestone urn graces the front yard. This lawn planter was returned to the mansion in 2010 after having been sold from the property in 1899, several years after Culbertson's death.

The interior of the residence features richly painted wall and ceiling frescoes with a plethora of colors, patterns and images in the Aesthetic Movement and Eastlake styles of the late nineteenth century. A spacious front hall terminates in a winding rosewood staircase rising three stories to the attic level. Crystal and brass chandeliers, ornate cast plaster ceiling medallions, interior window shutters and marble and wooden mantelpieces often fitted with French mirrors embellish the house's principal rooms and speak to the Gilded Age wealth that had now reached the shores of this most populous and influential of Indiana river towns of the day. A description of the house's drawing room from the 1869 newspaper account illustrates this:

> *We will enter into the magnificent drawing room, which is in front of the library, through a superb rosewood door from the main hall near the vestibule. And in this really palatial drawing room one is greeted by all that is perfect in art, elegance, and good taste. The room itself is 18½*

> *feet wide and 48 feet long. It is lighted by one large bay window and a swell front window, the latter on the main front and the former on the east side. Two rosewood doors open into it from the main hall and one from the library. The frescoeing and finish of the walls and ceiling are simply grand. To give one a proper idea of the mellow blending of the colors, the harmony of every tint, the perfection of border and solid body, with just enough of brilliance to relieve monotony and prevent gaudiness, would be an impossibility for the writer's pencil. Therefore we must be content to say that the artist had done a work worthy of a master's brush and pencil. The floor is covered by a magnificent Moquette carpet, imported from the celebrated house of Requilant, Roussell, & Chocques, Paris, through A.T. Stewart of New York. When the light from the gorgeous chandeliers is turned upon the carpet it brings out from the delicate, silky softness of the tufts cherubs and other figures which are only seen under the gas light. The curtains to the windows are the purest white lace, overhung with rich blue satin damask. The furniture is pure rosewood, beaded with gilt. Solid gilt chairs occupy spaces in the bay window. The covering of the furniture is blue satin damask. The mirrors are superb, of the richest and heaviest gilt, with molding finish and beautiful mountings of gilt ornaments. They reach from the floor to the ceilings. There is nothing in art that would add to their beauty or their elegance. The base of the mirrors is in the Corinthian style, with the upper finish in the Grecian. The ornaments are baskets of fruits and flowers. But to get a proper idea of the magnificence of this drawing room one must see it, for we cannot properly and fully describe it.*

A native of New Market, Pennsylvania, William S. Culbertson settled in New Albany and made his early fortune in the dry goods business, retiring in 1868 from that pursuit and investing wisely in other ventures, including the Kentucky and Indiana (K&I) Bridge Company, utilities and banking. He became one of Indiana's wealthiest and most powerful citizens. Active in civic affairs and philanthropy in New Albany and beyond, Culbertson used his considerable wealth to fund the establishment of a home for widows located at 704 East Main Street and referred to as the Culbertson Widows' Home. Later, he built a home for orphans on Ekin Avenue known as the Cornelia Memorial Orphan's Home, named in tribute to his second of three wives.[17] That structure was demolished in the 1960s.

William S. Culberston died in 1892, and the mansion was subsequently sold at auction to John S. McDonald for a fraction of its original cost—a mere $7,100. The McDonald family resided here until 1946, when the property was sold to a post of the American Legion. The legion used the house for its meetings and social gatherings until the early 1960s, when the property was threatened with demolition for a service station. Local preservationists, led by businessman Richard Stem, acquired the house in 1964 under the auspices of a newly formed group, Historic New Albany, Incorporated. In 1976, the State of Indiana accepted ownership of the mansion, operating it as a historic house museum under the supervision of the present Indiana State Museum and Historic Sites. The William S. Culbertson Mansion was listed in the National Register of Historic Places in June 1974.

Blessing-Malbon House

907 East Main Street

Nicholas Blessing had this frame town house constructed in 1848 adjacent to his cooper shop, which stood at the corner of East Ninth and Main Streets. Steamboat captain Solomon Malbon and his wife, Elizabeth, purchased the house in 1853. Captain Malbon became active in politics after retirement and eventually was elected mayor of New Albany. By the mid-1930s, the Clark family resided here. Mary Clark became the first woman appointed to the New Albany Board of Education.[18] Her sister, Annette "Nettie" Clark, was the head librarian of the New Albany Public Library from 1905 to 1944. During World War I, at the request of the Library War Service, the New Albany School Board allowed Nettie to serve at the Library of Congress in Washington, D.C., for which she was given responsibility for book service for sailors on all vessels and at small training stations.[19]

The two-and-a-half-story, side-gabled, frame, transitional Federal/Greek Revival structure has been well preserved on its exterior, retaining its nine-over-nine divided-light sash windows, louvered shutters and recessed entry with slender sidelights and arched fanlight window. A four-panel arched entry door is a later Victorian addition. The interior retains its original staircase with columnar-shaped newel post, slender attenuated balusters and cherry handrail. Flat paneled wainscot along the run of the stair is a modern addition but in keeping with the house's simple architecture. The front parlor retains its original woodwork and post-and-lintel wooden mantel, which is flanked by recessed arched bookcases. A Federal-style mantel survives and is found in the house's less formal family room located in a one story wing

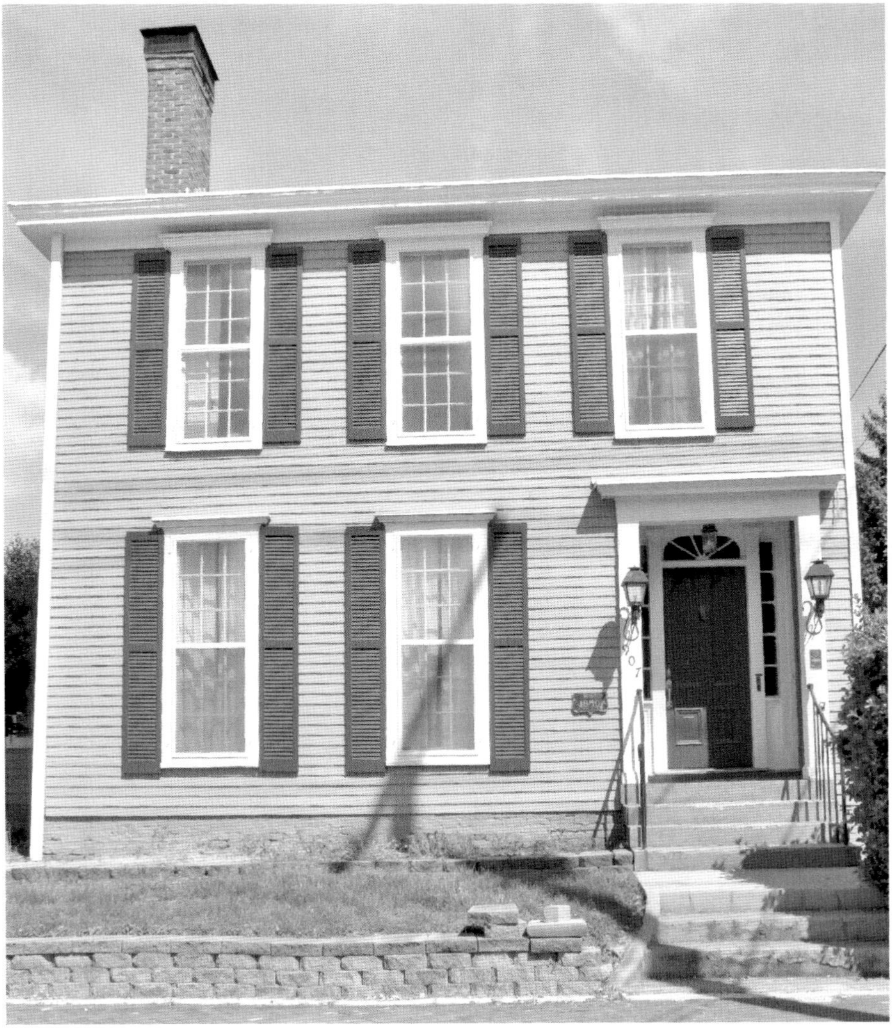

The 1848 Blessing-Malbon House is a transitional Federal/Greek Revival–style home. It was later occupied by steamboat captain Solomon Malbon. *Gregory Sekula.*

on the house's west side. The dining room contains a later Colonial Revival mantel with columns and a beveled-glass mirror. A built-in china cabinet is also found in this room. The upstairs front bedroom features an original Greek Revival wooden mantel.

Captain Charles Van Dusen House

913 East Main Street

This classic New Albany town house was built in 1853 for Captain Charles Van Dusen, a steamboat captain who owned the New Albany–built *Uncle Sam*.[20] Local tradition holds that Van Dusen desired his house to be built on high ground and that he had dirt hauled in to create the elevated lot that exists today.

After the death of Captain Van Dusen, John R. Nunemacher and his wife, Avesta Shields, purchased the house, and it remained in that family through 1927. The Numemacher's daughter Emma Shields Nunemacher was a prolific writer of poetry for many leading newspapers and magazines around the country in the late nineteenth and early twentieth centuries. In

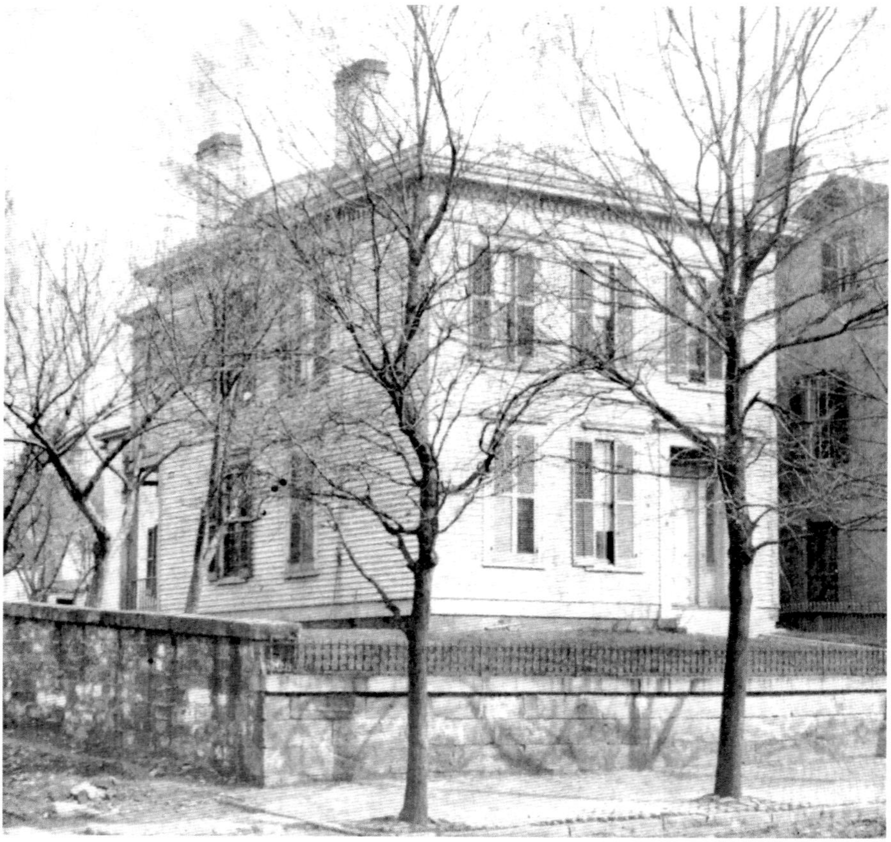

A circa-1880 stereo view of the 1853 Captain Charles Van Dusen House prior to the construction of its west side addition. *New Albany–Floyd County Public Library.*

1875, she married P.J. Carleton and moved to Indianapolis. She returned to New Albany following her husband's death and lived with her widowed mother and three sisters in this home. Emma Shields Carleton died at the age of seventy-four in 1924. Her obituary was published in the *New York Times* on December 31, 1924.

With its simple dentil work, wide frieze board cornice and recessed entry sheltering an original paneled door with narrow sidelights and three-part transom above, the Captain Charles Van Dusen House is a well-executed example of the town house form so prolific in New Albany during the mid-nineteenth century. A late-twentieth-century addition is found on the west side of the house, its setback position and shorter profile not detracting from the original mid-nineteenth century house.

James and Angelina Collins House

917 East Main Street

Built in 1852, this transitional Federal/Greek Revival–style brick town house was home to James and Angelina Maria Lorraine Collins. The couple was married in 1830. They moved to New Albany from Paoli, Indiana, and resided here for nearly thirty years. During that time, James Collins practiced law and was publisher of a family-owned newspaper. He also served in the Indiana General Assembly.

Angelina Collins, who had been a schoolteacher, is credited with writing the first published cookbook in the state of Indiana. *Table Receipts Adapted to Western Housewifery* was printed in 1851 by her neighbor John R. Nunemacher at his City Bookstore. A popular publication, the book was republished in 1857 in New York City under the title *The Great Western Cookbook; or, Table Receipts Adapted to Western Housewifery*. A devout Methodist and strong temperance advocate, Angelina Collins also authored a novel, *Mrs. Ben Darby; or, the Weal and Woe of a Social Life*, which chronicled in melodramatic fashion the hardships of a life of alcoholism. She also wrote poetry and was a passionate antislavery advocate. She died in 1885 at her son's home in Salem, Indiana.[21]

By 1865, Bela and Delphine Kent had purchased the house. Bela Kent was a partner in the wholesale grocery and produce establishment of Kent & Childs located in downtown New Albany. In addition to his business interests, Bela Kent once served as mayor of New Albany.

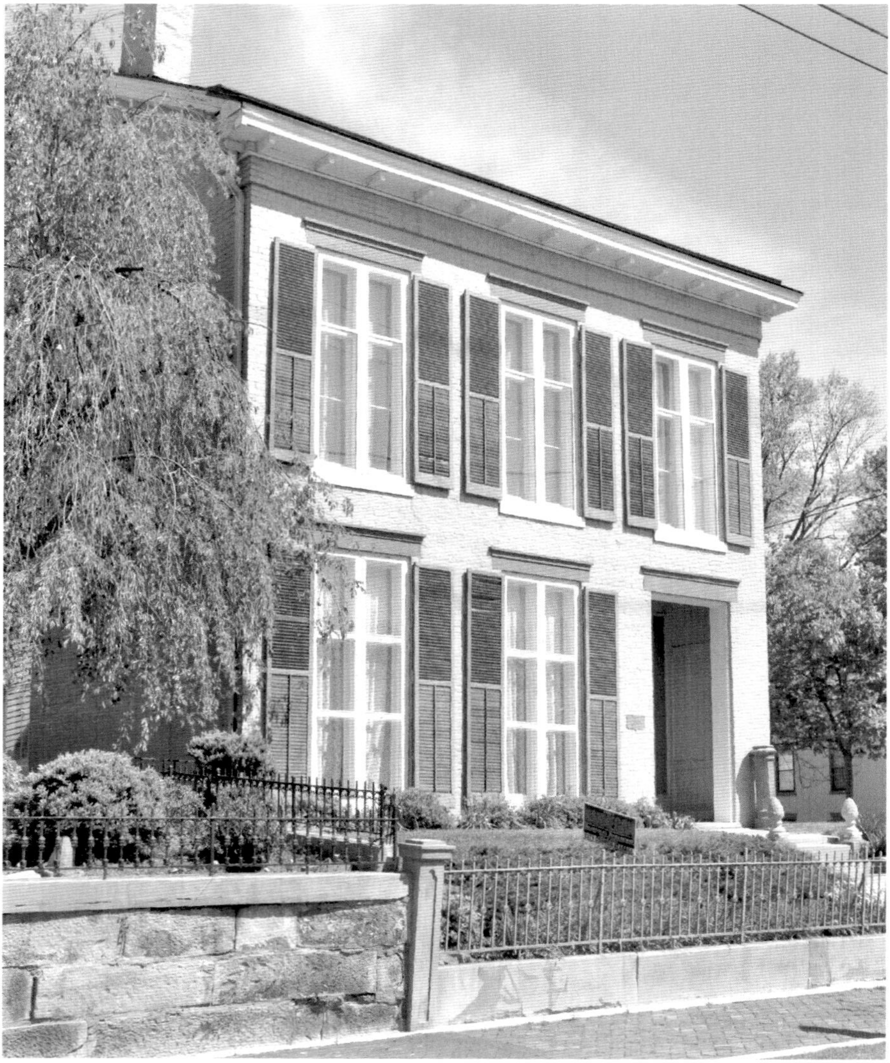

Schoolteacher Angelina Collins, writer of Indiana's first published cookbook, was the first occupant this home built in 1852. *Gregory Sekula.*

The James and Angelina Collins House, which is a documented work of Isaac P. Smith, features a simple bracketed cornice and unusual elongated façade casement-style windows. The windows on the first floor extend to the floor and give the house an elegant presence along East Main Street that is reinforced by the dwelling's elevated corner lot. Stone lintels embellish window openings on the façade as well as the recessed entry with its paneled and glass door.

Victor Pepin House

1003 East Main Street

The Victor Pepin House and the neighboring Kent-Ford House at 1015 East Main Street stand as New Albany's two finest examples of the towered Italianate Villa style. Their presence along East Main Street is made all the more dramatic by large lots that, taken together, compose an entire block of frontage along this historic street of standout residences. Constructed in 1854, this imposing brick mansion with central tower is based on a pattern book design by noted Philadelphia architect Samuel Sloan, whose publication *The Model Architect: A Series of Original Designs for Cottages, Villas, Suburban Residences, Etc.* was published in two volumes.[22] The house may be the work of William and James Banes, who are known to have built other dwellings in New Albany that were based on Sloan's designs. A shallow hipped roof with wide overhang on both the house and tower shelter a bracketed cornice. Brackets further adorn the house's front porch roof, which is supported by chamfered porch posts. Multi-light arched windows, arranged in pairs on the symmetrical façade, punctuate the main building block and give the house an airy presence. Further embellishment is achieved by an ornamental hooded balcony at the second-floor level of the tower and a group of three arched windows at the tower's third story.

The interior is on a grand scale. A large central hall with vestibule features period gasolier light fixtures, now converted to electricity, ornamented with dancing cherubs. The hall's signature feature is a winding staircase with walnut handrail and a turned newel post surmounted by a gilded statue of a classically draped woman holding a light resembling a torch. Deeply molded woodwork with shouldered architraves; hand-painted fourteen-foot-tall ceilings with plaster medallions and Neo-Grec and crystal chandeliers; parquet flooring; and marble, cast-iron and slate mantels adorn the spacious principal rooms on the ground floor. Heavy trim and cast-iron mantels adorn the second-floor bedrooms in the main block of the house. A partially open staircase leads to the tower room, which affords expansive views of the surrounding neighborhood.

Victor Pepin was the cashier of the New Albany Branch of the State Bank of Indiana located at Bank and East Main Streets in downtown New Albany. The Pepins only lived in the house for four short years before selling it to Sebre and Eleanor Howard for $25,000. This price included an additional fifty-foot lot on East Tenth Street. The Howards lost the house six years later

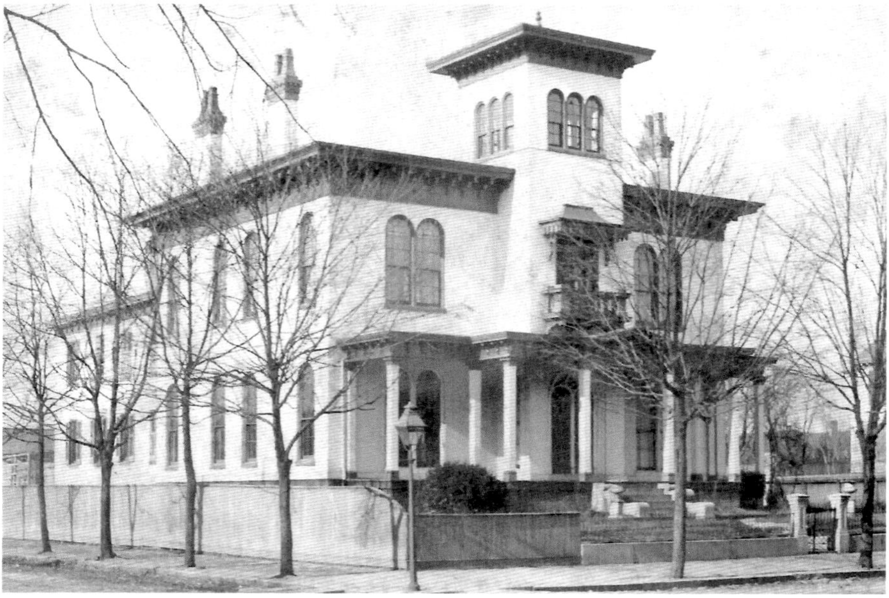

Constructed in 1854, the Victor Pepin House was based on a pattern book design by Philadelphia architect Samuel Sloan. *Cody Collection.*

to a bank foreclosure. In September 1863, John Cromie, a coal and lake ice dealer, bought the structure for $7,500. In 1887, August Barth purchased the home for $10,000. This began a tenure of nearly sixty-five years of the Barth family living here. Barth was the proprietor of the August Barth Tannery, located at East Tenth and Water Streets, just one block south of his house. He died in February 1902, but the tannery remained in existence until about 1985. Hugh Barth, the last Barth family member to live in the house, died in February 1950, and the home was then sold to the Turley family. The house became the Turley Nursing Home from the mid-1950s through the late 1960s. The property was later rented to Mary Muir as an antique shop, restaurant and residence before being purchased by several different owners in the intervening years. The current owner, Ron Smith, has rehabilitated the house as an events venue and bed-and-breakfast called the Pepin Mansion Historic Bed & Breakfast. A brick carriage home stands in the rear yard along East Tenth Street. Indiana Landmarks, a statewide historic preservation organization, holds a historic preservation easement on the property, which was donated by former owners Steven and Hays Hendricks, who owned the house from 1989 to 1996.

KENT-FORD HOUSE

1015 East Main Street

An architectural companion to its neighbor to the west and a likely Samuel Sloan design, this towered Italianate villa was built in 1854–55 for Phineas Kent, a well-respected New Albany lawyer.[23] The home later belonged to another prominent New Albany attorney, Randall C. Crawford. Around 1870, Captain John B. Ford, an entrepreneurial businessman who pioneered the production of plate glass in America, purchased the house.

Ford was born in Danville, Kentucky, in 1811 and apprenticed there as a local saddler at a young age. After running away from home following mistreatment by his employer, Ford eventually settled in Greenville, Indiana, where he acquired his own saddlery shop and became quite prosperous. While in Greenville, he also met his wife, Mary Bowker, who had also served as his teacher. By 1848, Ford had sold his saddle business and opened a general store. Following stints in the flour milling and furniture-making businesses, Ford moved to New Albany in 1854 and opened a factory to manufacture feed-cutting boxes constructed of wood and iron.

Needing a reliable source of iron for his box manufacturing business, Ford built his own rolling mill and foundry and, eventually, expanded his interests to the production of railroad and commercial iron products.

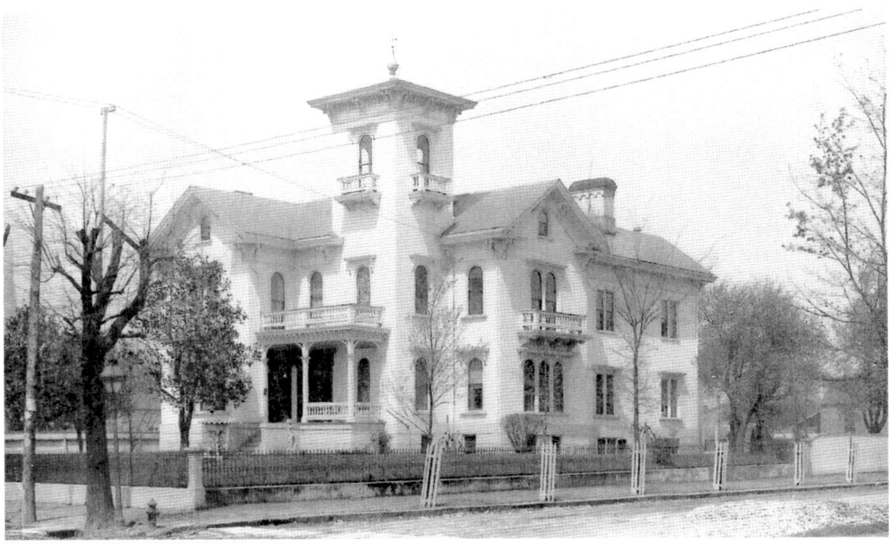

The Italianate Villa–style Kent-Ford House was built in 1854–55 for prominent lawyer Phineas Kent. *From* Art Work of New Albany, 1893.

By the late 1850s, however, he realized he could not compete with the industrial iron giants located in the iron regions around Pittsburgh, and he converted his factory into a shipyard to produce steamboats. New Albany's economy at this time counted steamboat manufacturing as one of its leading industries. Ford produced his own steamboat line and was addressed as "Captain Ford" by many of New Albany's residents. During the Civil War, many of Ford's boats were utilized by Union forces to transport troops down the Ohio River to help secure the Mississippi River from Cairo, Illinois, to New Orleans, Louisiana.

The decline of the steamboat industry due to advances in rail travel and transport after the war led John B. Ford to once again pursue other business endeavors. Capitalizing on the interest of Ford's son, Emory, who had visited several glass-making factories around Pittsburgh where he attended college, Ford and his son set up a small glass factory in New Albany known as the New Albany Glass Works, which produced bottles and jars. By 1867, the Fords had greatly expanded the factory and began to study the technology to produce plate glass, which until now was imported from Europe. In 1870, they had successfully mastered the technology and had the skilled workforce in place to produce the first plate glass in the United States.[24]

Financial troubles plagued the plate glass production, however, as the ability to transport the glass to distant population centers proved difficult and costly. John B. Ford eventually left New Albany and, after selling a patent on a glass sewer pipe and borrowing funds from a former employee and other investors, opened the New York City Plate Glass Company in 1880 with a plant in Creighton, Pennsylvania. In 1883, the business was reorganized as the Pittsburgh Plate Glass Company, which became one of the leading plate glass manufacturing facilities in the country.[25] Ford sold his interest in that company in 1897 but had also previously invested in a chemical company that supplied vital soda ash for the glass production. Located in Wyandotte, Michigan, Michigan Alkali Company, later Wyandotte Chemical Company, became one of the nation's leading chemical firms at the time of John B. Ford's death on May 1, 1903, at the age of ninety-one.[26]

The Kent-Ford House, now the parish house for St. Paul's Episcopal Church, is a two-and-a-half-story, L-shaped brick dwelling with low-pitched gable roofs and a three-story off-set tower with a shallow hipped roof ornamented with a metal finial at its peak. Paired brackets adorn the eaves of the structure. Arched windows with ornamental bracketed window hoods further reinforce the Italianate style of the house. The front entrance is highlighted by a one-story, flat-roof front porch with bracketed cornice, chamfered porch posts and a railing with heavily turned balusters typical of high style examples of the Italianate. A beveled- and leaded-glass front door, flanked by sidelights, leads to a large interior center hall plan house. Highlights of the interior include double parlors on the west side of the house featuring original mantels and heavy moldings. An open staircase in the tower features a heavily carved newel post and turned baluster railing. Behind the house sits a brick carriage house that was partially reconstructed following damage in a 2008 fall storm. That building has been repurposed as a community kitchen and multipurpose meeting space. The property is partially surrounded by an ornamental iron fence.

FERRY-MCDONALD-GREEN HOUSE

1014 East Main Street

Levi Ferry, a prominent New Albany businessman and insurance agent, purchased this property in 1865, and this imposing frame Italianate house was constructed the following year. In May 1869, the house was purchased by banker John S. McDonald for $10,500. Aside from his banking interests, McDonald was extensively involved in the pork packing industry in New Albany and was a partner in the New Albany Rolling Mills, located on West Water Street. After McDonald's death in June 1877, his widow, Nancy, remained in the house, except for a few years in the early 1880s, until her death in 1899. This ended a nearly thirty-year ownership of the house by the McDonald family.

During a brief period in the 1880s, the house appears to have been leased to General James A. Ekin and his family. General Ekin served in the Union army during the Civil War and worked in various leadership positions in the Quartermaster's Department of the United States Army. Importantly, Ekin also served on the military tribunal that heard the case against eight conspirators involved in the assassination of President Abraham Lincoln.[27] Ekin Avenue in New Albany bears his name today.

Henry Green purchased the property in May 1907, and it remained in the Green family through the 1940s. Green was vice-president of the

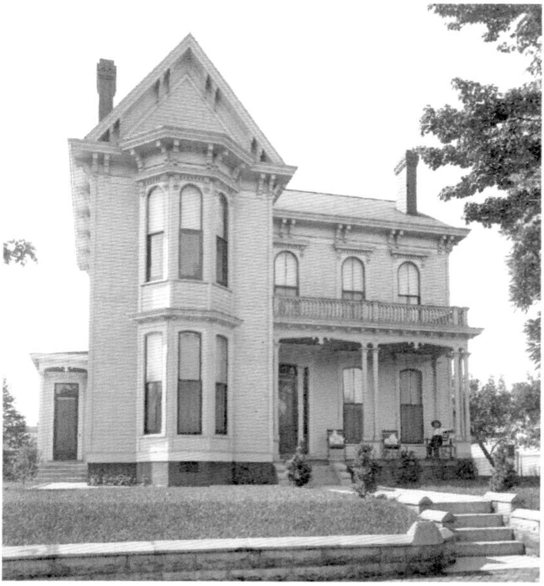

The 1866 Ferry-McDonald-Green House, as seen in this circa-1905 photo, is attributed to architects and master builders William and James Banes. *New Albany–Floyd County Public Library.*

Ohio Falls Iron Company, a complex that stretched over three blocks along West Water Street. His brother John, also associated with the business, and his sister Susannah (Sue) also came to live in the house with their brother shortly after he purchased the home. Sue Green was head nurse of the New Albany Chapter of the American Red Cross and the great niece of Florence Nightingale, founder of modern nursing.[28] After her death in June 1947, the home was divided into multiple apartments and remained so until the late 1970s. More recently, in the early 1990s through the early 2000s, the house served as a bed-and-breakfast and is presently a single-family home again.

With its gable-and-wing form, prominently sited front gable bay windows, paired bracketed cornice and hooded window and door surrounds, the Ferry-McDonald-Green House bears the hand of architects and builders William and James Banes, who designed the nearby William S. Culbertson Mansion, Culbertson Widows' Home and other notable residences in New Albany. Despite its past use as a multifamily dwelling, the interior of the house retains much of its original woodwork, open hardwood staircase in the front hall, mantels and even some of the original gasolier light fixtures hung from elaborate ceiling medallions, now converted to electricity. Several historic interior photographs of the house also survive, making the Ferry-McDonald-Green House one of the most historically documented houses in the city.

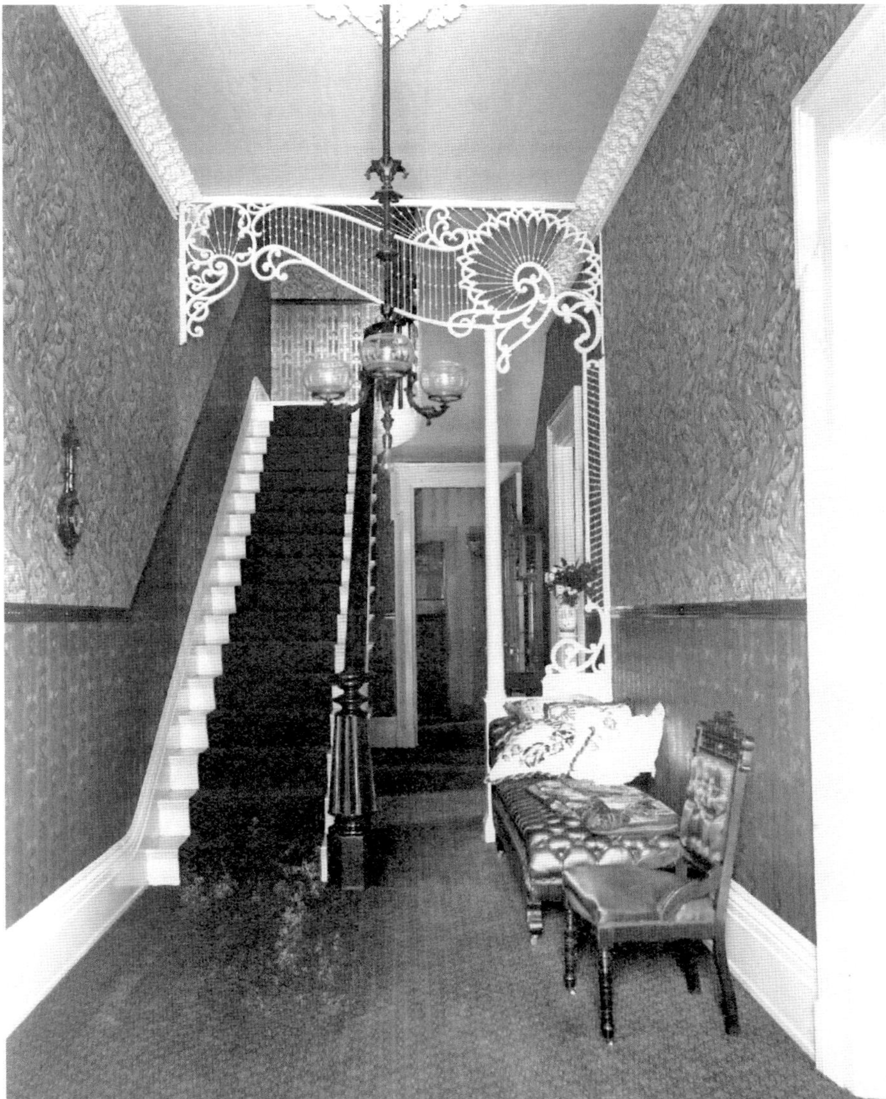

A circa-1905 image of the front stair hall of the Ferry-McDonald-Green House. *New Albany–Floyd County Public Library.*

KNOEFEL-SCHWARTZEL-LOFTON HOUSE

1103 East Main Street

Built for New Albany druggist and banker Charles Knoefel and his wife, Mary, this unique two-story brick house was constructed in 1896 by New Albany contractor John Nafius, who built the now demolished Vincennes and Shelby Streets School.[29] Knoefel was proprietor of Knoefel Drug Store and president of the New Albany Trust Company. Charles and Margaret Schwartzel purchased the property from the Knoefels in 1926. Charles Schwartzel was president of the New Albany Box and Basket Company and director of the Mutual Trust & Deposit Company. Their son-in-law, Isadore Marguet, also resided with them after his wife died. The house remained in the Schwartzel-Marguet family until the mid-1940s. By 1949, a service station was constructed and attached to the East Eleventh Street side of the house. It was not until 1979 that this inappropriate appendage was removed from the house when new owners Harry and June Lofton embarked

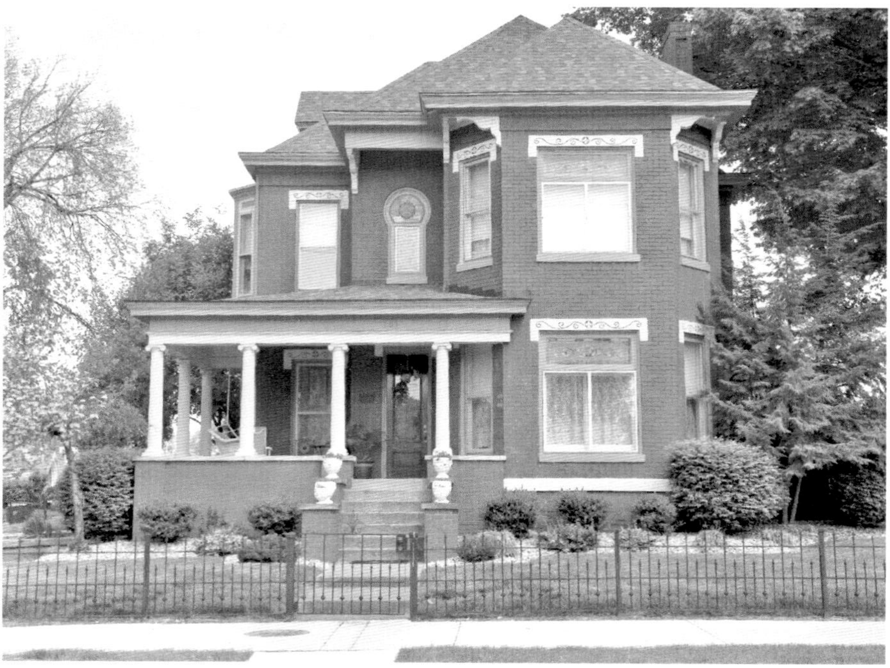

The Knoefel-Schwartzel-Lofton House is a superb example of the Queen Anne style of architecture executed in brick. *Gregory Sekula.*

on an ambitious restoration. Donna Stephenson purchased the property in 1999 and has continued to restore and maintain this East Main Street jewel.

The exterior of the Knoefel-Schwartzel-Lofton House features a pressed red brick exterior with a two-story projecting front bay window. Stone lintels with Eastlake-style incised carving ornament the house's door and windows. A partial front porch supported by fluted Ionic columns set on a stone-capped, brick knee wall shelters the front entrance. This porch replaced the house's original, wooden, rounded, front porch, which originally featured a conical roof section and second level supported by bracketed turned posts. The house's signature exterior feature is a unique "key hole" stained-glass window above the front porch. A copper-clad oriel window projects from the East Eleventh Street side of the house. Beveled- and leaded-glass windows are also found in the front bay, stairwell landing and dining room.

The interior of the house features original woodwork throughout, including pocket doors between the principal rooms and five-panel doors with ornate brass-plated hardware. Cherry-stained mantels in the front parlor and dining room feature foliated and classical motif carvings, beveled-glass mirrors and antique tile surrounds. Strip oak flooring with pattered parquet borders and an open staircase with paneled newel post and turned balusters add to the richness of the house's interior. A unique feature of the second floor is a corner tiled fireplace in the former nursery which retains an ornate cast-iron firebox insert.

Michael C. Kerr House

1109 East Main Street

Built in 1864, this imposing brick town house was first occupied by Michael C. Kerr. Born in Titusville, Pennsylvania, on March 15, 1827, Kerr attended schools in Pennsylvania before attending law school in Louisville, Kentucky. In 1852, he set up a law practice in New Albany and served as city attorney in 1854 and Floyd County prosecuting attorney in 1855. In 1856–57, he was elected to the Indiana House of Representatives. Beginning in 1865, Kerr was elected to five terms in Congress, eventually becoming Speaker of the U.S. House of Representatives on December 8, 1875. He died on August 19, 1876, in Virginia.[30]

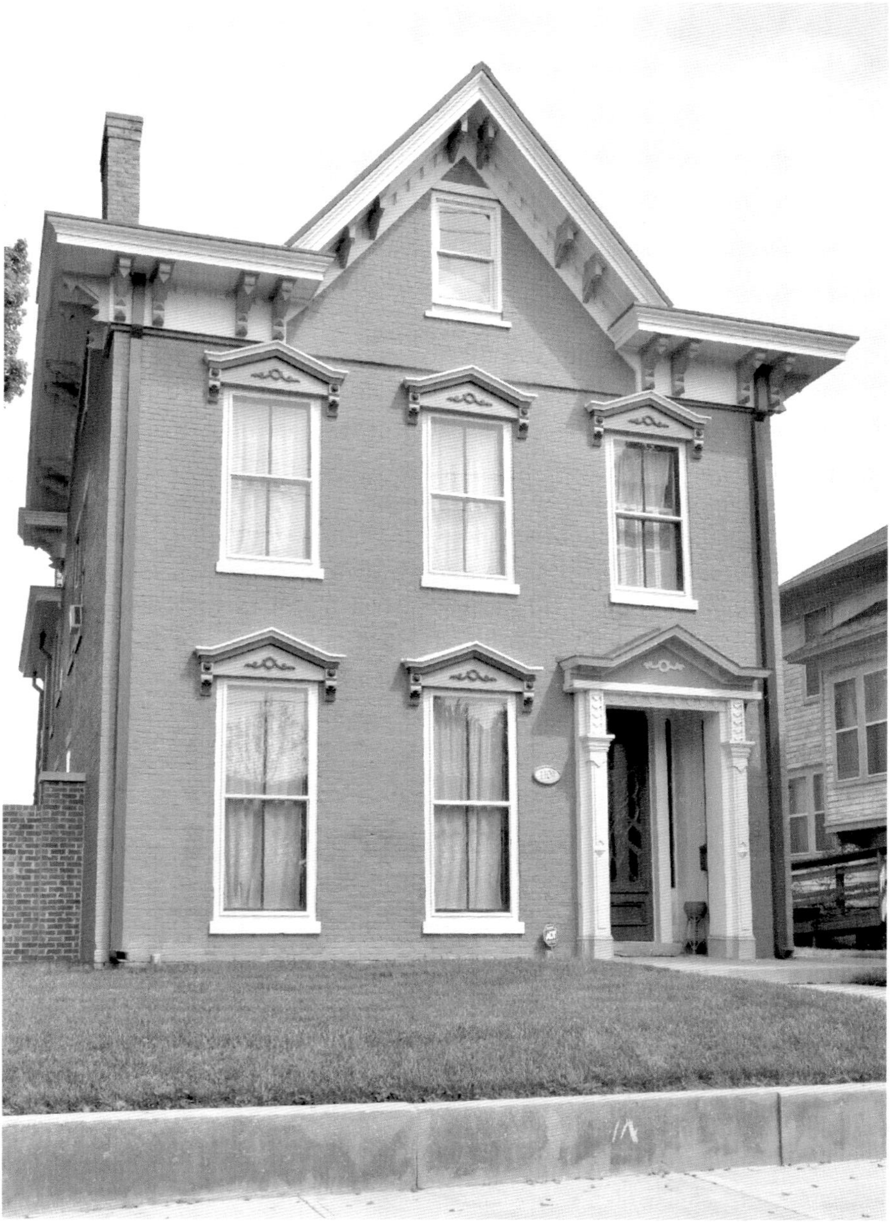

Speaker of the U.S. House of Representatives, Michael C. Kerr first occupied this 1864 Italianate-style town house. *Gregory Sekula.*

In 1886, the house was remodeled with the addition of the steeply pitched front gable, pediment and bracketed window hoods and front door surround, updated two-over-two window sashes on the façade and bracketed cornice. The house suffered greatly from deferred maintenance in the early 2000s and eventually was rescued from bank foreclosure by Eli and Alonna Beardsley in 2005. The couple embarked on an extensive rehabilitation of the house and earned a statewide preservation award in 2011 from the Indiana Department of Natural Resources, Division of Historic Preservation and Archeology.

SHIPMAN-MCCORD HOUSE

1206 East Main Street

One of Main Street's true mansions, the Shipman-McCord House is a sophisticated Italianate-style dwelling that was completed in 1866 for William Shipman, proprietor of the Phoenix Foundry, one of many shipbuilding suppliers in New Albany. Only two years later, Shipman sold his splendid estate to Robert G. McCord, who originally had been a partner of William S. Culbertson in a wholesale dry goods business on Pearl Street. McCord would later partner with businessman Lawrence Bradley in the same type of business.

McCord's largest business venture was the establishment of a woolen mill in 1866 with partners Washington C. DePauw, Lawrence Bradley and James Haines on Vincennes Street where New Albany High School is located today. By September 1869, the operation was merged with J.F. Gebhart's New Albany Woolen Mills, making the McCord and Bradley Woolen Mills "the largest establishment of the kind in the West."[31] The mill complex was subsequently destroyed in a tornado that swept through New Albany in March 1917—to date New Albany's most cataclysmic natural disaster after the flood of 1937.

The McCord family owned the East Main Street property until the early 1940s, when the house was divided into apartments. It remains a multifamily dwelling today. Despite being subdivided into apartments, the house retains its regal exterior appearance with its ornate cast-iron front porch, bracketed cornice, arched windows and projecting one-story bay window with iron balustrade above. An elaborate hooded entry with slender sidelights, arched transom window and front door with rare surviving etched-glass panel adds to the house's visual grandeur. The interior retains much of its fine

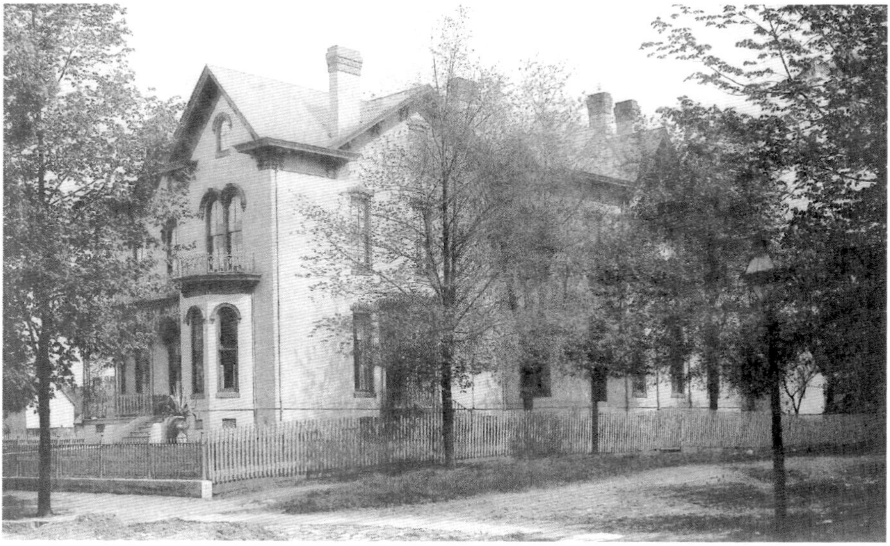

The 1866 Shipman-McCord House is one of New Albany's largest and most sophisticated Italianate-style dwellings. *From* Art Work of New Albany, 1893.

woodwork and the original hardwood staircase with turned newel post and classic balusters.

With its steeply pitched gables and gable-and-wing form, the house likely is the work of architects and master builders William and James Banes, who executed similar houses of brick and frame along East Main Street and other prestigious addresses in the city. The form of the house also conforms to a known pattern book design by Philadelphia architect Samuel Sloan from whom the Banes brothers are believed to have borrowed heavily. Of particular interest nearby for comparison is the frame residence of Samuel A. McClung, whose house directly to the west across East Twelfth Street is a bookend version in basic building form of the Shipman-McCord House.

JAMES MARSHEL HOUSE

1209 East Main Street

Constructed in 1863 in the midst of the Civil War, this imposing Italianate-style brick house was built for James H. Marshel, a wholesale dealer in coach and saddlery hardware and manufacturer of collars, harnesses and carriages.

The property remained in the Marshel family until 1875, when the house was sold to a New Albany physician, Dr. Elijah Newland. Subsequent owners were the McClean and Lapping families, both of whom were associated with the Wood-Mosaic Flooring Company that supplied parquet flooring throughout the country, including allegedly the White House in Washington, D.C.[32] The East Main Street home became a showroom for the display of different flooring types and patterns. Each room today features a different parquet design.

The exterior of the James Marshel House features a side-gabled roof with four large corbelled brick chimneys. A broad front façade features large double-hung sash set in shallow-arched windows with matching arched stone window lintels. A modillion block cornice is sheltered by a wide overhang at the house's second-floor cornice line. A center recessed entrance door with arched transom and flanked by sidelights is sheltered by a shallow arched molded entry hood supported by elaborate foliated brackets. A three-sided, one-story bay window topped with metal cresting is found on the house's east side.

The interior of the house features a wide central hallway illuminated by an original chandelier. An open staircase of mixed hardwoods is highlighted by a rosewood octagonal newel post topped by a figural spelter newel post lamp of a classical woman. Large first-floor rooms feature elaborate marbleized cast-iron fireplace mantels, original two-part molded wood trim and parquet floors,

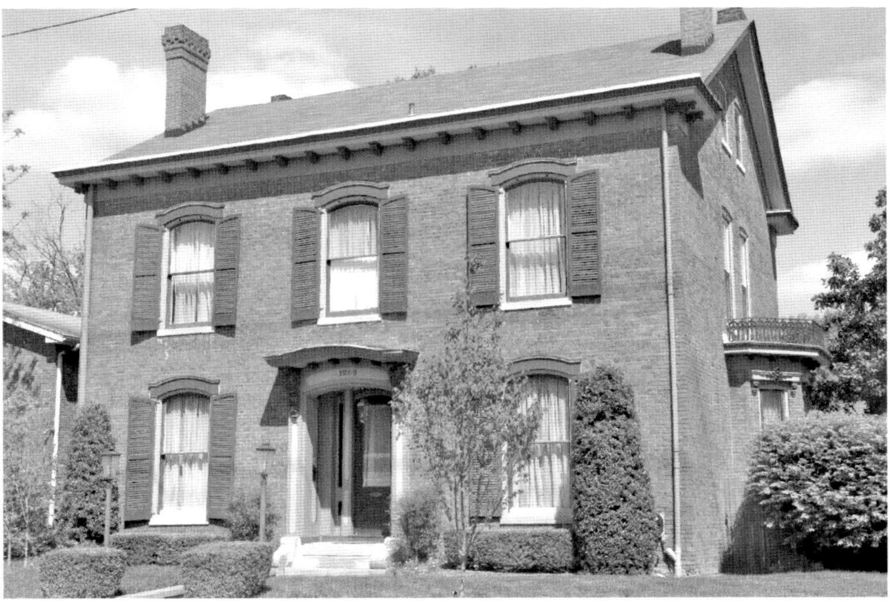

Constructed in 1863, the James Marshel House features a wealth of parquet flooring supplied by New Albany Wood-Mosaic Flooring Company. *Gregory Sekula.*

each room with a different design. Foliated cast plaster ceiling medallions, some of which retain original or antique light fixtures, are found in several rooms. Large gilded mirrors hang above the matching fireplaces in the house's large double parlor room on the east side. An oak paneled Arts and Crafts–style dining room with boxed beam ceiling provides an interesting contrast to the high style Victorian formality found in the rest of the house.

At the rear of the property is an original brick carriage house whose footprint has been enlarged with frame additions. Of particular interest is a Greek Revival door entrance that was salvaged by attorney Stephen Beardsley from the Conner-Jackson House at 1638 Dewey Street. This exceptional Greek Revival house was tragically razed in 1972. The lot on which it stood remains vacant today.

LOUIS BIR HOUSE

1218 East Main Street

This charming Queen Anne–style frame house was built around 1890 for the Louis Bir family. Bir, a prominent New Albany businessman, was proprietor of the Louis Bir Lumber and Manufacturing Company founded in 1882. The company, with its unforgettable slogan "Lum-Bir," supplied southern Indiana residents with building materials for almost ninety years. Its lumberyard was located on the northeast corner of East Thirteenth and Main Streets, a site now occupied by three brick bungalows at 1301 and 1305 East Main and 210 East Thirteenth Streets, that were built for other members of the Bir family. The two-and-a-half-story Queen Anne–style frame house at 1401 East Main Street is also a Bir home. The lumber business was later relocated to East Thirteenth and Dewey Streets, where it remained until 1970. This house remained in the Bir family until 1937, when it was purchased by the Bonnie Sloan Post of the American Legion. The house saw a variety of other commercial uses before being converted back to residential use by present owners Tim and Elizabeth Young.

Notable features of the Bir House include the full-width porch with early twentieth-century cast-concrete fluted Scamozzi Order columns and railing with heavy turned balusters. A two-story bay window features prominently on the house's East Thirteenth Street elevation and is adorned with brackets at the second-story eaves. The detailing is repeated on the second-story bay

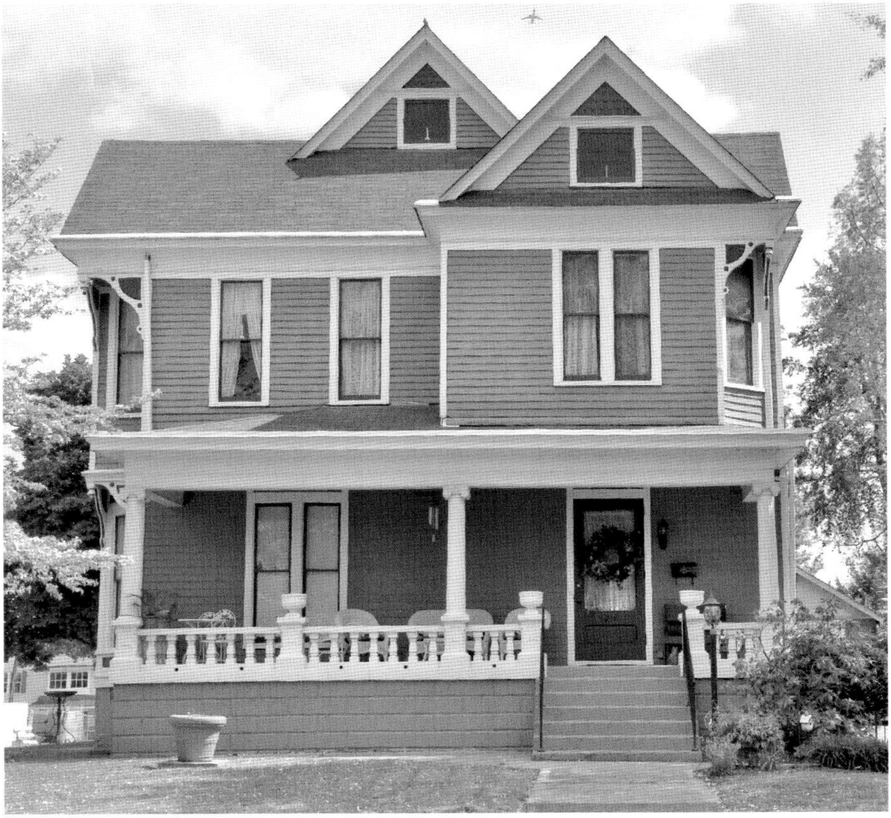

Lumber dealer Louis Bir had this frame Queen Anne–style residence built around 1890. *Gregory Sekula.*

window on the front façade. A notable feature is an oculus window on the house's west elevation containing stained glass in a floral motif. This window, along with a larger rectangular window above, illuminates the house's Eastlake style staircase in the front entry hall.

WARREN-MORRILL HOUSE

1309 East Main Street

Built in 1854, this brick town house was constructed by architect and builder Isaac P. Smith for Franklin Warren, mayor of New Albany from 1856 to

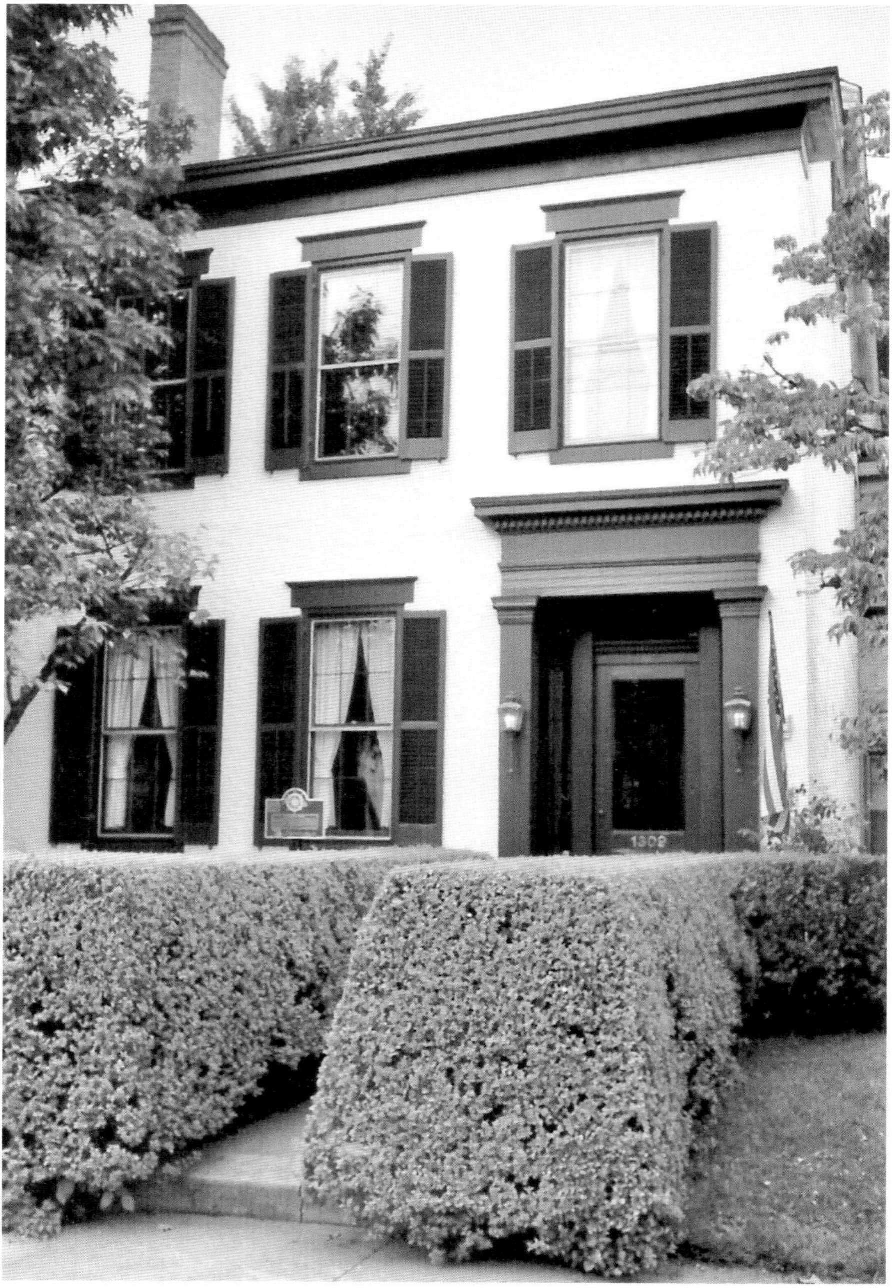

Franklin Warren, mayor of New Albany from 1856 to 1859, had this Greek Revival–style town house built in 1854. *Barksdale collection.*

1859. In addition to his political career, Mayor Warren was involved in the business venture of Plumer, Bushnel & Warren, iron dealers and ship chandlers. Warren later became a partner in the agriculture and seed store of Goulding & Warren. He was also a director of the First National Bank, one of New Albany's early banking establishments.

By 1865, Dr. Wilbur and Mary Crawford Morrill had purchased the home, and it remained in their possession for nearly forty-five years. Dr. Morrill was a dentist in New Albany. His wife was the daughter of prominent New Albany lawyer Randall C. Crawford. When essayist and poet Ralph Waldo Emerson lectured in New Albany on February 14, 1866, he visited with the Morrill family and spent the night here.[33]

Subsequent owners of the house included the Spalding and Conner families. In the early 1940s, James and Marie Montgomery became the owners of the house. James Montgomery was president of the Tribune Company, Incorporated, until his death in the late 1940s. Marie Montgomery remained in the home until her death in 1969. The home was later owned by Mike and Sally Newkirk. Sally Newkirk is executive director of the Carnegie Center for Art & History in downtown New Albany, which is housed in the city's former Carnegie Library.

The Warren-Morrill House is a notable example of a Greek Revival–style town house with its recessed side hall entry door framed with a heavy entablature and simple pilasters with crown detailing. Six-over-six wooden window sashes are highlighted by rectangular lintels and louvered shutters—a feature so often lost on historic homes. Original woodwork, mantels, period light fixtures and strip oak flooring contribute to the overall ambiance of this classic New Albany residence.

JOHN H. STOTSENBURG HOUSE

1407 East Main Street

Local attorney and later judge John H. Stotsenburg purchased this lot for $1,000 in July 1867 and, as was reported in the *New Albany Dailey Commercial* on August 4, 1867, ordered a house from Chicago, Illinois, to be erected on the site:

> *We have heard that the new residence of Mr. John H. Stotsenburg is to be built entirely in Chicago, with the exception of the sills. All the frame*

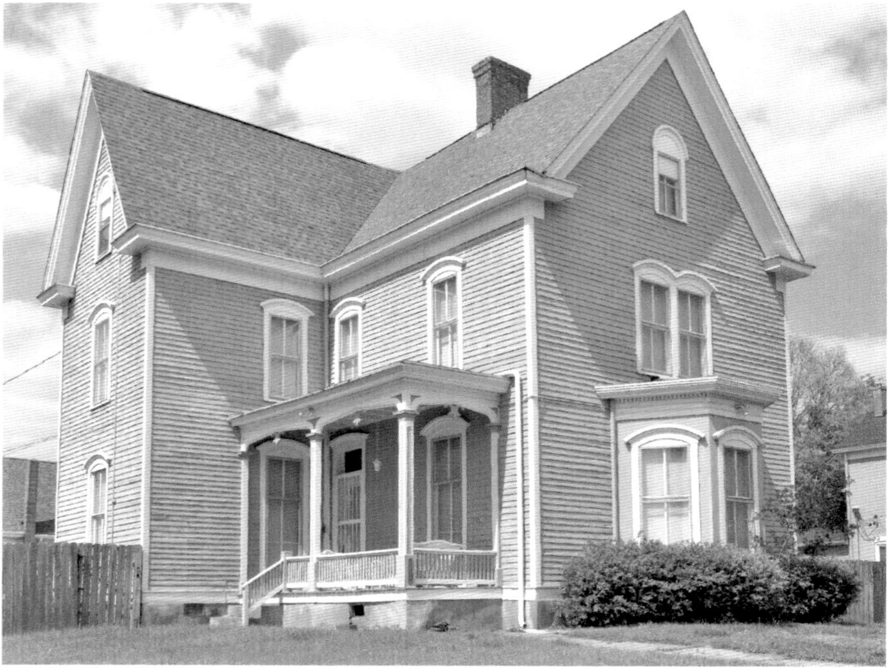

The John H. Stotsenburg House was ordered from Chicago, Illinois, and erected on this site in 1867. *Gregory Sekula.*

> *work, windows, doors, and indeed, everything connected with the building have been contracted for in that city. This shows what Yankee enterprise, combined with improved machinery, can effect for Chicago; it will also show our mechanics that they must look out lest these Northerners usurp their laurels.*

Judge Stotsenburg and his wife, Jennie, had been married in her hometown of Constableville, New York, in December 1857. The couple moved to New Albany shortly thereafter and raised four children in the house, including Colonel John M. Stotsenburg, who was a soldier in the regular army and was killed while leading his regiment in a charge in the Philippines. Their son Evan practiced law with his father and made his home here until his marriage to Zenobia Borden of Washington, Arkansas, in 1892. The couple had a new home built on prestigious Cedar Bough Place, a private street in New Albany. They only lived there a few years, however, before returning to the East Main Street house in February 1897. Evan's law firm of Stotsenburg & Weathers would eventually employ up-and-coming attorney Sherman

Minton in the early 1920s. Born in Georgetown, Indiana, Minton would later serve as a U.S. Supreme Court justice. Evan Stotsenburg would become Indiana's attorney general, a member of the Indiana Senate and House of Representatives and, in later years, Indiana's state highway commissioner.[34]

Jennie Stotsenburg died suddenly in December 1901 while on a trip to Washington, D.C., to visit her sister and daughter-in-law. Judge Stotsenburg remained in the residence, passing away in the house in June 1909 at the age of seventy-eight. Evan Stotensburg died in August 1937, and his widow remained in the house until the early 1940s when she moved to Sunset Drive in the fashionable Silver Hills neighborhood of New Albany. The home was then divided into apartments and remained so until Dana and Suellen Kolter purchased the structure in 1988 and returned the house to a single-family dwelling.

The two-and-a-half-story John H. Stotsenburg House is characterized by a steeply pitched cross-gabled roofline with a one-story bay window dominating the house's front façade. Segmental-arched hoods ornament the house's window openings, and a wide unadorned frieze board is located at the eaves. A front porch is embellished with squared columns supporting shallow arches with pendants. The front door, topped by a single-light transom, opens into a spacious entry hall featuring an open staircase with octagonal mahogany newel post and turned balusters at the railing. Strip oak flooring highlighted by an inlaid border is found in the entrance hall. Similar flooring is found throughout much of the house, and the original two-part molded woodwork and six-panel doors also remain throughout. A wide cased opening leads into the front parlor, which includes a large bay window with a built-in bench supported by delicate turned legs. The focal point of the room is a Colonial Revival wooden mantel with fluted Scamozzi Order columns. An older, Eastlake-style over-mantel with three-part mirror and panels with incised floral ornamentation rests on top of the mantel. The house's dining room contains a built-in china closet.

SCOTT-MCKIERNAN HOUSE

1417 East Main Street

David and Sophronia Scott purchased two lots from David Cadwalder in July 1864 for $1,600 and built this brick town house. As early as 1848, David Scott was a chair maker for Hugh Nesbitt of New Albany. By the time of house's construction, Scott was a partner with John W. Brindley in the business venture of Scott & Brindley, manufactures and dealers in furniture, located on West Main Street between State and West First Streets. The Scotts lived here only briefly before selling their home to George McKiernan in December 1866 for $8,000. McKiernan was secretary of the newly formed Jeffersonville, Madison & Indianapolis Railroad, a product of the 1866 merger of the Indianapolis & Madison Railroad with the Jeffersonville Railroad. This railroad came to New Albany in 1866 and was owned and operated by the Pennsylvania Railroad. Both the passenger and freight stations were located south of East Main Street between State and Pearl Streets.

The exterior of the Scott-McKiernan House features ornamental window hoods and a recessed front entry door. A large addition by prominent New Albany builders Stephen Day & Son was added to the east side of the structure in 1895 at a cost of $1,200. The addition features an engaged porch with brick arches that were subsequently enclosed as a sun porch. The recessed entry door leads to a front hall with an open staircase with octagonal newel post and turned spindles rising above a paneled wall. An arched, Queen Anne–style window with colored-glass squares framing a

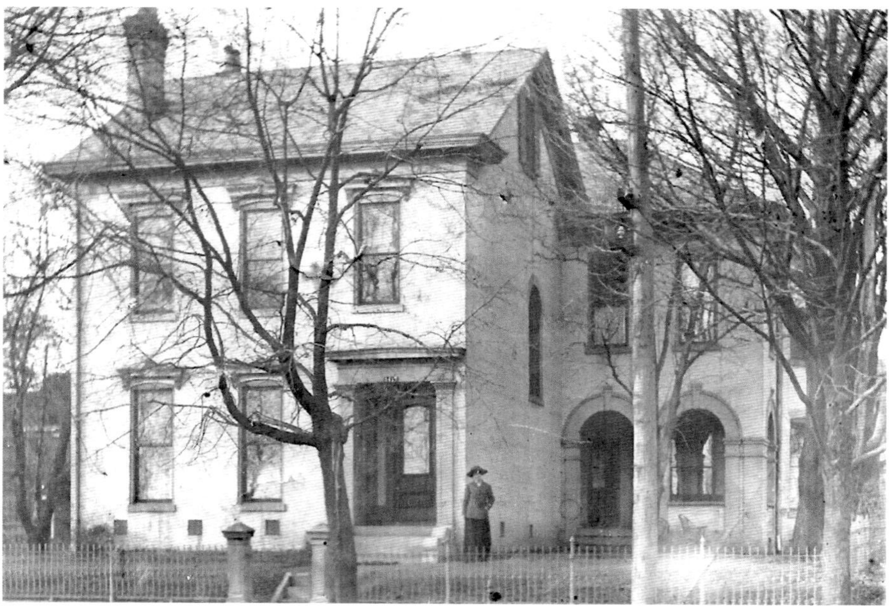

This 1913 postcard image of the Scott-McKiernan House shows the 1895 east side addition by New Albany builders S. Day & Son. *Barksdale collection.*

clear glass center pane illuminates the stairwell. The front parlor features a black marble mantel and two-part molded woodwork. Simple wooden post-and-lintel mantels in the Greek Revival taste are found in other rooms on the first and second floors.

Brown-Hunt House

1613 Dewey Street

Located in New Albany's Dewey Heights neighborhood, the Brown-Hunt House is a significant Gothic Revival–style residence that is believed to be a mid-nineteenth century pattern book house designed by famed landscape and building designer Andrew Jackson Downing (1815–52). The house, with its distinctive steeply pitched centered gable and hipped roof configuration, closely resembles in its basic form the cottage residences promoted and popularized by Downing in his landmark publication *Victorian Cottage Residences*, first published in 1842 with numerous editions through 1873. Similar pattern book examples can also be found in his 1850 publication, *The Architecture of Country Houses*.

The property on which the Brown-Hunt House sits was purchased by William Brown in July 1835 from Epaphras Jones, founder of the town of Providence, in which this lot lies. The town, initially conceived by Jones as a rival to New Albany, was founded in 1820 with building lots being advertised for sale by February 1821.[35] Jones had great expectations for the new community, with its main thoroughfare being Vincennes Street. He laid a series of streets perpendicular to Vincennes Street and began selling house lots. Unfortunately for Jones, the town was never officially incorporated. It later was annexed as part of New Albany.[36]

The Brown family never resided in the home but continued to own the property until it was sold to Mary Birtles in 1909. The Birtles family lived in the Dewey Heights area but apparently only used the house for rental purposes. Mary Birtles sold the home to Wesley M. Hunt in September 1918, and the Hunt family remained in the house until the late 1920s. Wesley Hunt was a telegraph operator for the B&O Railroad system. The house has subsequently had numerous owners in the intervening eighty years.

In the spring of 2008, the Brown-Hunt House, by then covered in aluminum siding and stripped of its exterior ornamentation, sustained

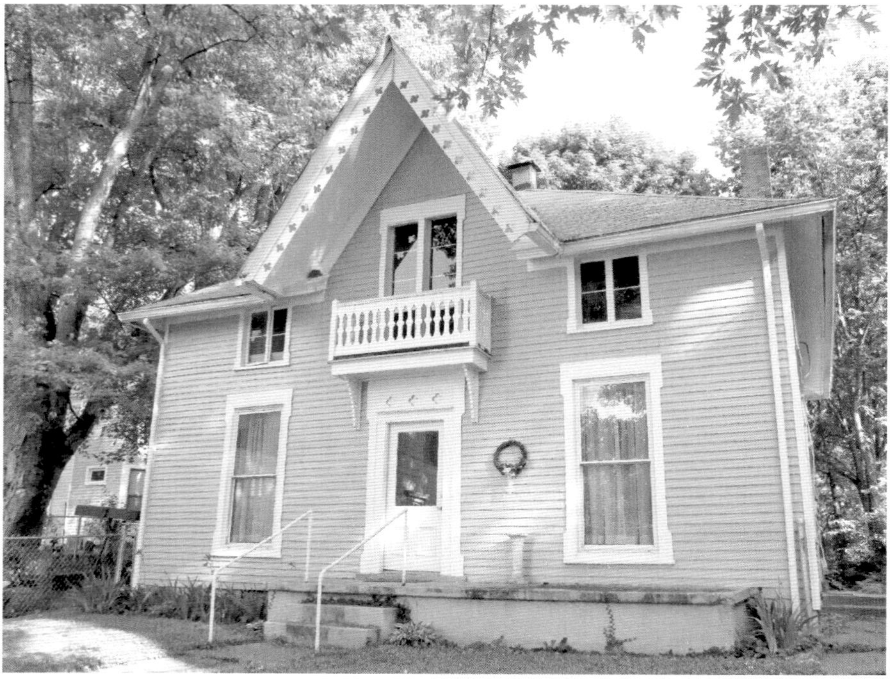

The Gothic Revival–style Brown-Hunt House is believed to be a mid-nineteenth-century pattern book house by building designer Andrew Jackson Downing. *Gregory Sekula.*

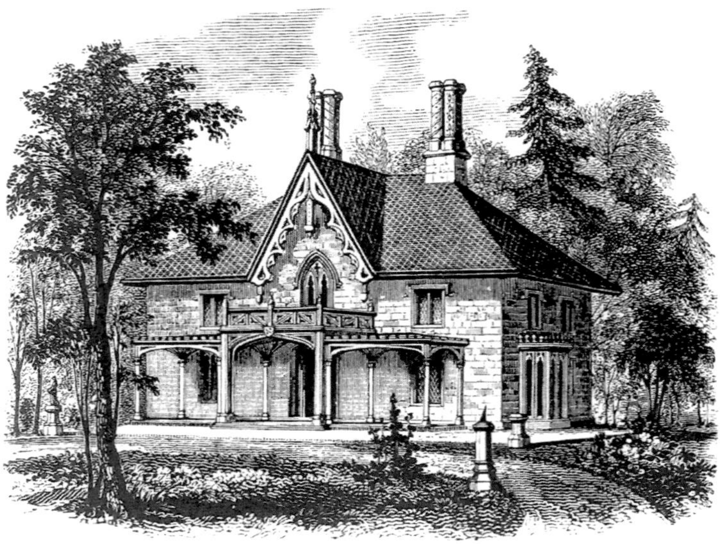

An image from Andrew Jackson Downing's *Victorian Cottage Residences* shows a close resemblance to New Albany's Brown-Hunt House. *Dover Publications, 1981.*

damage in a fire that gutted the second floor of the home. The property was subsequently donated to New Albany/Floyd County Habitat for Humanity, which sold the property after placing a preservation easement on the house with Indiana Landmarks, a statewide, nonprofit historic preservation organization. In 2014, after a buyer of the property failed to make timely repairs, Indiana Landmarks acquired the property and completed an interpretive exterior restoration of the house, removing the aluminum siding and installing decorative bargeboard with a quatrefoil design in the steeply pitched front gable of the home and rebuilding a decorative balcony above the front door based on visual evidence remaining on the siding. The house was subsequently sold to a buyer who is presently rehabilitating the interior for owner-occupancy.

DAVID HEDDEN HOUSE

1626 Dewey Street

The last remaining of three large estate properties that once graced the south side of the 1600 block of Dewey Street, the David Hedden House is an imposing Italianate-style residence that is believed to be the work of famed architects and builders William and James Banes. In plan, the house exhibits the gable and wing form characteristic of the Banes brothers' work, but its footprint extends to the west with an additional two-story section where a formal stair hall wing is incorporated. The house bears a striking resemblance to a pattern book house by noted Philadelphia architect Samuel Sloan whose Italian Villa–style dwellings may have been the design inspiration for several New Albany houses built by the Banes brothers. In the case of the David Hedden House, the Banes design does not include a three-story square tower seen in Sloan's example highlighted in his two volume publication *The Model Architect*. The David Hedden House also incorporates a more modest one-story brick wing on the east side of the residence. This one-story eastern section of the house bears earlier construction techniques, suggesting that it may be the remnants of an earlier dwelling on the site built by Epaphras Jones who established this area as a new town called Providence in 1820.

David Hedden purchased the property known as Mount Pleasant in 1852 and eventually built a larger residence here in 1867.[37] Hedden had

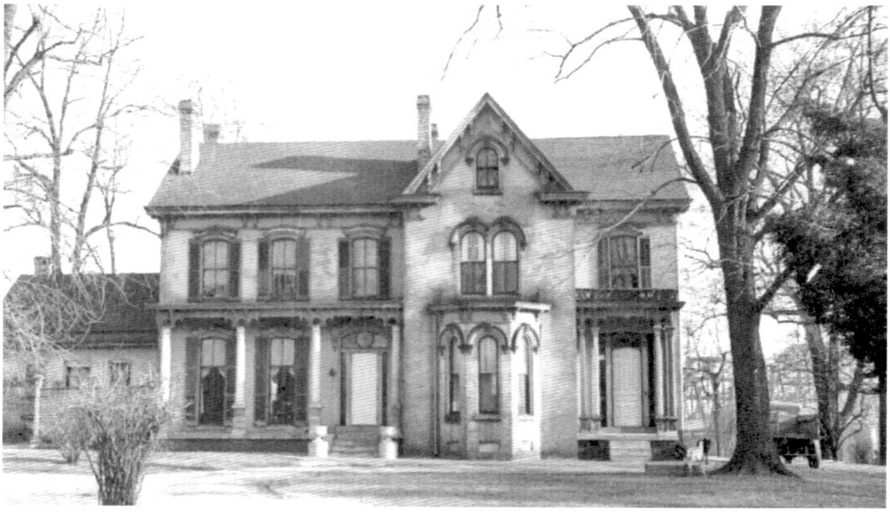

The 1867 David Hedden House, shown in this circa-1945 photo, is the last large estate property along New Albany's Dewey Street. *New Albany–Floyd County Public Library.*

arrived in New Albany in 1820 and began working in several dry goods houses in town. He eventually had his own company located in downtown New Albany. He also farmed and owned land off Charlestown Road that became known as Hedden's Grove. This tract was eventually sold and platted for residential development along two main streets named Hedden Court and Hedden Park. Today, that residential enclave is listed in the National Register of Historic Places.

The David Hedden House features solid masonry construction with a steeple pitched front gable with a one-story bay window with paired bracketed cornice and arched windows with heavily molded window hoods. Paired bracketing continues along the main cornice line of the two story sections of the house. Full and segmental arched windows with molded hoods further define the street-facing façade of the house. Two main entrance doors with sidelights and arched transoms are sheltered under one-story porches with bracketed cornices. Early twentieth-century cast-concrete columns replace what originally were chamfered square porch posts.

Highlights of the interior of the David Hedden House include a stair hall with winding walnut staircase ornamented with a figural newel post light of the goddess Diana. Arched cast-iron fireplaces are found in the double parlors and dining room. Two-part molded woodwork, paneled pocket doors and twelve-foot ceilings on the first floor endow the house with a sense of grandeur.

3

East Market Street

Like its neighbor East Main Street to the south, East Market Street developed as a fashionable residential address as the town grew and prospered in the 1830s and 1840s. In downtown New Albany, Market Street became the hub of the city's local commercial activities, boasting two covered block-long open markets located in the center of the street in the blocks flanking State Street. In the blocks extending to the east of downtown, in particular, commercial buildings gave way to residential quarters. A few large, estate-like properties were built in the 1840s and 1850s, followed by more dense development along the street throughout the remaining decades of the nineteenth and early twentieth centuries as streetcar lines were constructed and additional building lots were platted. Portions of East Market Street are included in the National Register and locally designated Mansion Row Historic District. The following are some of the residences of note along East Market Street.

John Conner House

805 East Market Street

Attributed to architect and master builder Isaac P. Smith, this elegant brick house was built around 1845 for clothing merchant John Conner.

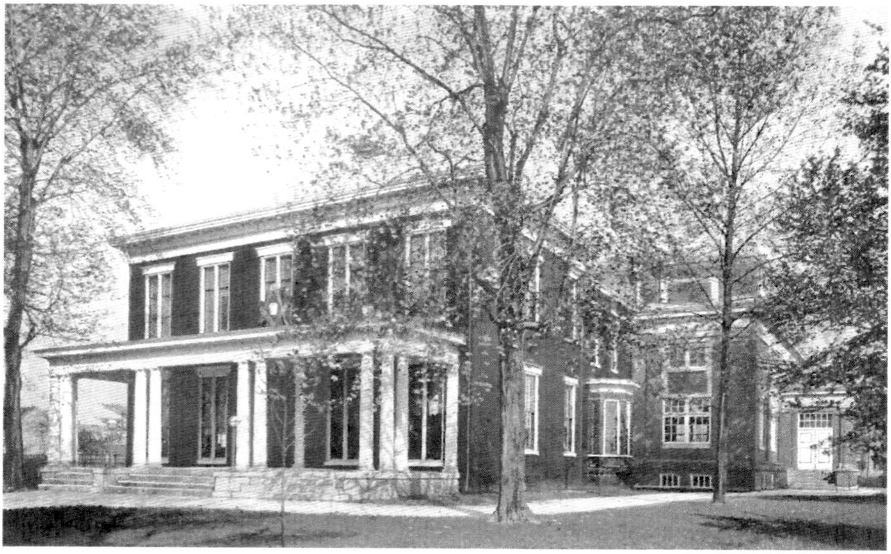

A circa-1920 postcard image of the John Conner House shown after the completion of the Masonic Temple Association's auditorium. *Barksdale collection.*

His business, Conner and Company, was located on East Main Street in downtown New Albany. Conner's sizable "estate" lot, running from Market Street north to Spring Street, was comparable in size to the neighboring estate of James Brooks, whose imposing brick Italianate villa was erected immediately to the east. The Masonic Temple Association purchased the entire estate in 1919 for $20,000 and a year later erected a substantial brick institutional auditorium on the back of the house.

In form and over all architectural expression, the John Conner House closely resembles the Joshua Bragdon House at 517 East Main Street and the now demolished Abbey Butler House at 1612 Dewey Street. While these two comparable residences were of frame construction and the John Conner House is masonry, the three houses share similarities with a shallow hipped roof covering the main building block along with paired elongated windows arranged symmetrically on the façade. Full-width porches span the façades of each and shelter a central entrance door framed with heavy entablature and pilasters. In the case of the Bragdon and Conner houses, paired column groupings support the porches, reinforcing the Greek Revival style favored by Smith.

Brooks-Bradley-Hess House

815 East Market Street

Prominent New Albany lawyer James Brooks purchased the entire half block of real estate bounded by East Spring Street, East Ninth Street, East Market Street and a mid-block alley in 1854–55 and had his estate built here with its formal entrance facing East Market Street. Completed in 1857, the two-and-a-half-story brick house remains one of New Albany's finest examples of the Italianate Villa style with its bracketed cornice, contrasting limestone quoins at the building corners, limestone trim work highlighting rectangular and segmental arched window openings. A secondary entrance was incorporated into an original one-story square bay window on the East Ninth Street side of the house when it was purchased and adapted as a pediatrics office for Dr. Patrick Hess in the early 1960s.

The house likely is the work of the prolific builders William and James Banes. It appears to be modeled after a pattern book design by Philadelphia architect Samuel Sloan, for whom the Banes brothers appear to have borrowed heavily in their body of local domestic work.

First owner James Brooks Esq. was the founder and first president of the New Albany and Salem Railroad, later to be known as the Monon,

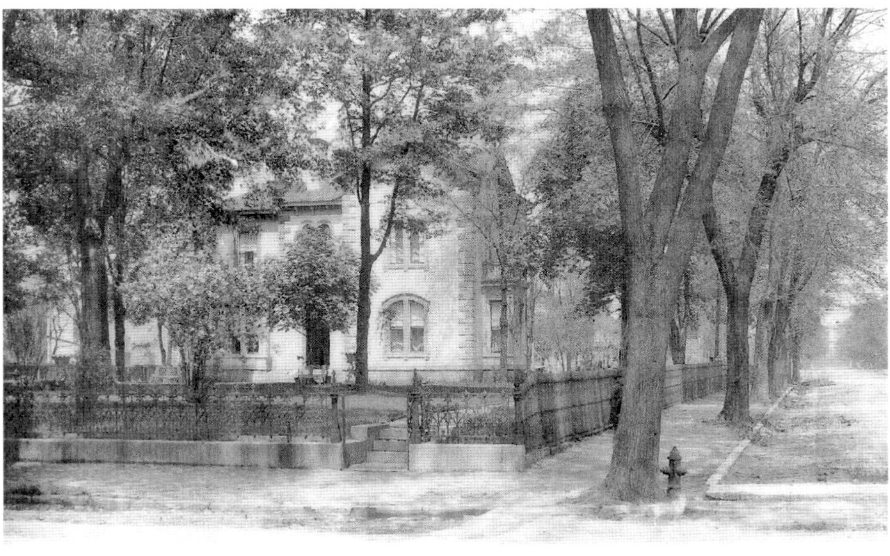

Lawyer James Brooks, founder and first president of the New Albany and Salem Railroad, had this Italianate villa built in 1857. *From* Art Work of New Albany, 1893.

also called *The Hoosier Line*.[38] Brooks had been involved in other business pursuits as well. In the mid-1840s, he was a partner in the Brooks & Paxton Company, merchants in china-, glass- and queensware. Then by the late 1840s, he was partners with Jesse J. Brown in the Brooks & Brown Company, dealers in china-, glass-, queensware and cutlery. By the late 1850s, he had his own wholesale establishment, selling chinaware, glassware, queensware, hardware and cutlery from a downtown New Albany location on the north side of East Main Street between State and Pearl Streets.

The Brooks family lived in the house for only seven years, losing the property at sheriff's sale. The estate was sold to Lawrence Bradley for nearly $12,000. Bradley was a wholesale dealer in dry goods, boots, shoes and hats with business partner Robert G. McCord. McCord, Bradley & Company was located on Pearl Street in downtown New Albany. Bradley later pursued a banking career, serving as president of the Bank of Salem for nearly a decade and then as president of New Albany's Second National Bank for over twenty years. He also served as president of the New Albany Woolen and Cotton Mills, which was located on the site of present-day New Albany High School on Vincennes Street. He later was secretary and treasurer and then president of the New Albany Cotton Batting Mills.

With his growing prosperity, Bradley made several improvements to the house, including an addition on the northwest corner of the residence and the installation of an ornamental iron fence around the house. Sadly, in July 1901, Bradley lost the house to sheriff's sale, and the Second National Bank took over the property. As early as April 1902, the bank began to sell off parcels of the estate and demolish the north and northwest wings of the house. This led to the subdividing of lots to the north along East Ninth Street where four homes were constructed. Further development occurred to the south of the house, including the erection of a house and service station at the northwest corner of East Ninth and Market Streets, which blocked the Brooks-Bradley-Hess House's original entrance view from East Market Street. The estate's original servant's wash house survives and is located behind the Charles and Cora Zink House at 317 East Ninth Street. Portions of the original carriage house behind the George Kraft House at 323 East Ninth Street also remain and have been incorporated into an early-twentieth-century garage.

By 1937, the original house had ceased to remain a residence. Subsequent owners included the Knights of Columbus and the union hall for the Plumber's and Steamfitter's Union, Local #605. In September 1963, Dr. Patrick Hess purchased the property and opened his pediatrics office here. It remained his medical office for over thirty years until his retirement in 1995. An accomplished artist, Dr. Hess later used the house as an art gallery. He is also credited with purchasing and demolishing the later properties to the south of the house to reclaim the original front view of the estate. In 2010, the Brooks-Bradley-Hess House was purchased by Louisville resident Myrna Hinkebein, who embarked on a sensitive rehabilitation of the house for conversion to professional offices.

The interior of the Brooks-Bradley-Hess House retains many notable features from its original construction and subsequent remodeling in the early twentieth century. The etched-glass front door and hallway staircase illuminated by a skylight above are two of the house's original features that have survived intact. Parquet flooring, stained- and beveled-glass windows in the dining room, cast-iron and wood mantels and a reclaimed coffered ceiling in what may have been originally used as a library are other interior features of note.

Crawford-Moosmiller House

820 East Market Street

Now the home of the nonprofit Arts Council of Southern Indiana, this two-story brick town house was constructed sometime after 1852 by John B. Crawford. He, in turn, sold the house to Adam Knapp in December 1855. Knapp was a partner in the business concern of Knapp and Gohmann, dealers in wholesale groceries, liquors and tobacco. The business was located on Pearl Street.

By March 1863, Merchants National Bank president Jacob Hangary owned the property. Upon his death in January 1880, his daughter and son-in-law, Mary A. and Colonel John S. Day, purchased the home. Colonel Day was involved in New Albany railroads at an early age, having worked his way from the freight office to superintendent of the Louisville, New Albany & Chicago Railroad, later known as the Monon. After retirement, he managed extensive lumber interests and was an original investor in the New Albany Steam Forge Company. Day was also active in local and state politics, serving twice on the New Albany City Council and two terms in the Indiana Senate. He died in July 1893.

Following the death of Colonel Day, his widow remained in the home and was joined by her daughter and son-in-law, Mary and Paul E. Moosmiller. Paul E. Moosmiller was an architect. Around 1901, he designed a separation of the house into two individual residences, with the former rear wing becoming 221 East Ninth Street. At the same time,

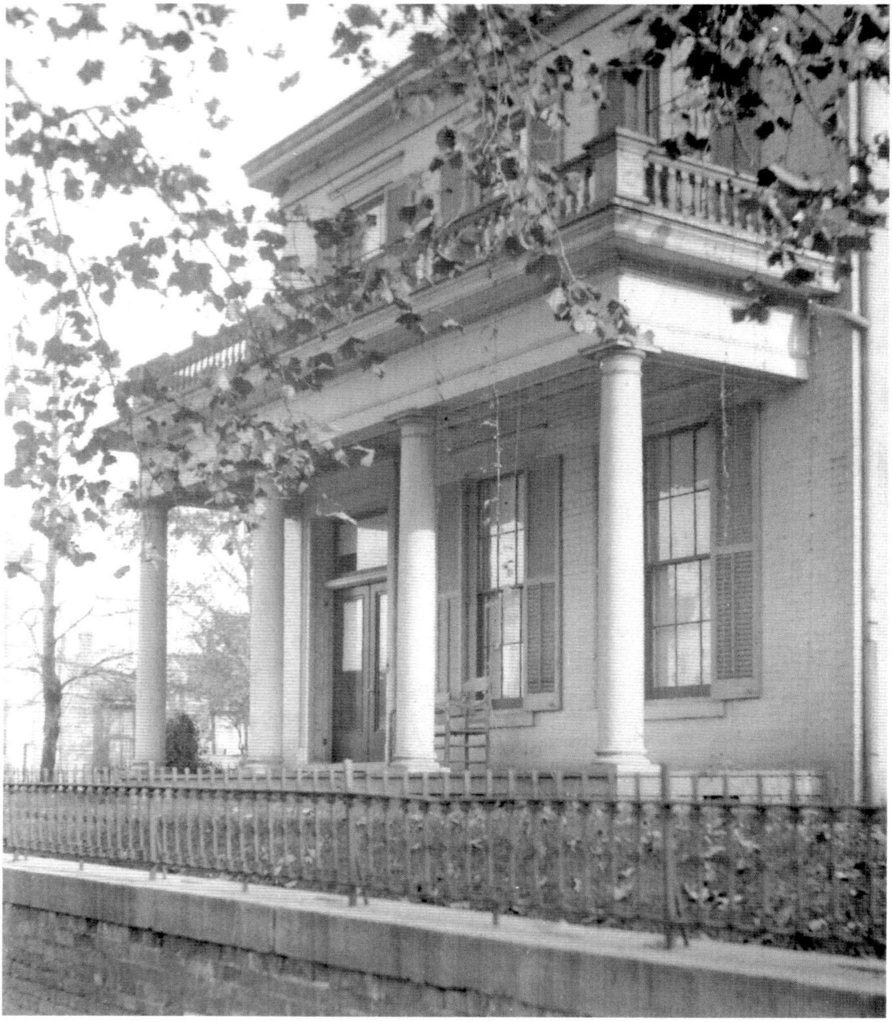

A circa-1935 photo of the Crawford-Moosmiller House showing the Classical Revival–style porch added by architect Paul E. Moosmiller. *Arts Council of Southern Indiana.*

Moosmiller designed a new west wing for this home, along with a room extension on the east containing a new staircase to the second floor. A Classical Revival–style front porch was also added to the house but was subsequently removed in a 1970s renovation by then owners Sam and Paula Robinson. The couple saved the house from certain destruction after years of vacancy and vandalism. In 2005, the Arts Council of Southern Indiana was able to obtain the house as its headquarters through a successful capital campaign, including gifts from several major donors.

Howard-Morrison-Briggs House

1118 East Market Street

Situated on a lot at the southwest corner of East Twelfth and Market Streets, this outwardly Italianate-style house was originally a more modest four-room brick dwelling that was built between 1853 and 1855 by carpenter John Howard as his personal residence. James and Rachel Morrison purchased the property for $4,000 in December 1856. James Morrison was a partner in the company of Norman, Morrison & Matthews, publishers of the *New Albany Daily Ledger*. He was also a member of the New Albany City Council, the New Albany Board of School Trustees and, later, was elected to the Indiana legislature. Senator Morrison died in January 1862. The property remained in the Morrison family until it was sold to John S. Briggs, a dealer in building materials and hardware, and his wife, Mary, in April 1884 for $3,000. Three months later, on July 21, 1884, the *New Albany Daily Ledger* wrote:

> *Mr. John S. Briggs is removing into the residence recently purchased by him on Market and East 12th Streets. Mr. Briggs has enlarged and improved the property and when completed, it will be one of the most convenient and handsome residences in the city.*

Some of these improvements included the addition of a bracketed cornice, a two-story bay window on the Market Street façade with ornamental pressed metal window hoods and an extension of the house at the south that gave the building its present L-shaped footprint. A large porch, facing East Twelfth Street and supported by fluted Composite-order columns, shelters the house's original Greek Revival entrance, which is defined by broad pilasters and heavy entablature.

Briggs was also president of the Light, Heat & Power Company, and upon his death in January 1895, his widow was appointed the company's president. She remained in the home until her death in May 1938. In the early 1940s, Doctors James and Helen Lange purchased the house for use as their residence and medical office. The Lange's son-in-law, Dr. George Weber, continued the mixed use of the house until the mid-1960s when the medical office was moved to an accessory structure on the property.

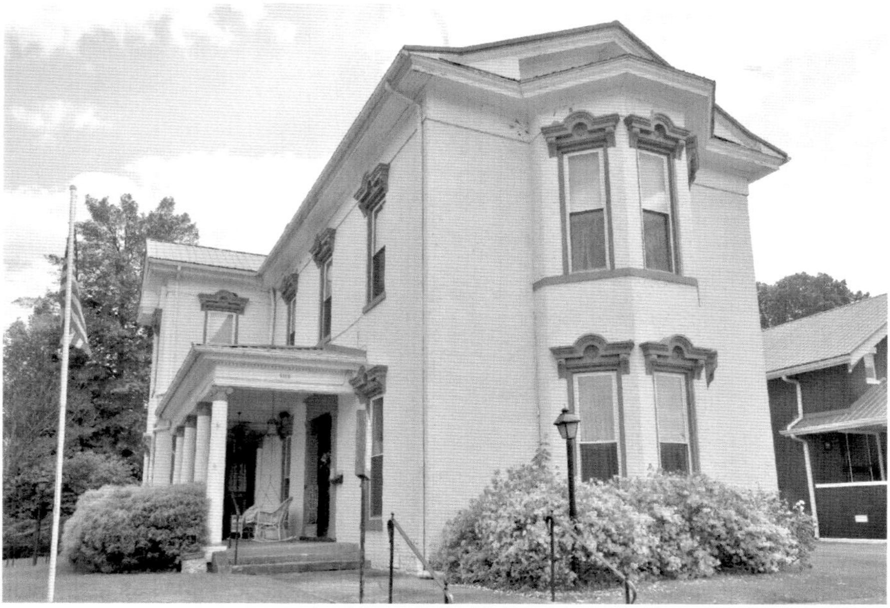

The outwardly Italianate-style Howard-Morrison-Briggs House was originally a modest, four-room brick dwelling built between 1853 and 1855. *Gregory Sekula.*

Despite the mixed-use nature of the house over the past seventy years, the interior retains many fine architectural details, including heavily molded woodwork and the original front staircase with its mixed hardwood railing with turned balusters and octagonal newel post executed in oak. An Eastlake-style back stair—the product of the 1880s remodel—also remains. The principal rooms have twelve-foot ceilings that feature elaborate gilded plaster cornice moldings with garland and cherub motifs. Cast-iron mantels, two of which are marbleized and embellished with Eastlake and Aesthetic Movement design, are also found in the house. A rare surviving feature is an elaborate gasolier light fixture in the front parlor embellished with foliated leaves in a gilt bronze finish.

BOARDMAN-MEEKIN HOUSE

1220 East Market Street

Richard Boardman purchased the corner lot on which this house stands in August 1881 and by 1883 had also purchased the adjoining property to the east at 1216 East Market Street where a two-story gable-front frame house had been erected in 1880 by William and Carrie Kesler. Boardman would eventually reside at the neighboring house. The dwelling he built around 1882 on this corner lot was also a two-story gable-front frame structure of similar design. This house, however, incorporates side entry porches at the front and back with Italianate features, including bracketed chamfered posts.

Richard Boardman originally held a clerical position in the printing establishment of John R. Nunemacher, owner of the City Bookstore in downtown New Albany. For twenty-five years, and up until his death at age fifty-nine in February 1911, he was manager of the Great Atlanta & Pacific Tea Company (A&P), located at 226 Pearl Street. Boardman was formerly a New Albany city councilman, being elected to an at-large position in 1906. He also served as a member of the board of police commissioners. His widow, Medora Boardman, remained in the home until her death at age eighty-five in November 1933.

By the printing of the 1935–36 *New Albany City Directory*, George Jouett Meekin was residing in the house. Jouett, as he was commonly referred, was a Major League Baseball pitcher. During his career—which spanned from 1891 to 1900—he played for the Louisville Colonels, the Washington Senators, the New York Giants, the Boston Beaneaters and the Pittsburgh Pirates. In 1894, he achieved acclaim by winning thirty-three games for the Giants and helped lead the team to a postseason championship.[39] Meekin lived in the home until his death in December 1944. Burial was in New Albany's Fairview Cemetery. In July 2002, the Floyd County Historical Society led an effort to have a permanent grave marker noting his prolific baseball career placed at Fairview. A year later, in July 2003, the Floyd County Historical Society placed a historical marker at his former residence.

George and Mary Borgerding House

1414 East Market Street

George and Mary Borgerding purchased the lot on which this house stands in February 1889 from Jacob Zinsmeister, who erected his stately, brick, Second Empire–style residence next door. The George and Mary Borgerding House was completed in the latter part of 1889. George Borgerding was associated with several New Albany manufacturing

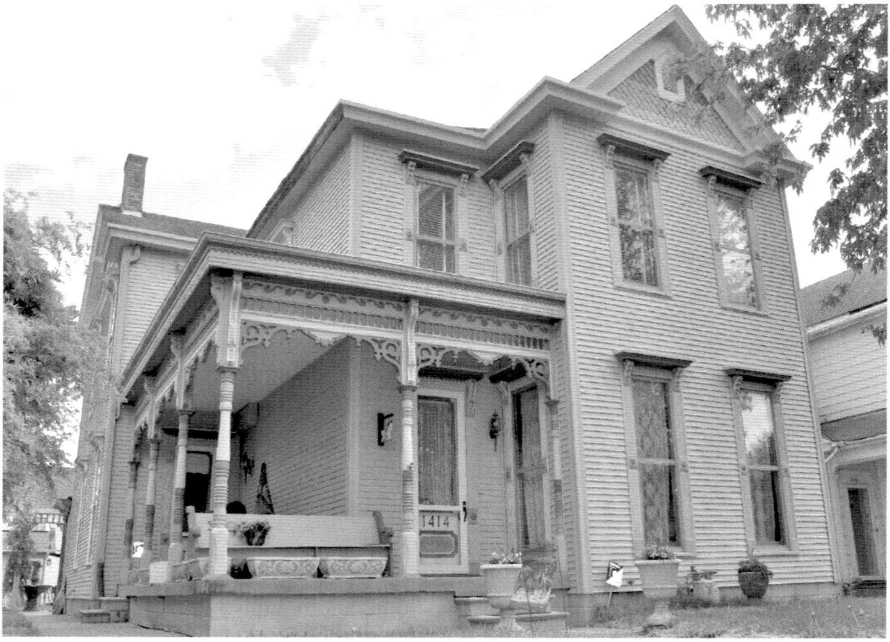

The 1889 George and Mary Borgerding House exhibits a wealth of exterior detailing characteristic of the Queen Anne style. *Gregory Sekula.*

concerns, working as a bookkeeper until 1893, when he became the cashier at the New Albany National Bank. In January 1919, he became president of the Mutual Trust & Deposit Company. Tragically, Mary Borgerding met an untimely death in January 1922 as a result of a motorcar accident. The couple had been enjoying the bright winter sunshine on a late afternoon drive on Green Valley Road when George Borgerding pulled to the side of the road to let another vehicle pass. In doing so, he lost control of the vehicle and struck a tree. Both were injured in the accident with Mary dying a few days later of her injuries at New Albany's St. Edward Hospital.[40]

The Borgerding's son, William, and his wife, Susan, came to live in the home with George after his wife's death. George Borgerding remained with Mutual Trust until his death from a heart attack in November 1937 at the age of eighty-one. The younger Borgerding was associated with both the Indiana Veneer & Panel Company and the Crescent Paneling Company. He remained in the house until his death in August 1964, ending seventy-five years of occupancy by the Borgerding family.

Queen Anne in style, the George and Mary Borgerding House is a rambling frame residence with patterned shingles in its broken pediment gables. Decorative molded window hoods and a wraparound porch with turned posts and patterned and spindled spandrels provide the ornamentation that is the hallmark of the Queen Anne. On the interior, original woodwork, a beautifully detailed open staircase, pocket doors between the double parlors, inlayed strip oak floors and numerous fireplace mantels evoke the grandeur of the Victorian era.An outstanding feature of the interior is a magnificent archway leading from the entry hall to the front parlor.

JACOB ZINSMEISTER HOUSE

1420 East Market Street

In 1866, Frank Zinsmeister Sr. relocated from Louisville, Kentucky, to New Albany where he established a grocery and produce store. Sons Jacob and Frank Jr. worked in the family business but by 1881 had left their father's store and established their own wholesale grocery company. Business flourished, and a second store was opened in Louisville.

Jacob and Anna Zinsmeister purchased the lot on which this grand house stands in February 1889 and had the house constructed the same year for

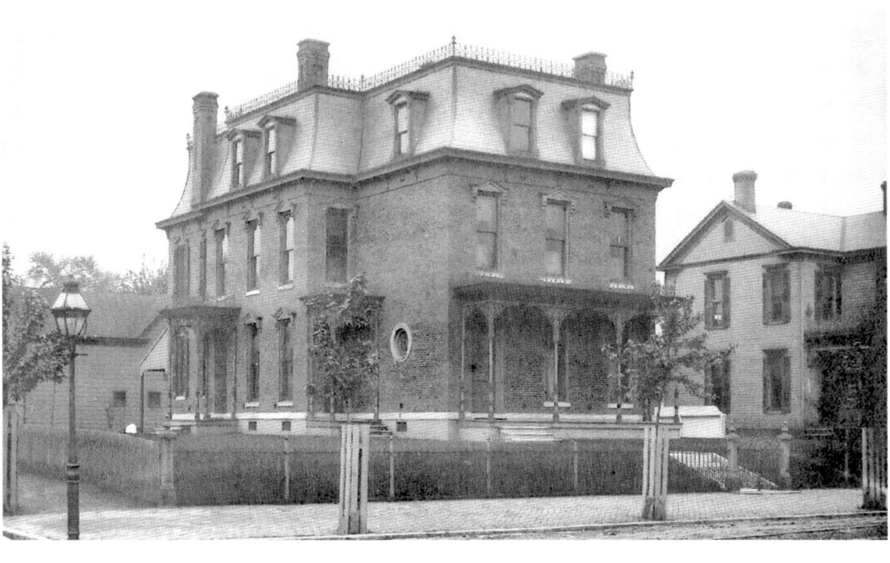

Known as "Little Culbertson," the 1889 Jacob Zinsmeister House is one of New Albany's finest examples of the Second Empire style. *From* Art Work of New Albany, 1893.

$8,000.[41] The 1890–91 *New Albany City Directory* lists the couple as living at this address. In 1910, the business partnership between the two brothers dissolved, and Jacob Zinsmeister purchased the Louisville store and moved his family there in 1916.

S. Otto and Florence Voyles purchased the house in 1917. Otto Voyles lived here until his death in 1953. His wife remained in the house until her death in 1962. Voyles was president of the Calumet Fertilizer Company located on the south side of East Main Street west of Silver Street. This company later became known as the Tennessee Corporation. During the Voyleses' residency, the house's original cast-iron front porches were replaced with the large wraparound porch supported by Composite Order fluted columns that remains today. An original cast-iron side porch survives on the East Fifteenth Street side of the house.

Affectionately referred to by locals as "Little Culbertson," the Jacob Zinsmeister House exudes Second Empire style with its hallmark slate-covered mansard roof with shallow arched dormers. Ornamental iron cresting originally embellished the roofline. The house's bracketed cornice, towering corbelled chimneys, cut limestone door surrounds and ornamental Eastlake-style window hoods create a cohesive design that gives the house a monumental presence along East Market Street, suggesting the work of a skilled architect and builder, such as the Banes brothers. The lavish interior includes Corinthian columns between the entry hall and front parlor and plaster cornice moldings throughout the first floor. Pocket doors separate the parlor from the dining room. Parquet floors and handsomely detailed mantels provide further embellishment to this grand dame of East Market Street.

4

East Spring Street

East Spring Street developed as one of New Albany's major east–west thoroughfares throughout the latter half of the nineteenth century. Major institutional buildings including the Floyd County Courthouse, the U.S. Post Office and the opera house were located at East Spring Street intersections in downtown. As one traveled farther east, the city's Carnegie-funded public library, high school, St. Edward Hospital and numerous churches and social clubs made East Spring Street one of the city's most important addresses. Streetcar lines and a bridge over Silver Creek at the far eastern end of the town connected New Albany to the neighboring town of Clarksville, Indiana, and made Spring Street one of the New Albany's major entry points.

Portions of the East Spring Street neighborhood, extending from the former St. Edward Hospital at East Seventh Street east to East Eleventh Street, were placed in the National Register of Historic Places in 2002. Efforts are underway in 2014–16 to expand the boundaries of the East Spring Street Historic District to roughly Vincennes Street to the east. Portions of neighboring East Elm Street to the north and East Market Street to the south will also be included in the expanded National Register historic district boundaries. The following residential properties are some of the more noteworthy residences along East Spring Street.

MITCHELL-WOLFE HOUSE

613 East Spring Street

This fine, outwardly Italianate-style brick town house actually began as an earlier brick house built by James Mitchell, a New Albany brick mason. Mitchell purchased the west half of this lot in 1837 and the remainder in 1846. It is believed that the house was likely constructed the following year.

The house saw several different owners until Judge Simeon K. Wolfe purchased it in July 1870 for $9,000.[42] Judge Wolfe was born near Georgetown, Indiana, on February 14, 1824. As a young adult, he moved to Corydon, Indiana, and became a shoemaker. He also began the study of law and entered the law office of a Judge Porter in Corydon. After attending law school in Indiana, he was elected state senator from Harrison County in 1851. From 1857 to 1865, he also served as editor of the *Corydon Democrat* newspaper. After moving to New Albany in 1870, he was appointed judge of the circuit court of Floyd and Clark Counties in 1880 to fill an unexpired term of the late Judge John S. Davis.[43]

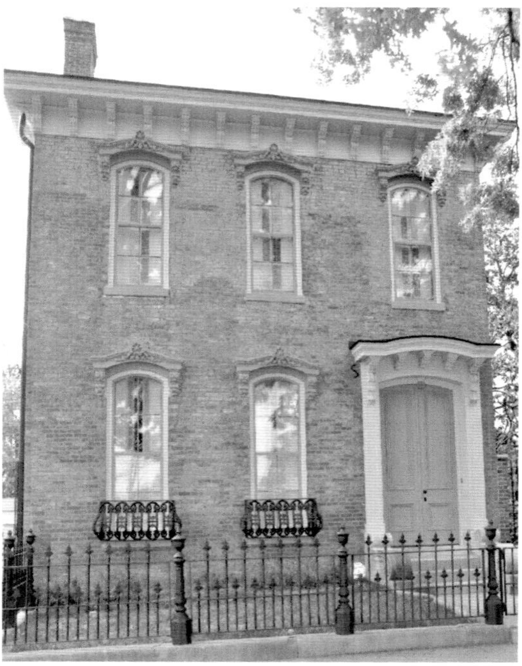

The Italianate-style façade of the Mitchell-Wolfe House was added after 1870 by the second owner, Judge Simeon K. Wolfe. *Gregory Sekula.*

It was Wolfe who enlarged the East Spring Street house, adding rooms on to the front of the residence and outfitting the façade in the latest fashionable style of the day. Improvements included arched window sashes with elaborate window hoods, a bracketed cornice and front entry with paired arched doors sheltered by a bracketed, shallow, arched door hood. Such embellishments make the Mitchell-Wolfe House one of New Albany's finest examples of the Italianate style in traditional town house form. More recent enhancements include the iron balcony grilles on the house's elongated ground story windows, period-appropriate iron fence at the sidewalk edge and an iron gate with a gas lantern.

Charles and Cora Zink House

317 East Ninth Street

This one-and-a-half-story Queen Anne–style dwelling was erected for Charles and Cora Zink, who purchased this lot in July 1903 for $1,460 and had the house built soon thereafter. It stands on ground once connected to the estate of lawyer James Brooks, whose Italianate villa stands directly to the south. Charles Zink was the co-owner of the Laub-Zink Furniture Company in downtown New Albany. The furniture store specialized in "Made in New Albany" products and was one of the most successful furniture retailers in southern Indiana.[44] In July 1917, Thomas and Sophia Jackson purchased the home and would remain there through June 1945. Thomas Jackson was

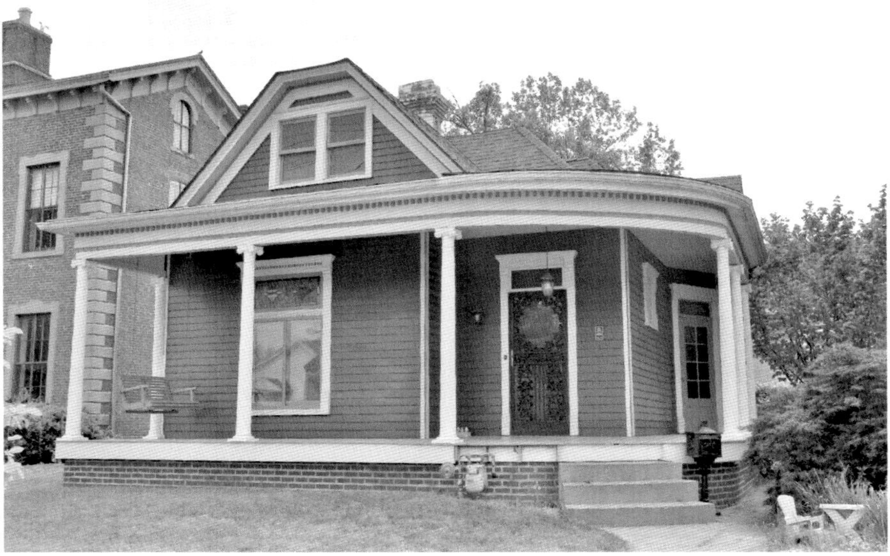

After an August 2008 fire, the exterior of the Charles and Cora Zink House was meticulously restored by owners Jim and Tabitha Sprigler. *Gregory Sekula.*

the New Albany postmaster from 1922 to 1933. John Burke, along with his sisters—Mary, Anna and Agnes—were the next owners of the property. It remained in the Burke family into the late 1960s.

Norman and Virginia Perkins purchased the house in April 1970 and owned it for over thirty years. Norman Perkins was an agent with the National Life & Accident Insurance Company. He died in October 1998, and his widow sold the house in December 2003 to present owners Jim and Tabitha Sprigler. The Spriglers were in the process of an extensive exterior restoration of the house in August 2008 when tragedy struck. While workman were removing layers of paint from the building's clapboard exterior, heat equipment ignited a fire, and within minutes, the house's roof structure was consumed in flames.[45] After an extensive rehabilitation, the house was once again occupied in 2010.

The exterior of the Charles and Cora Zink House features a complex roofline with a clipped gable facing the street. A large wraparound porch with Classical Revival detailing and fluted Scamozzi Order columns creates an inviting presence along East Ninth Street. The post-fire interior retains some of the house's original trim, Classical Revival mantel and parquet flooring but also incorporates a new open staircase to the second floor cleverly situated to open up the house's floor plan and maximize second-floor living space.

THOMAS AND EMMA ARMSTRONG HOUSE

417 East Ninth Street

With its steeply pitched gable roofs, fanciful bargeboard gable trim, bracketed porch and corbelled brick chimneys with clay chimney pots, the Thomas and Emma Armstrong House stands as New Albany's finest expression of the Gothic Revival style. Ben Cline, builder and owner of a local lumberyard, constructed two small houses in 1867 on this lot owned by Thomas Armstrong. Armstrong—along with his wife, Emma, and their three children—occupied this home while other family members occupied the other house. Prior to the printing of the 1871–72 *New Albany City Directory*, the second house was moved to a lot on East Fifth Street near Elm Street.

One of New Albany's most prominent businessmen, Thomas Armstrong was a general freight agent with the Louisville, New Albany & Chicago Railroad before becoming involved with the flour and grain milling industry

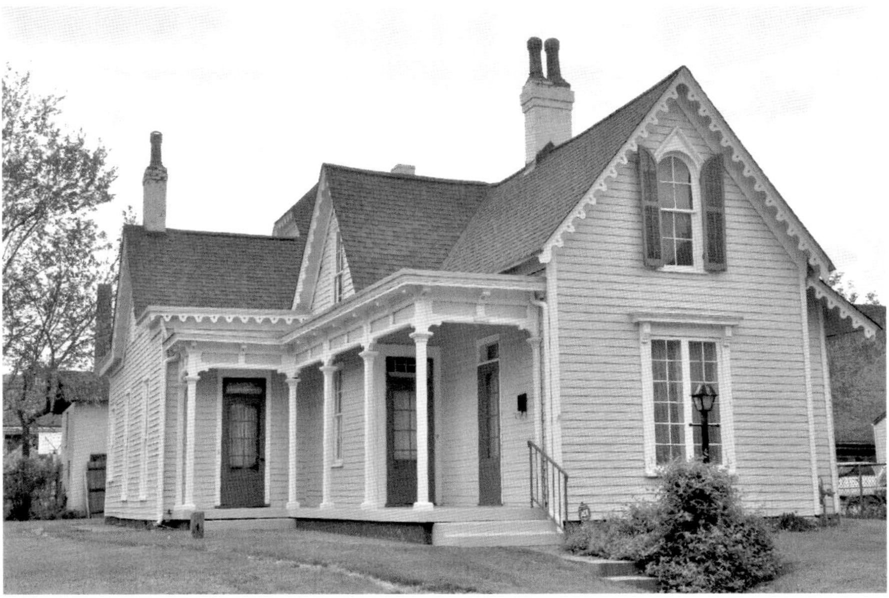

The Thomas and Emma Armstrong House, built in 1867, stands as New Albany's finest expression of the Gothic Revival style. *Gregory Sekula.*

in New Albany. After working with several well-established mills, he founded the New Albany Milling Company, located at State and West Elm Streets.

Armstrong was active in the civic, commercial and social affairs of the city and was an ardent supporter of the Republican Party. He was elected mayor of New Albany and also served as a member of the New Albany School Board of Trustees.[46] Thomas Armstrong passed away in March 1917 and Emma Armstrong in March 1940. Daughters Kate, retired from operating the milling company, and Julia, a teacher at the DePauw Free Kindergarten, remained in the home until their deaths in June 1968 and August 1974, respectively. This ended a residency by the Armstrong family of 107 years.

JOHN AND MINNIE MEYER HOUSE

907 East Spring Street

This distinctive brick bungalow was built in 1913 for John and Minnie Meyer. The Meyers had purchased the property in 1899 and lived in a house that formerly occupied the lot. They vacated that house in 1911 and moved in with Minnie's brother and sister-in-law, Fred and Rose Colby, at 1219 East Elm Street while the new house was being built.

John Meyer was a native of Germany and moved from Chicago to New Albany in 1896. He purchased the Paul Reising Brewery Company in 1899, located on West Spring Street. His brother-in-law, Fred Colby, was also secretary of the brewing company. Meyer sold the brewery in 1905 and became involved in an ice manufacturing business, Louisville's Ice and Cold Storage Company. Prior to establishing the Cannelton Sewer Pipe Company in 1913, he was president of a furniture manufacturing company that supplied the magnificent woodwork and parquet flooring for his new East Spring Street residence. John Meyer passed away in June 1915 and his wife in August 1925. Upon her death, their nephew John Colby inherited the house.

After the marriage of John Colby to Thelma Miller in October 1940, the Colbys set up housekeeping here. John Colby was a retired director of Can-Tex Industries at Cannelton, Indiana, and died in March 1968. His widow remained in the house until the mid-1970s. She later remarried and passed away in Florida in December 1996. Interior designer Barry Wooley

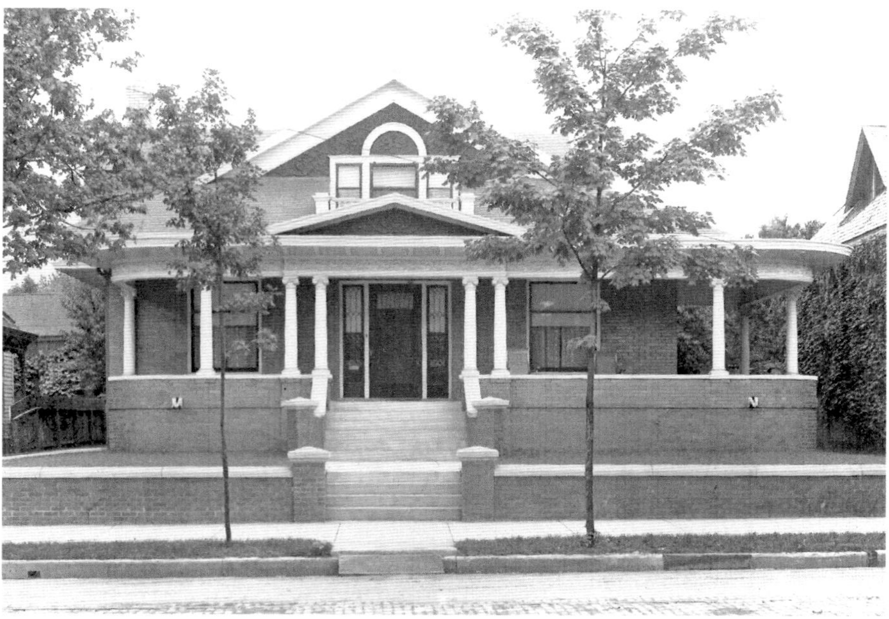

This 1913 photo of the John and Minnie Meyer House shows the residence shortly after its completion. *Fangman Collection.*

and artist and faux painter Jude Loew have resided in the home since the late 1990s and have restored and enhanced the house's interior and exterior.

The John and Minnie Meyer House is notable for its expansive wraparound porch supported by paired fluted columns sheltered under wide overhangs with exposed rafter tails. The front gables of the house and porch are decorated with pressed metal foliated ornamentation whose contrasting paint colors give the residence a truly elegant appearance. Leaded- and beveled-glass windows are found in the entry door and sidelights as well as in the front parlor. Natural oak woodwork, original crown moldings, a quartersawn oak mantel in the front parlor, pocket doors and a dining room with an abundance of Arts and Crafts detailing from the boxed beamed ceiling to the built-in buffet and fireplace make the Meyer House interior one of the finest early twentieth-century interiors in the city.

Frank Zinsmeister Jr. House

1001 East Spring Street

Frank Zinsmeister Jr. and his wife, Emma, purchased this property in 1911 and demolished an earlier structure that stood on the lot. Here they erected this fine two-and-a-half-story brick residence and two-story garage in 1912, the latter of which was later subdivided from the main house and converted into a residence. Its address is 414 East Tenth Street. Brothers Frank Jr. and Jacob Zinsmeister formed a partnership in 1881 and opened the wholesale grocery concern of Jacob Zinsmeister and Brother on State Street. Business flourished, and a second store was opened in Louisville. In 1910, the business partnership was dissolved, with Frank Zinsmeister Jr. retaining the New Albany store and brother Jacob Zinsmeister purchasing the Louisville outlet.[47] Frank Zinsmeister Jr. died in February 1918, and his widow remained in the home until her death in January 1957. For many years, the house was a well-known costume shop called the Costumery. It closed in 2015, and the house was recently purchased for single-family use.

The Frank Zinsmeister Jr. House exhibits restrained yet sophisticated Classical detailing ranking it as one of New Albany's finest expressions of the early twentieth-century Colonial Revival style. The main rectangular building block of the house, sheathed in a gray Roman brick, is capped by a jerkinhead roof with a large, centrally located, hipped and shingled

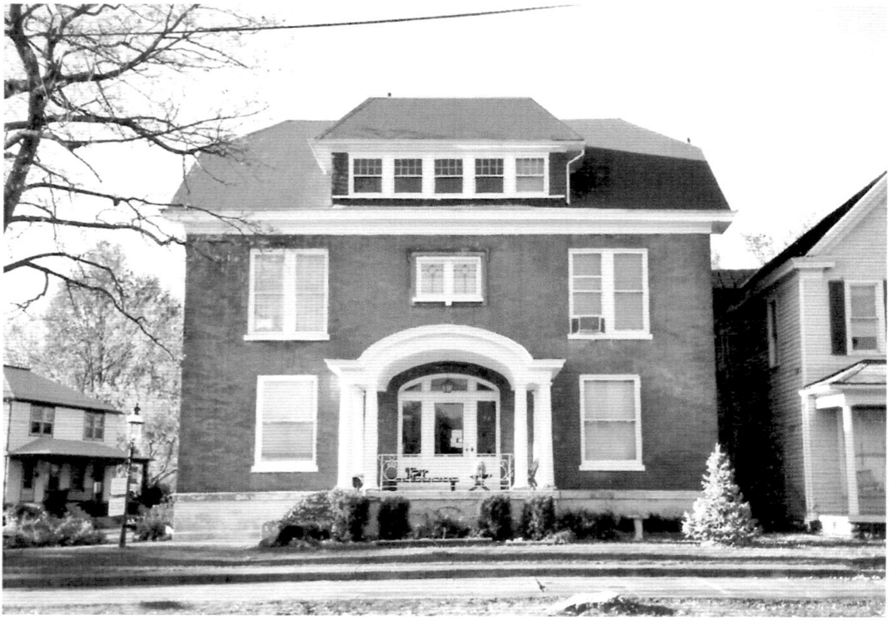

Restrained, yet sophisticated classical detailing is exhibited in the Colonial Revival–style Frank Zinsmeister Jr. House. *Barksdale collection.*

dormer dominating the sloped roof on the main façade. A band of five eight-over-one windows fills the dormer. Symmetrically placed windows on the front façade bookend the house's most distinguishing exterior feature—an arched, barrel-vaulted entry portico supported by paired fluted Doric columns. The porch shelters the house's main entry door with three-part arched transom windows mimicking the curvature of the porch roof. Wide leaded-glass sidelights flank a beveled-glass entry door that leads into a wide center hall with a monumental open staircase with a stained handrail and turned balusters and newel post. The signature feature of the stairway is an oriel window at mid-landing with a bay of leaded-glass windows. Pocket doors on the first floor lead to the large double parlor on the west side of the house with its leaded window band, bay window, built-in bookcases and fireplace with wooden paneled mantelpiece. On the east side of the hall is the dining room, with its boxed beamed ceiling, original plaster ceiling lights and built-in china cabinet with bowed paneled and leaded-glass doors and a beveled mirror. A finished third floor contains a ballroom for entertaining.

BICKNELL-WILCOX HOUSE

1010 East Spring Street

George A. Bicknell Sr., father of the prominent judge George A. Bicknell Jr., took up residency here next door to his son's home at 1006 East Spring Street around 1857. George Sr. and his wife, Emeline, purchased this lot in June 1853, but it doesn't appear that the home was constructed until a few years thereafter. Emeline Bicknell passed away in March 1868, and George Bicknell Sr. sold the property to Dr. Seymour Wilcox in September 1868 for $4,200, moving next door to live with his son until his death at age eighty-six in November 1871.

After arriving in New Albany from Franklin, New York, Dr. Wilcox and his wife, Julia, used the west side of the home as their family residence, while the east side functioned as his physician and surgical office. The doctor passed away at age ninety in January 1909, and his widow remained in the home until her death in June 1923. Their son, Frank Wilcox, also a doctor, moved his physician's office into the house shortly before the death of his father. He and his wife, Portia, lived in the home

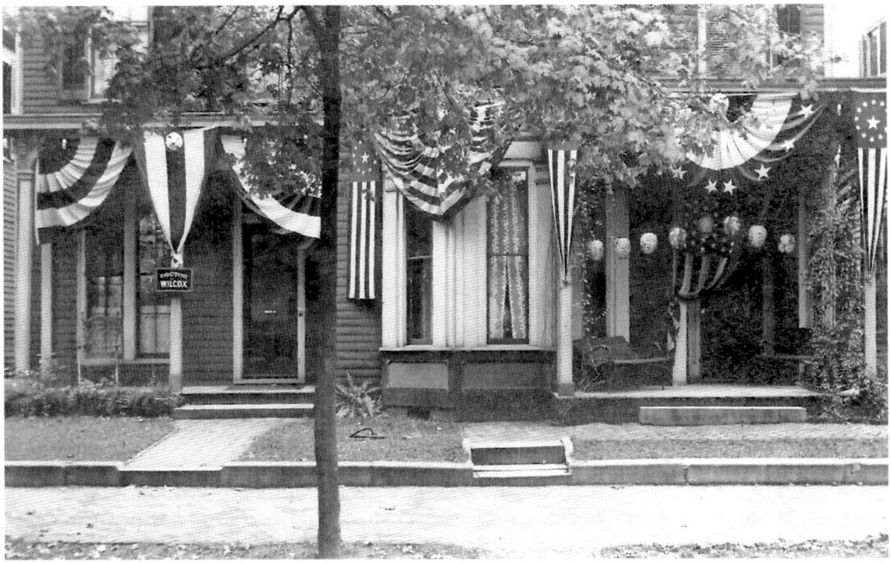

The porch of the Bicknell-Wilcox House is decorated for New Albany's 1913 Centennial Celebration. *Barksdale collection.*

after the passing of the elder Wilcox in 1909. Dr. Frank Wilcox died in April 1924 following a surgical operation for an intestinal ulcer. Portia Wilcox remained in the home until her death in December 1950. The property was transferred out of the family in November 1953, ending eighty-five years of Wilcox ownership.

Italianate in style, the Bicknell-Wilcox House features a wealth of exterior detailing with its paired bracketed cornice, a broad first-floor façade bay window and entry and side porches with chamfered posts and pendant decorations. The main block of the house exhibits the iconic town house form, but the footprint is expanded with a two-story secondary block on the house's east side that may have been an addition by Dr. Wilcox to accommodate his mixed use of the property.

TRINITY METHODIST EPISCOPAL CHURCH PARSONAGE

1100 East Spring Street

New Albany architect Arthur R. Smith designed this 1901 house as the parsonage for the now demolished Trinity Methodist Episcopal Church, which stood nearby at East Thirteenth and Spring Streets. Phillip Kahl was the house's contractor. This site was home to the former John Street Methodist Episcopal Church. Members of this congregation, along with those from the Centenary and Wesley Chapel Methodist Churches, established Trinity Methodist Episcopal Church in 1888.[48] The church continues its ministry today as Trinity United Methodist Church and is located on Charlestown Road in a contemporary structure.

The parsonage was sold to Dr. Jefferson Streepey in April 1946 and was used as his physician's office. His brother, Dr. Robert Streepey, also had his dental practice here. The two offices remained in the house through the mid-1960s. The Marketing Company is the present occupant.

Constructed of red pressed brick, the two-and-a-half-story dwelling features asymmetrical massing with a hipped roof with flared eaves with decorative rafter tails. Towering brick chimneys punctuate the roofline. A two-and-a-half-story bay window dominates the façade and rises above the eave line, terminating in a conical roof that ties back into the main roof slope. A rectangular stained-glass window highlighted by fluted stone pilasters adorns the bay at the second story. A two-story bay rises on the

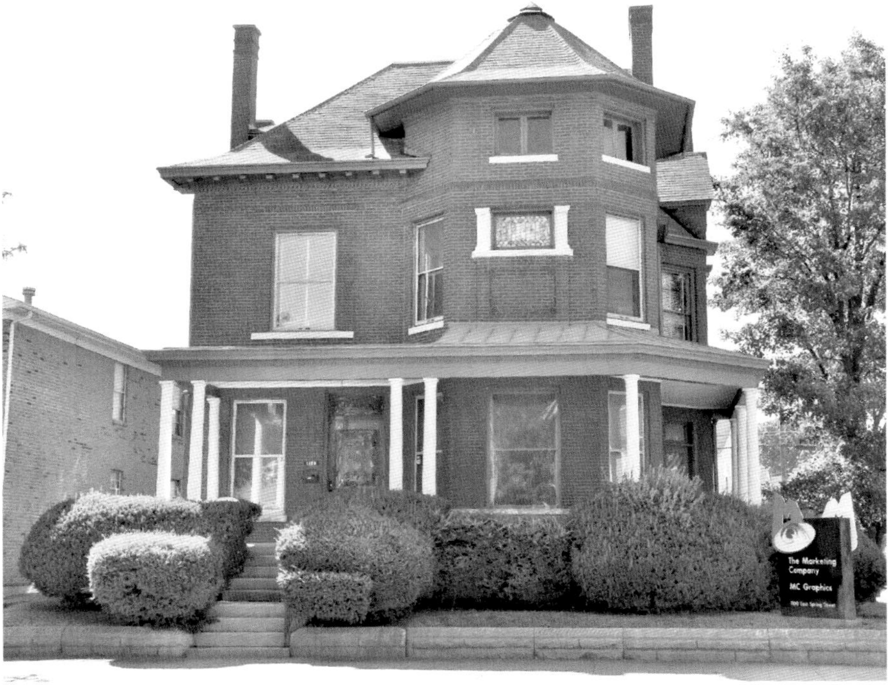

New Albany architect Arthur R. Smith designed this house as the parsonage for the now demolished Trinity Methodist Episcopal Church. *Gregory Sekula.*

East Tenth Street side of the house. A wraparound porch supported by paired columns shelters a quartersawn oak front door embellished with a beveled- and leaded-glass window.

James and Mina Forman House

1109 East Spring Street

James and Mina (Kammerer) Forman had this buff brick veneer residence built sometime after 1925 on the former site of the late nineteenth-century Queen Anne mansion built by Merrill Weir. Mr. Forman was the secretary of the Conrad-Kammerer Glue Company located on the south side of East Main Street, west of Silver Street.

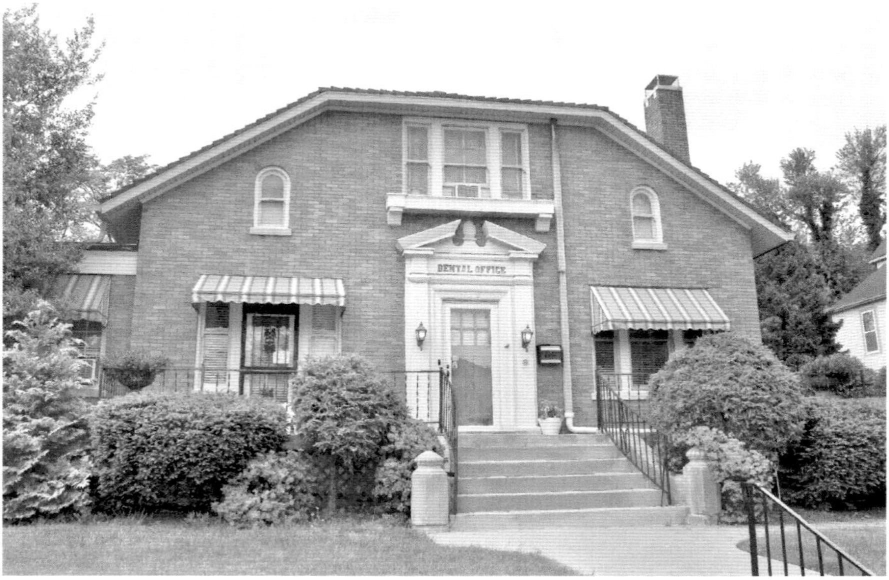

A present view of the James and Mina Forman House with its distinctive jerkinhead gable clay tile roof. *Gregory Sekula.*

In May 1950, the house was sold to Dr. Wilson E. Stemm and his wife, Ella, who used the structure as both their residence and Dr. Stemm's dental office. The couple passed away in 2009. Today, the property is still in Stemm ownership with son, Dr. W. Stephen Stemm, maintaining his dental practice here.

The house features a distinctive jerkinhead gable clay tile roof with shed roof side dormers. The symmetrical façade features an elevated terrace with a broken pediment framed front door surround. The stone steps leading to the terrace with their distinctive molded railing terminating in hexagonal newel posts are remnants of the original Weir mansion. Above the front door is a tripartite window with a bracketed window box below. Single arched windows frame the center window grouping on the second floor.

CONNER-CANNON HOUSE

1203 East Spring Street

James Wesley Conner Jr., former owner of 611 East Spring Street, was the first resident of this commodious Queen Anne–style dwelling completed in 1901. Conner was associated with the Roberts & Conner Veneering Company and, later, managed the New Albany Lumber Company. Prior to his work in the veneer industry, he owned a printing office and stationery store at 330 Pearl Street. The house remained in the Conner family until 1919, when it became the residence and office of physician Dr. James Baxter. Dr. Baxter was a former president and secretary of the Floyd County Medical Society. He also served at one time as the head of staff at the old St. Edward Hospital, which originally operated on East Spring Street. Portions of the old St. Edward Hospital have now been converted to affordable housing units known as St. Edward Court.

In September 1954, the property was sold to Dr. Daniel Cannon and his wife, Marilynn. Dr. Cannon also used the house as his physician's office until he purchased the house next door at 1201 East Spring Street for that purpose. Dr. Cannon began his medical career in 1948 and retired in 2002. He was a captain in the United States Medical Corps and served as the Floyd County coroner for eighteen years.[49] Marilynn Cannon was a registered nurse and a member of the Floyd County Medical Auxiliary. She was also the founder of the Southern Indiana Dyslexia Association.[50] Marilynn Cannon passed away in March 2011 and Dr. Cannon in December 2013. Jason and Hannegan Roseberry purchased the home in March 2013. The couple has been working to restore the house to its former grandeur.

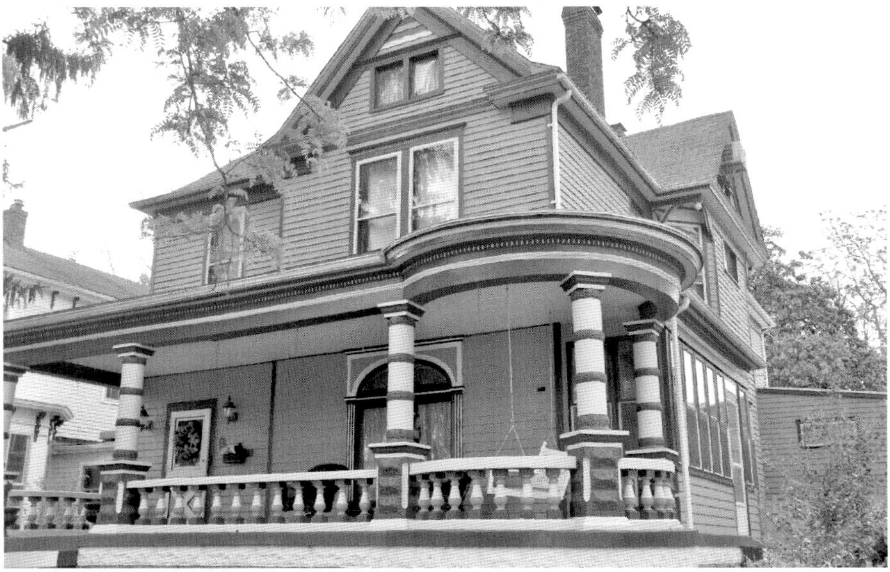

The Conner-Cannon House was completed in 1901 in the Queen Anne style for James Wesley Conner Jr. *Gregory Sekula.*

The two-and-a-half-story, vernacular, Queen Anne–style house features a large wraparound porch supported by segmental cast-concrete columns set on rusticated block piers. A conical roof projection at the corner of the porch reinforces the house's Queen Anne style. Two-story bay windows on the east and west sides of the house provide further visual interest to the structure's exterior. A large arched stained-glass window above the first-floor front window provides a hint of the rich interior of the Conner-Cannon House.

An abundance of natural oak woodwork embellishes the first-floor principal rooms from the paneled staircase with built-in bench and hall tree to the columned oak mantels with beveled-glass mirrors. Paneled and glass-light pocket doors are found between the principal rooms, and strip oak parquet floors with different three-dimensional patterns are found in each room. Beveled- and jewel-faceted stained-glass windows further enrich the interior spaces in the stair hall, parlor and dining room. A family room addition, added by the Cannon family, wraps around the back of the house and incorporates salvaged stained- and leaded-glass windows. Original trim, oak mantels and converted gas light sconces are found on the second floor.

JUDGE ALEXANDER DOWLING HOUSE

1217 East Spring Street

Built in 1870, this imposing frame house was originally the home of Judge Alexander Dowling. It was Dowling who expanded the house's original footprint in 1888 by adding a large rear addition, which necessitated the relocation of the house's original interior staircase. A beautiful stained-glass window in the Aesthetic Movement taste was incorporated into the new staircase landing and can be appreciated on the East Thirteenth Street side of the house. The dwelling remained in the Dowling family until the death of Judge Dowling in 1917. It was then purchased by the Edward Jackson family and remained in their possession until 1936. Jackson was proprietor of the E.E. Jackson Saloon in downtown New Albany. He later ran the Opera House Bowling Lanes at the northeast corner of East Spring and Pearl Streets. He died at the age of sixty-one in 1932. His wife, Una, remained in the house until she sold it in 1936. By 1937, the home had been repurposed as the Mullineaux Funeral Home—a fate common to many larger historic homes throughout the country beginning in the Depression

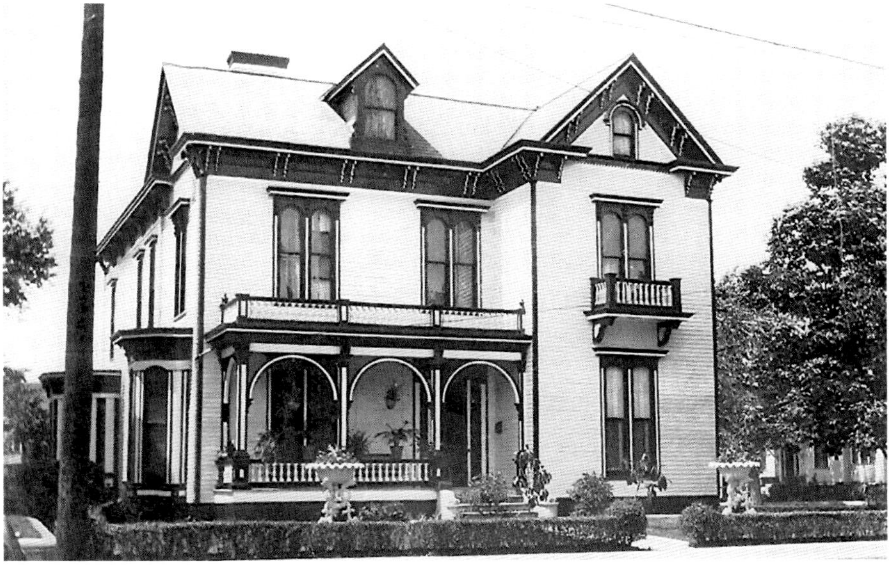

A circa-1925 view of the Judge Alexander Dowling House before the removal of its porch and other features for conversion to a funeral home. *Carl Platt collection.*

era. Despite changes in business ownership, the house remains an active funeral home today.

Early images of the house that survive before its front porch was enclosed and, later, expanded for the funeral home business, show a classic gable-and-wing building form with an abundance of Italianate detailing from the bracketed cornice to the two-story side bay window on the house's east side, to the paired arched front windows with bracketed window hoods. Two one-story bay windows were also found on the west side of the dwelling, one of which survives. The building's form and detailing link the structure to the work of architects and master builders William and James Banes, who were responsible for several other gable-and-wing houses, including the Ferry-McDonald-Green House at 1014 East Main Street and the Culbertson Widows' Home at 704 East Main Street. The William S. Culbertson Mansion is the most celebrated work of the Banes brothers.

Despite its conversion to a funeral home, the Judge Alexander Dowling House has retained much of its original wood trim from the 1870s period of original construction. Parquet flooring and the open staircase with figural newel post light, as well as an elaborate mantel in the house's former dining room, are likely remnants of the 1888 updates to the house.

5

MIDTOWN

The area, referred to geographically today as Midtown, is a relatively recent namesake for an area of the city extending east of East Fifth Street to Vincennes Street and from East Market Street north to Beeler Street. The neighborhood encompasses some of the earliest plat extensions to the city and consists generally of middle- and working-class housing. Grander residences are found in concentration along East Elm Street, while more modest housing is located along East Oak Street, Culbertson Avenue, Ekin Avenue and the numbered cross streets in between.

The Midtown designation was created in 2009 as part of a rebranding effort by city officials and neighborhood leaders and residents who were interested in promoting revitalization of an inner-city urban neighborhood that had fallen on hard times with a high concentration of vacant and foreclosed homes and depressed property values. The area was a designated target area for federal Neighborhood Stabilization Program (NSP) funding that was awarded to the City of New Albany in 2009. Rehabilitation of vacant housing and construction of new housing units began in earnest in the neighborhood in 2010, with over thirty rehabilitation and new construction projects occurring over a two-year period. Additional housing rehab and new construction are occurring incrementally as part of a revolving fund created from homes sales of NSP properties.

For purposes of this publication, Midtown refers to the geographic area bounded by East Ninth Street on the west, Vincennes Street on the east, East Elm Street on the south and Ekin Avenue on the north. The following are some of the historic homes of note in the Midtown neighborhood.

JOHN AND CATHERINE VERNIA HOUSE

912 East Elm Street

John and Catherine Vernia were residing in the two-story Queen Anne–style dwelling at 1310 East Elm Street when they purchased this lot—including an older house that stood on the property—for $1,950 in July 1908 from the heirs of John McBarron. The Vernias demolished the existing house and immediately began construction on this spacious American Foursquare, which was completed by 1909. With its Classical detailing and second-floor front façade bay window, the new home is of similar design to the Klosse-Leist House at 1006 East Elm Street and was likely constructed by the same builder.

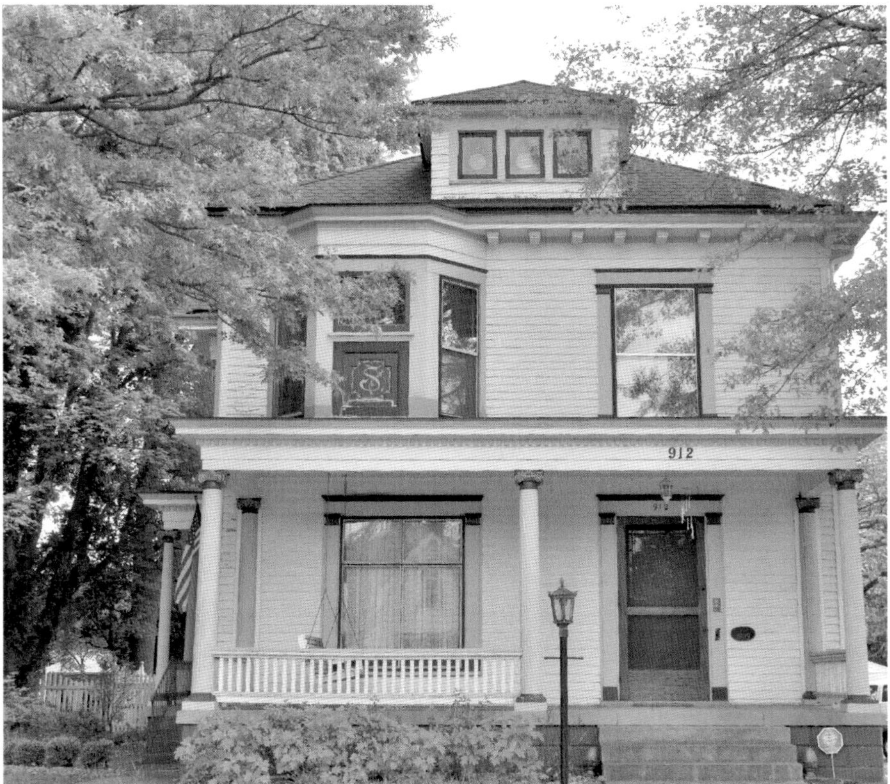

This Classical Revival–style home was built circa 1909 for monument dealer John Vernia and his wife, Catherine. *Gregory Sekula.*

John Vernia was the founder of New Albany's John Vernia & Son Monuments, established in 1876 and located at 501 Pearl Street. He also served on the New Albany City Council and owned numerous investment properties throughout the city. Following his death in September 1918 at the age of seventy-two, his widow remained in the home with her daughter and son-in-law, Laura and Joseph Foley, until her death at age eighty-one in February 1933.

Soon after Catherine Vernia's passing, the Foleys' daughter and son-in-law, Katherine and Eugene Fenger, came to live in the home. Laura Foley remained there until her death in February 1951 at age eighty. Eugene Fenger was an employee of the L&N Railroad for over fifty years. He passed away at age eighty-six in December 1981. His widow continued living here until her death in January 1985, ending over seventy-five years of residency for three successive generations of the Vernia family.

Attorney Bill Smith and his wife, Janet, purchased the property in 1987 and spent twenty years rehabilitating and upgrading the residence before they relocated to Florida. One notable enhancement by the Smiths was the conversion of the attic space into a contemplation chapel. Other interior features of the house of note include a paneled oak front entry door with beveled- and leaded-glass; an open oak staircase in the front hall that is illuminated by an arched stained-glass window at the landing level; natural oak, cherry and pine woodwork throughout the house; a corner fireplace in the front parlor with quartersawn oak mantel with scroll work and a beveled-glass mirror and inlaid strip oak flooring throughout the first floor.

Galbraith-Dishman-Hedden House

916 East Elm Street

This two-story frame house has an interesting history as it is one of the earliest documented house moves in New Albany. The two-story gable-front structure was built for William Galbraith around 1865 and originally stood on Lower Second Street between Main and Water Streets. In 1876, following the laying of railroad tracks along the Ohio River in the house's vicinity, then owner Frank Dishman, son-in-law of William Galbraith, and his wife, Martha, contracted with a moving company in Chicago to move the house in at least two pieces to its present East Elm Street site.

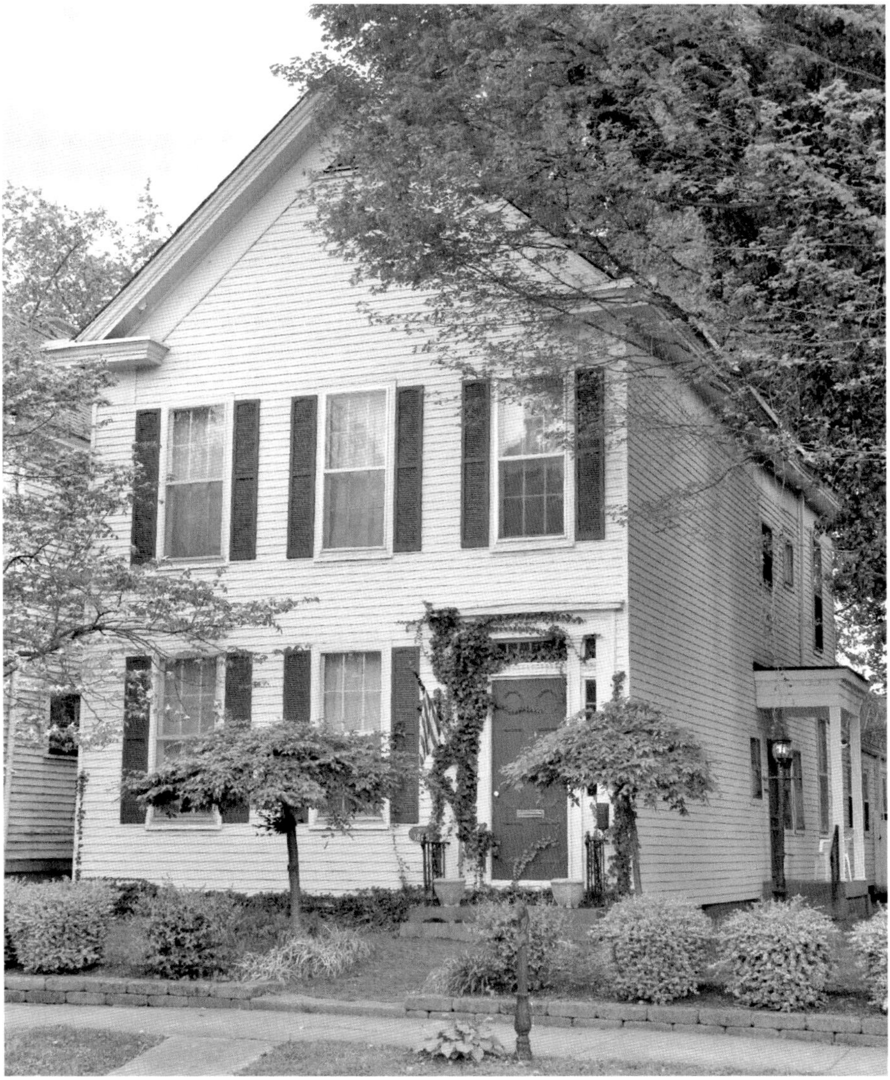

The circa-1865 Galbraith-Dishman-Hedden House was moved to its present site from Lower Second Street in 1876. *Gregory Sekula.*

The *New Albany Daily Ledger* reported the slowly progressing move by wooden beams on rollers pulled by mules in a series of brief accounts beginning on February 24, 1876, and continuing through March 20, 1876. The March 10 account was particularly noteworthy and captured the excitement of this event:

March 10, 1876—Mr. Dishman's house is slowly wending its way up the street, and still continues to attract crowds of idlers. One enthusiastic young lady declared that she saw smoke coming out of one of the chimneys, and said the family was still living in it, cooking and eating the same as ever. The rollers mashed in a large rock over the culvert across Main street at State, showing the immense weight resting on them.

Following the death of the Dishmans, the house was inherited by their daughter and son-in-law, Sarah and Earl Hedden. A notable exterior feature of the house includes its Greek Revival entrance with paneled door, slender sidelights and three-part transom window. A prominent interior feature includes an open staircase in the front hall with cherry handrail and newel post with ash spindles. Original woodwork survives throughout most of the house, with the breakfast room possessing alternating ash and walnut panels.

CONNER-MOSER-RICKE HOUSE

917 East Elm Street

Surrounded by the city's finest example of cast-iron fencing, the Conner-Moser-Ricke House is a notable Italianate Villa–style dwelling attributed to noted New Albany architect and master builder Isaac P. Smith. The main two-story block of the house features wide overhanging eaves with a bracketed cornice and paired windows. Scratch marks on the brick suggest that the building originally had a stucco finish and may have been scored to resemble blocks of cut stone, which was a popular treatment of the period. Built in 1856 for John T. Conner, the house was sold within two years to John Gordon Jr., who was a partner in the New Albany firm of Gordon, Castlen & Gordon, wholesale dealers in iron, hardware and metals. It is believed that Gordon had the intricate cast-iron fence installed during his residency. In May 1869, Joseph J. Terstegge purchased the property. Terstegge was proprietor of J.J. Terstegge, a manufacturer, wholesale and retail dealer in boots and shoes. He was also partners in a foundry business that evolved into the Stratton & Terstegge Company.

Charles Schwartzel purchased the house in 1924 as a wedding gift to his granddaughter Margaret and her husband, Karl Moser. The Mosers made many improvements to the property, including an update of the entrance

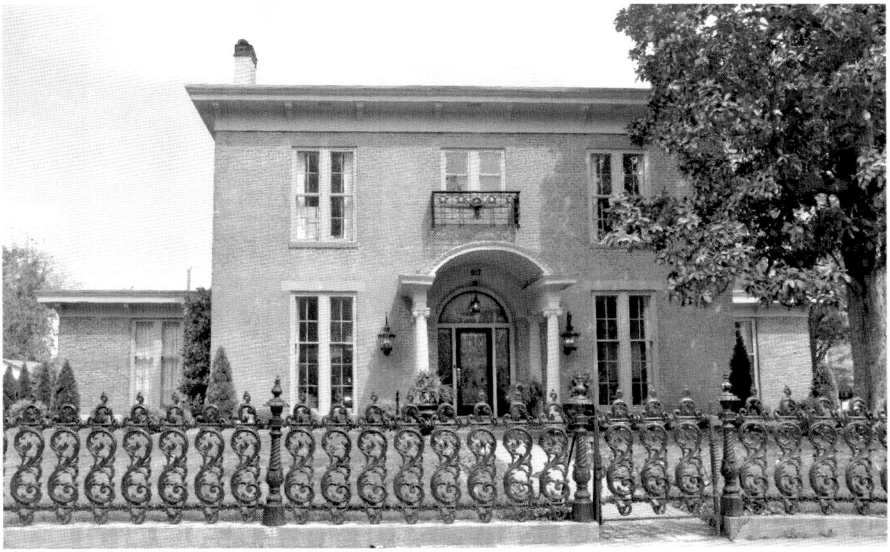

Attributed to noted New Albany architect and master builder Isaac P. Smith, the 1856 Conner-Moser-Ricke House was built for John T. Conner. *Gregory Sekula.*

with its arched Colonial Revival porch supported by fluted Composite Order columns and Arts and Crafts–style leaded-glass windows. The Mosers hired the Charles Hegewald Company to replicate the design of the fence and extend it around the side of the property. Another gift of Schwartzel was a mural painted above one of the front parlor fireplaces by local artist James Russell that now hangs in the hallway.[51] In 1937, the house became the home to Charles and Mary Marguet. Charles Marguet was associated with New Albany Box and Basket Company.

In late 2006, Larry Ricke and his wife, Ann, purchased the home from Margaret "Beebs" Marguet and initiated a substantial rehabilitation. The Rickes rebuilt an existing one-story wing on the west side of the house and built an east wing to match it. The front entrance received new leaded- and beveled-glass windows, and ironwork was added under the house's second-floor façade center window to enhance the elegance of the structure. Larry's sister Barbara Ricke, the owner of Barbara Ricke Interiors of Lexington, Kentucky, provided exterior and interior design upgrades to the house, incorporating lavish moldings, lighting and finishes. A notable historic feature of the interior is a second-floor Art Deco bathroom with lavender Carrara glass. The original Italianate hardwood staircase also remains intact and is illuminated at mid-landing by an art glass window from the 1920s remodeling.

Neat-Hoffer House

1010 East Elm Street

Addis and Sophia Neat purchased this new home from William Aikin in January 1885 for $1,800. "Mr. Neat was one of the best known citizens of New Albany and substantial businessmen of Louisville," reported the *New Albany Evening Tribune* of September 5, 1904. Addis Neat was involved in the retail and wholesale drug business, both in New Albany and Louisville.

In May 1892, Tobias and Mary Hoffer bought the property for $2,500. For a time, Tobias Hoffer was proprietor of the T. Hoffer & Company, whiskey distillers and wholesalers. The firm was located at 106 East Market Street and, later, at 119 East Main Street. Tobias Hoffer passed away in May 1921 at the age of fifty-eight. Mary Hoffer remained in the home through the mid-1930s, while her daughter, Stella, continued her residency here until the late 1930s. By September 1942, the Hoffers sold the house, ending just over fifty years of ownership by the family.

Recently rehabilitated after years of neglect, the Neat-Hoffer House is a one-story gable-and-wing plan house similar in form to the Kesler-Farnsley House at 1306 East Elm Street, among others. The house has few exterior

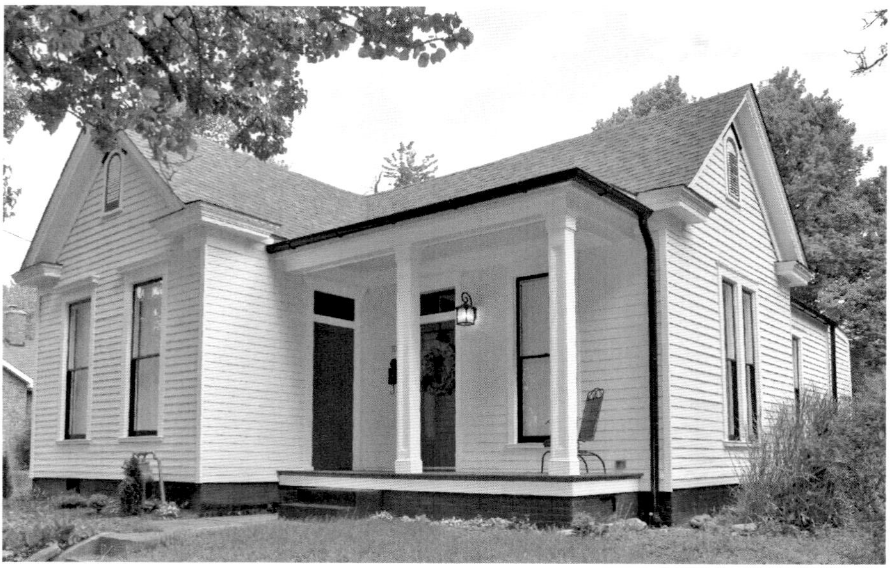

The 1885 Neat-Hoffer House is a one-story gable-and-wing plan frame house built for New Albany and Louisville, Kentucky druggist Addis Neat. *Gregory Sekula.*

embellishments but retains its original elongated window sashes with simple molded hoods and wooden front doors with full-length glass. Square paneled posts support the partial front porch and replaced a slightly more elaborate post treatment with shallow arched spandrels.

HARVEY AND MARY SCRIBNER HOUSE

1113 East Elm Street

Harvey and Mary Scribner had made their home next door at 1109 East Elm Street since July 1869. Around 1889, they completed this new, Queen Anne–style house on the lot immediately to the east. Harvey was the grandson of Joel Scribner, one of the founders of New Albany. He was the cashier for the New Albany National Bank and was also engaged in the book, stationery and wallpaper business. He passed away in January 1900 at the age of seventy-one. The Scribners had moved from their East Elm Street house shortly before the death of Harvey Scribner. Mary Scribner then moved in with her mother, Mrs. Silas Day, at 419 Bank Street. Mary Scribner died in July 1932 at her home at 1621 Ekin Avenue, where she had resided for nearly twelve years.

An outstanding feature of the Scribner House is its elaborate gabled front porch supported by turned posts and decorated with brackets and sawnwork ornamentation, including an arched spandrel resembling a stern wheel of a steamboat. The detailing found in the house's front gable is similar to other Queen Anne–style dwellings found in the Uptown section of New Albany, including the Keyes-Harris House at 1923 Ekin Avenue and the Merker-Klerner-Fix House at 1821 East Elm Street, thus suggesting the hand of a single designer and/or builder.

ZOLLMANN-COLBY HOUSE

1219 East Elm Street

William Zollmann purchased this property in September 1897 for $1,550 from the heirs of Charles Sloemer. An earlier one-story shotgun-style dwelling had stood on the property along with the present carriage house in the rear yard at the alley. In 1902, the present house was completed, the construction date verified by an inscription written on the wall by a wallpaper hanger who signed and dated it, "Ed Huckleberry, 1902." Zollmann and his business partner, Edward Riely, were proprietors of the Boston Shoe Store, located at 304 Pearl Street.

The Zollmann family remained in the house only until March 1905, when it was purchased by Fred and Rose (Everbach) Colby for $4,500. Fred Colby was secretary at the Paul Reising Brewing Company, where his brother-in-law, John Meyer, was owner. He also was a retired executive of the Cannelton Sewer Pipe Company and a telegraph operator for Western Union. Family oral tradition maintains that Colby, a German immigrant, had made the first crystal radio in the area in 1915. He was later ordered to dismantle it due to anti-German sentiment during World War I. The home remained in the Colby family through mid-1980s.

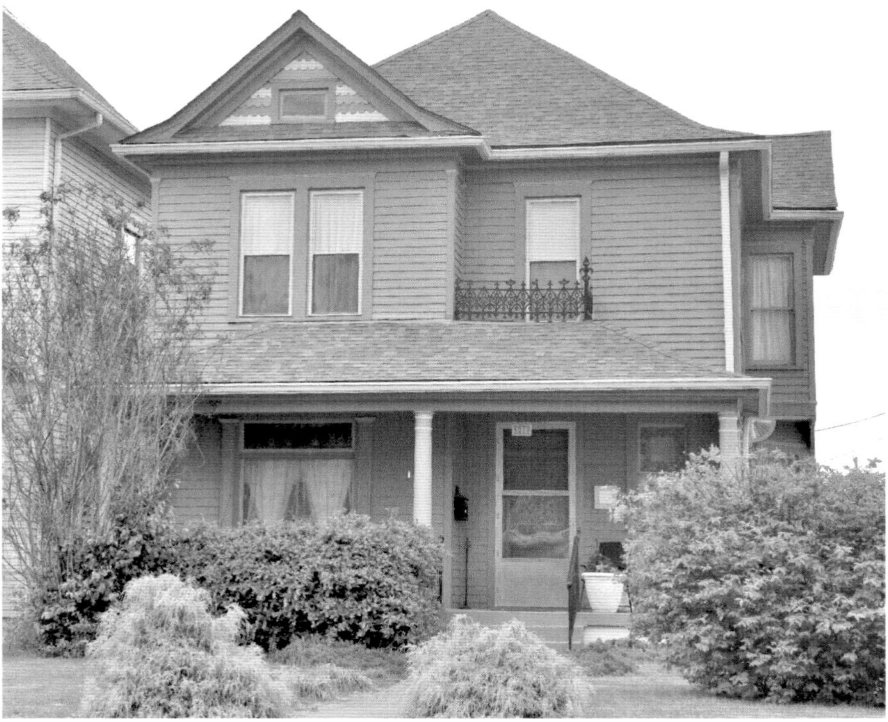

Replaced by an earlier structure, the 1902 Zollmann-Colby House exhibits numerous embellishments of the Queen Anne style. *Gregory Sekula.*

The exterior of the Zollmann-Colby House home exhibits many of the decorative embellishments typical of the Queen Anne style. The complex roofline with steeply pitched hipped roof with lower cross gables features flared eaves and gables ornamented with fishscale shingles. A full-width front porch is topped by wrought-iron cresting and supported by wooden Tuscan columns. Several window sashes on the house have decorative glass, including a notable diamond-shaped window on the East Thirteenth Street side of the residence and the oak front door with its beveled- and leaded-glass. The interior features an entrance hall with a paneled staircase with egg-and-dart molding, paneled newel post and built-in bench. The present front parlor originally was divided into two rooms, its wall and double doors removed and, later, installed in a Louisville, Kentucky home. An oak mantel in the parlor, built-in china cabinet in the dining room and hardwood floors are additional features that add to the house's Victorian charm.

ANSON BANES HOUSE

1523 East Elm Street

It appears that this house was completed shortly after the wedding of Anson Banes to his young bride, Laura Johnston, on January 1, 1880. Banes was a house carpenter and was very likely the builder of his own home. He began his construction career with his father, James, and uncle William Banes, who were responsible for many of New Albany's most notable residences, including the William S. Culbertson Mansion at 904 East Main Street, among others.

Anson Banes passed away at age sixty in March 1918, followed by his widow in December 1922. The Banes's daughter, Mabel, who had always lived in the house with her parents, continued her residency here until her death in November 1959 at age seventy-six. This ended almost eight decades of ownership by the Banes family, and the home subsequently went through several different owners. Window changes on the front façade and the application of asbestos siding over the original clapboard obscured the house's original design in these intervening years. Thankfully, the house was rehabilitated by the Louisville-based New Directions Housing Corporation in 2012 under a federal Neighborhood Stabilization Program (NSP) grant awarded to the City of New Albany.

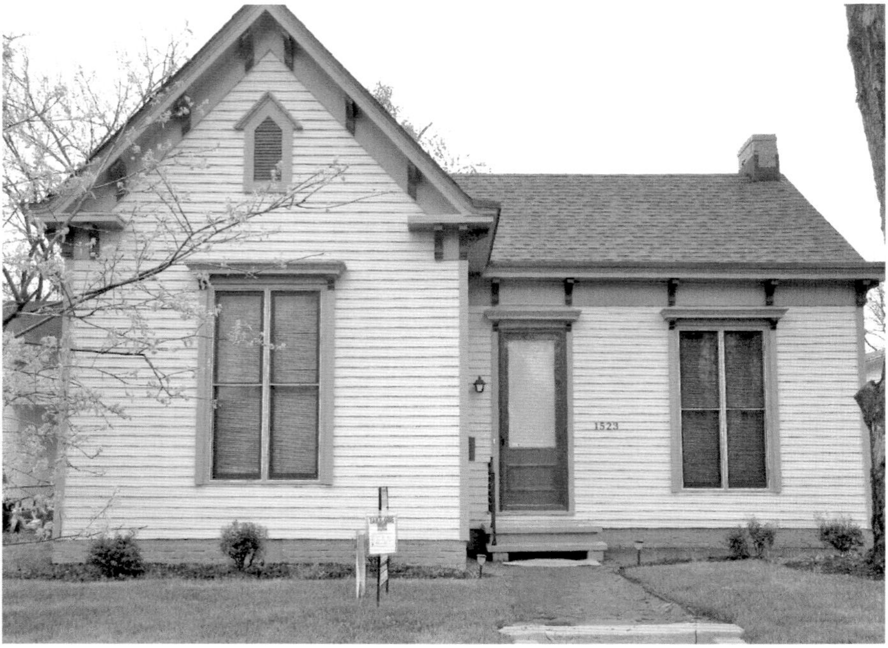

This gable-and-wing form circa-1880 house was built by house carpenter Anson Banes, whose father and uncle built many of New Albany's finest residences. *Gregory Sekula.*

This thoughtful rehabilitation reintroduced the house's original paired window configuration on the façade and reclaimed the clapboard siding hidden beneath the asbestos shingles.

In plan, the Anson Banes House follows the gable-and-wing form favored by the Banes brothers and relates this house to other known or attributed Banes residential commissions, including the Culbertson Widows' Home at 704 East Main Street and the Herman and Johanna Rockenbach House at 1811 Ekin Avenue. A steeply pitched gabled roof, cornice embellished with wooden brackets, a gabled attic vent and paired windows with bracketed window hoods give this modest cottage an air of sophistication, suggesting the hand of a trained designer and builder. On the interior, the NSP rehabilitation preserved the house's two remaining original wooden mantels and strip oak flooring with parquet border in the front room.

ALEXANDER AND CLEOPATRA MARTIN HOUSE

920 East Oak Street

This one-and-a-half-story gable-front brick house was built for Alexander and Cleopatra Martin in 1859–60. Alexander Martin was a professor at the New Albany Female Seminary before entering service in the Civil War in 1861. While in service, he became captain of the 38th Indiana Volunteers, Company H, under Benjamin F. Scribner. Captain Martin was wounded in the Civil War and came home to New Albany to recuperate.[52] On the night of May 18, 1863, there was fear of a race riot in New Albany when Captain Martin intervened on behalf of an African American man to protect him from being stoned by an angry mob near the Martin's house.[53]

Less than two years later, Captain Martin died at his home in April 1865 at age thirty-two. Cleopatra Martin, a prominent member of Third Presbyterian Church, remained in the house, along with her son, Charles, and his wife, Mattie, until her death in June 1909. After Mattie Martin's death in August 1925, Charles Martin sold the property in March 1930, ending over seventy years of ownership by the Martin family.

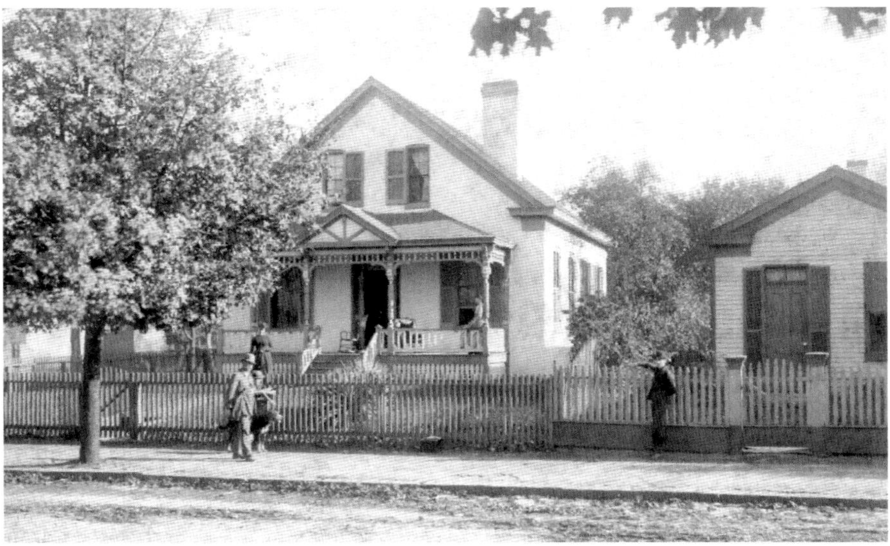

This circa-1890 image of the circa-1860 Alexander and Cleopatra Martin House shows the elaborate Victorian porch, now enclosed. *Roberts Collection.*

Presently owned by Pearl Street Baptist Church, the house has been used as a clothes closet ministry. The house's ornate Victorian porch, likely added in the 1880s or 1890s, still survives largely intact behind wooden partition walls used to expand the building's storage capacity.

CARDINAL RITTER HOUSE AND BAKERY

1218 East Oak Street

Elmer Joseph Ritter was one of six children of German immigrants Nicholas and Bertha Ritter. He was born in this combination house and bakery building in 1892. Ritter attended nearby St. Mary's Catholic Church and School and eventually went on to St. Meinrad Seminary in southern Indiana, where he studied for the priesthood. After a relatively short stint as a parish priest, Ritter rose quickly through the ranks of the church, becoming first the bishop and later archbishop of Indianapolis. He later was named archbishop of St. Louis. In the 1930s and 1940s, Ritter championed for the rights of disenfranchised groups, including African Americans, by confronting the Ku Klux Klan and challenging long-held beliefs about justice and equality. Ritter proactively desegregated the parochial school systems in Indianapolis in 1937 and, later in St. Louis in 1947. Both efforts occurred before the U.S. Supreme Court's landmark case *Brown v. Board of Education* made integration the law of the land. In 1961, Ritter was elevated to cardinal by Saint John XXIII, making him Indiana's only Roman Catholic cardinal to date. Cardinal Ritter became an influential voice in the Church's Second Vatican Council, supporting changes in the church that continue to this day.[54]

Recognizing the importance of Cardinal Ritter, Indiana Landmarks negotiated the purchase of the Cardinal Ritter House and Bakery in the summer of 2002 after the property had been condemned and was threatened with demolition. The preservation group began a stabilization of the property. Engagement with local residents and leaders of the community led to an effort to create a new nonprofit organization with the purpose of preserving the Ritter House and educating the public about Cardinal Ritter's legacy. The Cardinal Ritter Birthplace Foundation was formed in 2004. The following year, the foundation purchased the property from Indiana Landmarks and mounted a successful capital campaign to

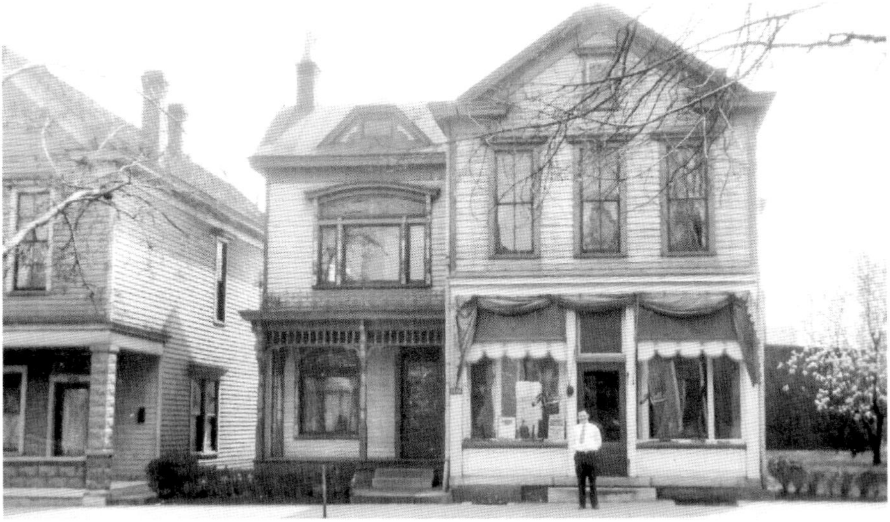

The Cardinal Ritter House and Bakery, shown in this circa-1930 photo, was restored through the efforts of Indiana Landmarks and the Cardinal Ritter Birthplace Foundation. *Cardinal Ritter Birthplace Foundation Collection.*

repurpose the house and bakery as an office building for social service organizations. The transformation of this once-derelict house into a beacon of hope for the Midtown neighborhood and beyond is one of the most compelling historic preservation success stories in New Albany.

The Ritter House was constructed in two stages, with the gabled storefront section having been built in the 1870s and the wing to the east built some twenty years later in the early 1890s. A brick ell at the rear of the house originally housed the bakery operations. A large frame multipurpose wing was added behind the bakery section in 2011. The two-story frame historic section of the house features a rebuilt storefront with large plate-glass windows with transom windows above. The residential entrance with its paneled and patterned-glass door is sheltered by a porch supported by turned bracketed posts with decorative spandrels in between. Ornamental iron cresting embellishes the porch roof. A three-part window with arched stained glass above illuminates the very room where Ritter was born. On the interior, diagonally laid quartersawn oak floors and molded woodwork with ornamental cornerblocks evoke the house's Victorian origins. A tiled fireplace with oak mantelshelf in the parlor and an open paneled oak staircase, illuminated by two stained-glass windows, reflect the modest grandeur of the original home.

SAPPENFIELD-BALDWIN-MCGRATH HOUSE

1509 East Oak Street

Built in 1887, this visually delightful Queen Anne–style home was originally occupied by Lydia Sappenfield, who purchased the property from the John A. Hutton Trust in September 1887. Sappenfield, who was the widow of John, lived in the home only through 1891. The house was then sold to Susan Baldwin and remained in the Baldwin family until 1904. It was the Baldwins who added the elaborate side porch to the house with its turned posts, bracketed and paneled cornice and sawnwork detailing.

Following ownership by the Albert and Day families, the house was purchased in 1924 by Michael McGrath and remained in the family for over sixty years. During the McGrath ownership, the house's cast-concrete front porch was added. The hipped roof porch is supported by tapered paired posts resting on formed rusticated concrete block bases. Molded concrete balusters form a railing between the piers. The front porch shelters an unusual arched Palladian window with decorative hood trim embellished with applied carvings. Above the front porch, a paired window at the second floor level is further embellished with a decorative gabled molded window hood. A bracketed cornice provides further exterior decoration at the house's main eave line.

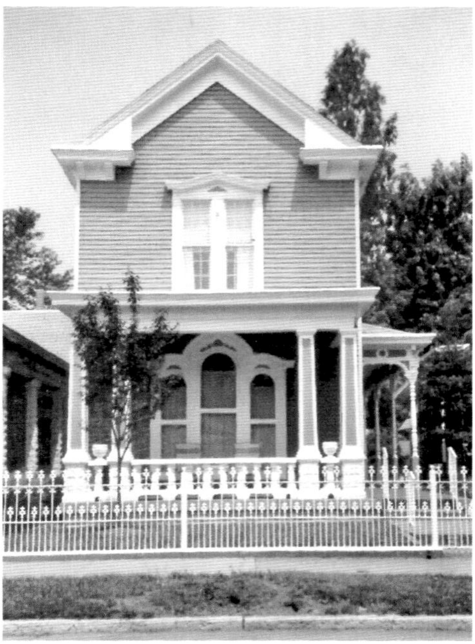

The 1887 Sappenfield-Baldwin-McGrath House, shown in this circa-1995 image, exhibits a wealth of architectural detailing spanning the 1880s to the 1920s. *Barksdale collection.*

The interior of the Sappenfield-Baldwin-McGrath House retains some of its original 1887 trim work, as well as some early twentieth-century "upgrades," including an open paneled oak staircase, plate rail in the dining room and an oak mantelpiece and an Arts and Crafts–style stained-glass window in the front parlor.

JOSEPH AND LOUISE KREMENTZ HOUSE

1527 East Oak Street

This notable American Foursquare plan residence with red tiled roof and buff brick exterior was completed in 1927 as the residence of Joseph and Louise Krementz and their daughter and son-in-law, Matilda and John J. Brown. The Krementz family purchased this property in May 1926 for $4,500 and demolished a two-story frame house that had stood on the lot. Elements of the Victorian house—including trim, doors and hinges—were salvaged from the earlier house and incorporated into the new residence, primarily on the second floor. Hand-painted wall murals originally were located in the living and dining rooms but have been painted over in recent years. Rich woodwork, a tiled fireplace in the living room with wood mantel shelf, built-in cabinetry in a breakfast room and vintage light fixtures from the 1920s have, thankfully, been preserved on the first floor.

Joseph Krementz owned Krementz Meat Market at 615 Vincennes Street, and his son-in-law served as manager. He died at age seventy-two in October 1932, and John Brown, then a salesman for the Louisville Grocery Company and an accomplished musician, passed in May 1935 at age fifty-two.

WILLIAM AND ELIZABETH DAY HOUSE

1515 Ekin Avenue

Constructed next door to the Day family home at 1517 Ekin Avenue, this classic frame bungalow was built for William Day and his bride, Elizabeth "Elsie" Schieman, in 1917 prior to their wedding in August of that year. William Day was the son of Stephen Day, whose family business—Stephen Day & Sons—was one of the most respected and prolific house building contractors in New Albany at the turn of the twentieth century. Day was employed in the family business, along with his father and brothers, Adolph, Clem and Herman. Construction of this house was delayed due to the March 23, 1917 tornado that devastated portions of New Albany just north and east of where this house is situated. The Day family used its building expertise to assist many New Albanians whose homes had been damaged or destroyed in the cyclone disaster.[55]

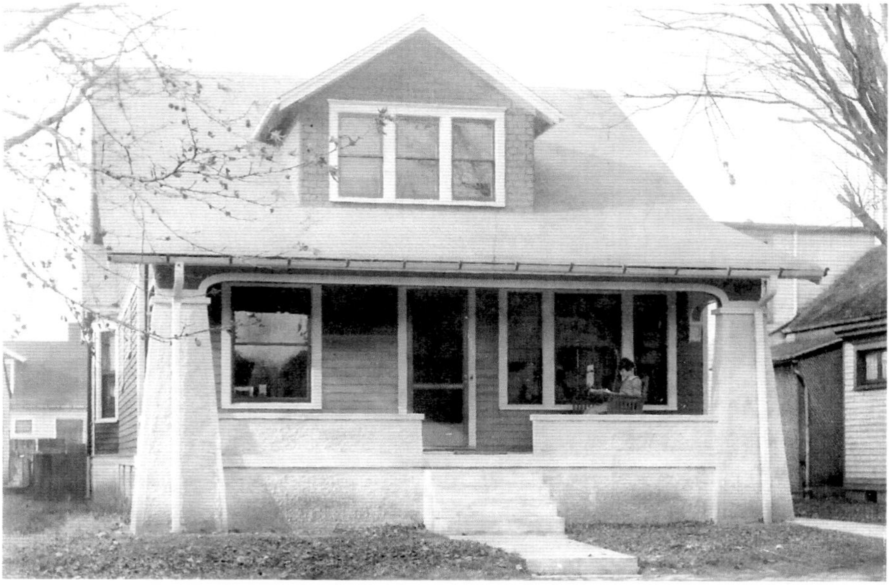

This dormer-front bungalow, depicted in this circa-1920 postcard, was built for William and Elizabeth Day in 1917. *Will Day collection.*

With its side gable roof, central gable dormer and tapered masonry porch supports, the William and Elizabeth Day House is similar in form to the Catherine and Anna Guthrie House at 1105 East Spring Street and the Martin and Fannie Herter House at 920 East Spring Street, thus suggesting additional residential commissions by Stephen Day & Sons. The interior of the William and Elizabeth Day House features a wealth of natural woodwork with different woods utilized in the various rooms.

Adolph and Josephine Day House

1608 Ekin Avenue

Adolph and Josephine Day had this two-and-a-half-story frame house built in 1902 after purchasing the lot from Holy Trinity Catholic Church in March of that year. "Dolph," as he was known, was the managing partner in the family contracting business of Stephen Day & Sons, perhaps the city's most prolific house builders in the early twentieth century. The company had been started by Stephen Day, who moved to New Albany from Lanesville, Indiana, in 1888. Stephen Day—along with sons Herman, Clem, William and Adolph—had their lumberyard nearby on East Fifteenth Street, and several family members built residences in the immediate area. Dolph married Josephine Ziegelbauer on May 12, 1896, and resided in a modest home at 1601 Ekin Avenue before building this house. The couple raised their eight children here. Dolph passed away on November 13, 1930, and his wife passed away less than three months later on January 31, 1931.

The Adolph and Josephine Day House is a vernacular Queen Anne style–dwelling with a hipped roof with lower cross gable roofline. A signature feature of the Day-built Queen Anne is the second floor oriel window that graces the front façade of house. In the case of 1608 Ekin Avenue, simple brackets support the oriel window. A cottage-style window below the oriel has a handsome leaded-glass transom window above. A partial front porch with a projecting gable is supported by brick piers and is enclosed as a sun porch. At least five other houses in New Albany are similar in form and style to the house at 1608 Ekin Avenue, including 716, 720 and 724 Vincennes Street; 1518 Shelby Place (a documented Day commission); and 1104 East Market Street. All six houses were constructed between 1898 and 1907 and likely are all Day commissions.

FRANCONIA-YOST HOUSE

921 East Eleventh Street

Charles Franconia purchased this lot in July 1885 for $275 from Henry Fawcett, who had platted this area in May 1882. Franconia owned a grocery at the corner of Beeler and East Eleventh Streets. He had this shotgun-style frame house built shortly after purchasing the lot. In November 1901, the house became the home to the Michael and Agatha Yost family, who moved to New Albany from Lanesville, Indiana.

The house was originally a one-story shotgun structure. The rear "camelback" portion was added shortly after the Yosts took possession and Agatha's brother, Stephen Day, the popular building contractor who moved to New Albany in 1888, most likely built the addition. Yost family members occupied the house for thirty-seven years, selling it in September 1938. In the 1960s, James and Rita Sarles owned the house. James Sarles was the

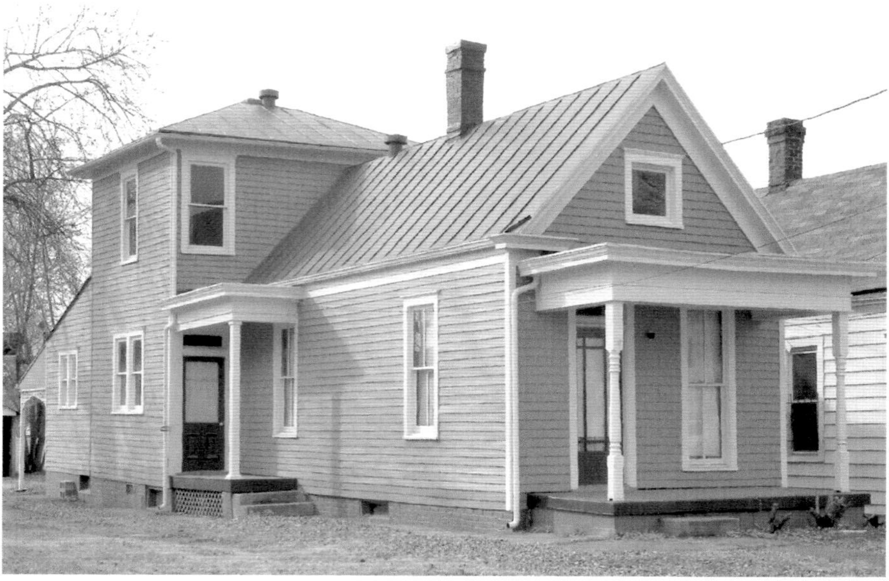

Known as a "camelback" shotgun-style house, the Franconia-Yost House received its second-floor addition by Stephen Day & Son around 1901. *Ray Day Collection.*

proprietor of the Texaco Service Station at the corner of Beeler and East Eighth Streets, which was directly behind their house.[56]

The Franconia-Yost House is representative of a housing type that was prolific for the working-class population throughout New Albany in the last quarter of the nineteenth century and first quarter of the twentieth century. The shotgun house, so named for its succession of rooms and the absence of hallways, was typically one story, with its narrow end facing the street. Rear rooms on the house were often slightly wider, which enabled a second entrance to be accommodated at the side of the house. In the case of the Franconia-Yost House, additional living space was achieved by adding a second floor to these larger rear rooms. Such shotgun houses have come to be known as "camelback" shotguns. Often associated with the South, the shotgun housing type was popular in the Louisville, Kentucky area, including the Indiana cities of Jeffersonville, Clarksville and New Albany located across the Ohio River. New Albany arguably may have Indiana's largest concentration of shotgun houses. Once threatened with demolition and subsequently donated to Indiana Landmarks, the Franconia-Yost House is one of several shotguns that was rehabilitated in Midtown as a result of the NSP grant program. Indiana Landmarks holds preservation covenants on this tiny gem in the Midtown neighborhood.

6

Cedar Bough Place

The residential enclave known as Cedar Bough Place was developed around 1889 by Andros Huncilman, a local real estate developer and landowner who owned the five-acre tract of land on which the subdivision was constructed. Huncilman chose to make Cedar Bough Place a private street and consequently deeded building lots that extended to the centerline of the street. Thus, homeowners along the elongated block held an ownership interest in the street in addition to their own property. This private street designation remains to this day.

Listed in the National Register of Historic Places in 2008, the Cedar Bough Place Historic District is a single block neighborhood consisting of twenty-five single-family dwellings that were constructed between 1891 and 1920. The neighborhood was considered a middle class stronghold when built and has remained so today, with numerous houses rehabilitated for single-family home ownership in recent years. The following is a sampling of some of the notable residences found "on the Bough."

Day-Tuley-Stemm House

801 Cedar Bough Place

This handsomely detailed one-and-a-half-story brick bungalow, anchoring the south entrance to Cedar Bough Place on the west side of the block,

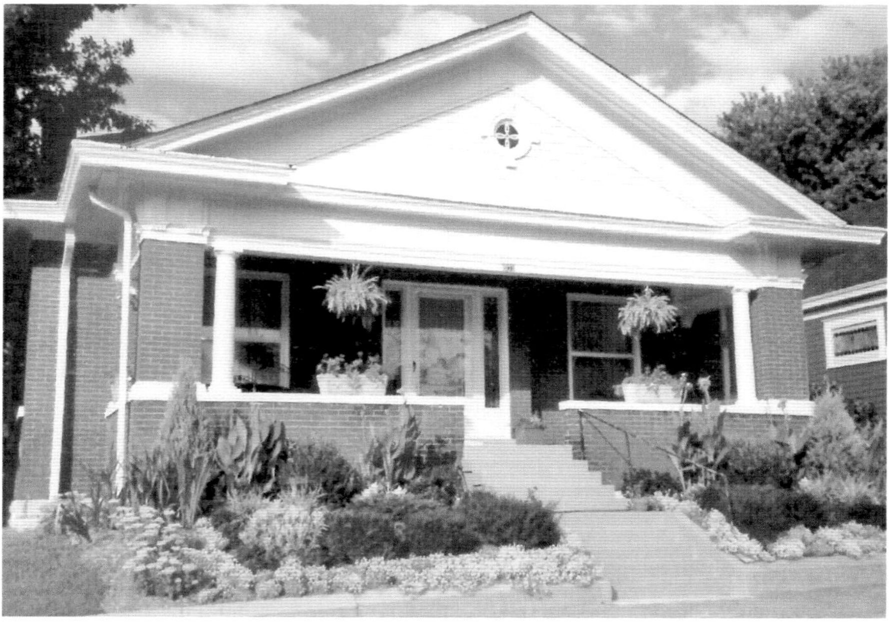

The Day-Tuley-Stemm House, shown in this circa-1995 image, was constructed by builder Isaac Craig in 1910 for Charles Day. *Barksdale collection.*

was built in 1910 by builder Isaac Craig and first occupied by Charles Day, secretary and treasurer of the Day Leather Company. The Day family owned the property for nine years. It was then sold to the Tuley family, who occupied the house until September 1942, when it was sold to Frank and Susan Stemm. The family moved to "the Bough" a year before Frank Stemm retired from the Quartermaster Depot in Jeffersonville, Indiana. The Stemms had four children: Wilson, Robert, Clara and Jeanne. Susan Stemm passed away at age seventy-seven in March 1964; at the time of Frank Stemm's death in June 1981 at age ninety-eight, he was recognized as one of the nation's last surviving veterans of the Spanish-American War.[57]

The Day-Tuley-Stemm House features an abundance of classical details on its exterior. The house's façade is dominated by a broad, gabled, full-width porch supported by brick corner pier columns with fluted Tuscan columns in antis. The porch's gable end features an entablature ornamented with simplified triglyphs positioned over the brick piers. A four-light oculus window with keystone surround is centered in the gable end. The house's main entrance features a single-light wooden door flanked by leaded- and stained-glass sidelights. Hipped dormers punctuate the house's truncated hipped roof, and a one-story bay window with diamond patterned leaded-glass window expands the rectangular footprint of the house on its south elevation.

Hemmer-Hock House

808 Cedar Bough Place

Anchoring the entrance to Cedar Bough Place on the east side of the street, this frame dwelling was originally the home of grocer Charles Hemmer, whose business, C.H. Hemmer Grocery, was located at 527 East Fourth Street. Hemmer and his wife, Mary, purchased this then-vacant lot in March 1904 and had the house built in 1905. Charles Hemmer died in June 1910, and his widow remained in the home until her death in May 1933.

In March 1944, Bernard Hock purchased the house. Hock was an accomplished table tennis champion, being inducted in both the Indiana and U.S. Table Tennis Hall of Fame. He formed his own company, the Hock Table Tennis Company, manufacturing equipment, including paddles.[58] The basement of the home was a popular gathering place for local youth interested in learning the sport. Bernard Hock was once associated with the Hock family business, Fidelity Roofing and Siding Company, still in existence today.

The vernacular Queen Anne–style house features a hipped roof with lower cross gables sheltering projecting bay windows. A wraparound porch with dentil-work cornice and fluted Roman Doric columns shelters the house's main entrance door with its leaded-glass window in a floral design. The interior of the house includes natural oak woodwork, hardwood floors and stained glass in the front vestibule, parlor and dining room bay windows. A corner oak fireplace in the parlor is adorned with laurel wreath appliques and full-length Corinthian-style columns and an oval beveled-glass mirror.

Bull-Wright-Coleman House

830 Cedar Bough Place

Constructed in 1892 for $5,000, including the price of the lot, this spacious Queen Anne–style dwelling is among the largest of the houses built on Cedar

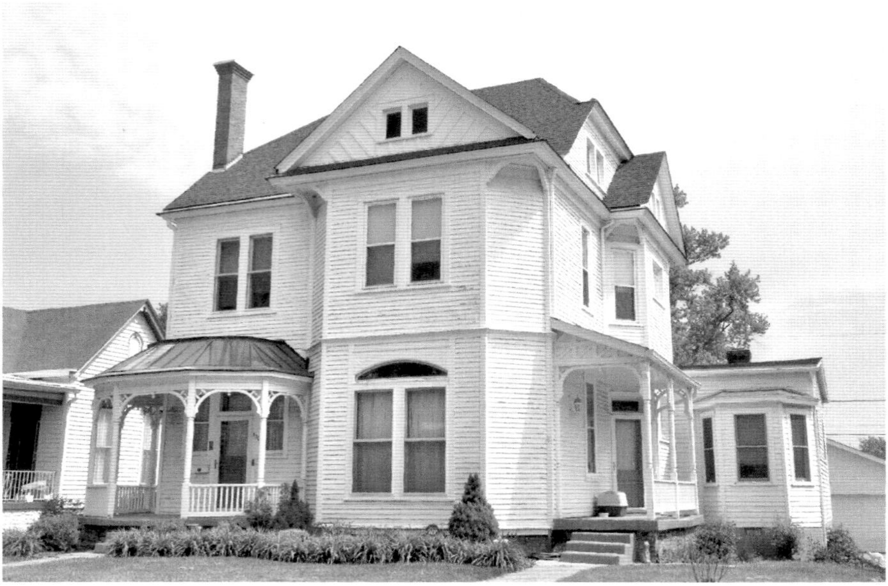

Constructed in 1892, the Bull-Wright-Coleman House features many distinctive Queen Anne elements, including some Stick-style decoration. *Gregory Sekula.*

Bough Place and was first occupied by Louisville commission merchant Benjamin Bull. Bull and his wife, Alice, lost their home to a sheriff's sale in February 1901. The property was purchased by Allen and Addie Wright. Allen Wright was vice-president of the Louisville branch of Cliver, Wright & Rainey, a cotton brokerage business. The Wright family occupied the house until February 1919, at which time it was sold to Dr. Arthur N. Coleman, a local dentist. Dr. Coleman had his office at 319 Pearl Street. The Coleman family had lived in the Coleman-Guthrie House at 838 Cedar Bough Place before purchasing this house. The Colemans remained here until the early 1950s. The house has seen numerous owners in the intervening years until 1984, when the present owners, Jackie and Joyce Meyers, purchased the house. The couple has worked to lovingly restore the house, maintaining its Victorian character.

The Bull-Wright-Coleman House features asymmetrical massing typical of the Queen Anne style. Its complex roofline is made distinctive by the presence of jerkinhead side gables. A projecting, bracketed, two-story bay window on the front façade is capped by a gabled roof with Stick-style decoration. The first floor of the bay features a framed grouping of paired windows with a segmental arched stained-glass transom above. A distinctive feature of the façade is the polygonal-shaped entry porch supported by turned posts and ornamented with arched brackets terminating in a drop-pendant decoration.

BRADLEY-GWIN-JANES HOUSE

831 Cedar Bough Place

The Bradley-Gwin-Janes House is one of New Albany's finest examples of Queen Anne architecture. Construction of this two-and-a-half-story dwelling was begun in 1891 shortly after Lawrence Bradley purchased the lot. The cost of combined lot purchase and construction was $5,250. The 1892–93 *New Albany City Directory* indicates that Charles L. Bradley was the house's first occupant. Bradley was the superintendent of the New Albany Cotton Batting Mills. By 1895–96, Lawrence L. Bradley is listed as living at this address. His occupation is identified as cashier for the Second National Bank and, later, as owner of a New Albany general brokerage and insurance company. Although there is no record of the Bradley family living in the house after 1896, the family owned the property until December 1905, when Earl Gwin purchased the home "on the Bough" for $3,500. Gwin was also cashier for the Second National Bank and lived here through 1915, selling the property to William Janes for $5,000 in January 1916. Janes is listed in city directories of the period as a chemist. The Janes family subsequently occupied the house for over forty-five years. In March 2006, the Bradley-Gwin-Janes House suffered a devastating fire. Fortunately, the blaze was quickly contained at the rear of the structure, although smoke and water damage occurred throughout. Subsequent owners embarked on restoration of this dwelling in 2007 through 2013.

Believed to be the work of New Albany architect Milton C. Pritchett, who may have also designed the nearby Browning-Dennis House at 843 Cedar Bough Place, this two-and-a-half-story frame house exhibits a wealth of architectural detailing on both the exterior and interior. The exterior façade is dominated by a steeply pitched gable roof ornamented with scalloped shingles. A projecting gable at the roof peak, supported by oversized wooden brackets, shelters a central oriel window in the attic space ornamented with diamond-pattern windows. The house's exterior is sheathed in clapboard siding with a scalloped shingle belt course between the first and second

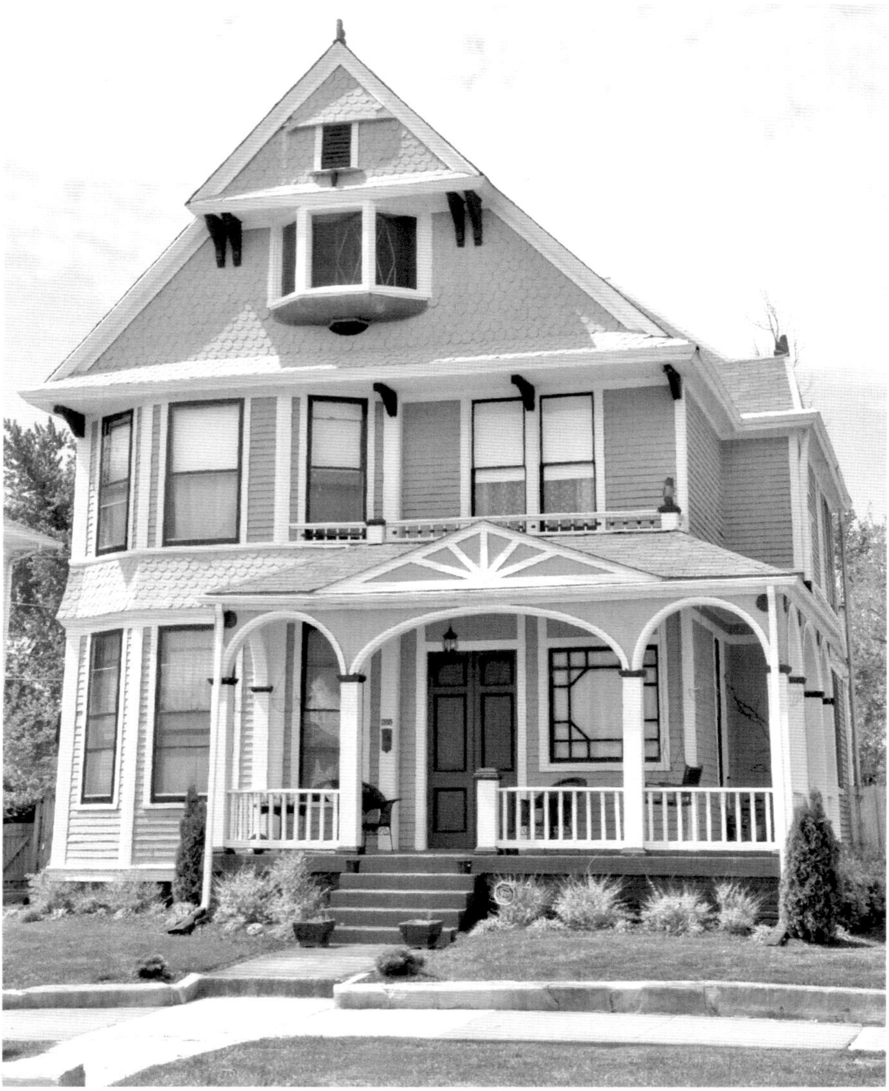

The two-and-a-half-story frame Bradley-Gwin-Janes House is thought to be the work of New Albany architect Milton C. Pritchett. *Gregory Sekula.*

stories. Two-story bay windows on the east and south side elevations help to enliven the main building mass. A partial wraparound porch supported by square posts with arches in between is decorated with sunflower appliques. The roof, which originally boasted an ornamental slate design, retains some of its original metal finials.

The interior features parquet and patterned oak floors, ornamental mirrored fireplace mantels in the front parlor and dining room with decorative tile hearths and pocket doors. Original door and window casings survive. The front entry contains an unusual open staircase with paneled wall and cherry tapered newel posts. An inglenook in the front hall contains a built-in window seat with a large beveled- and clear-glass window above with ornamental wooden muntin pattern. Stained-glass windows illuminate the main staircase landing, the dining room bay window and a second-floor bedroom. A butler's pantry off the dining room contains original built-in cabinetry.

FERDINAND T. AND MARY KAHLER HOUSE

837 Cedar Bough Place

This unusual Craftsman bungalow was constructed around 1920 for Ferdinand T. and Mary Kahler. The Kahlers purchased the adjoining house at 839 Cedar Bough Place and this lot in 1903 and lived in the adjoining house until this structure was completed.

Kahler founded the Kahler Manufacturing Company, a downtown New Albany woodworking enterprise, located at Pearl and Oak Streets, that manufactured table tops, kitchen cabinets and interior woodwork for residences and offices.[59] An inventor who held five U.S. patents, Kahler also was an entrepreneur. He reorganized the American Automobile Manufacturing Company as the Ohio Falls Motor Company in 1912 and then reorganized that company into the Falls City Motor Car Company in 1913. These New Albany companies produced the "Ohio Falls" and "Pilgrim" motorcars. The Kahler Company later contracted with Henry Ford in 1917, to become one of the suppliers of Model T chassis for the Ford Motor Company.[60] Kahler's manufacturing facility was located just a few blocks from his home near the north Y intersection at Grant Line and Charlestown Roads. That factory was destroyed in the March 23, 1917 tornado that devastated northeastern portions of the city. After attempts from auto leaders in Detroit to lure Kahler to build a plant there, he responded by rebuilding a new plant in the same location, doubling its size and workforce.[61]

Ferdinand Kahler died in November 1927 at the age of sixty-two, and his widow remained in the home until her death in September 1932 at age sixty-eight. Other prominent New Albany families that subsequently resided

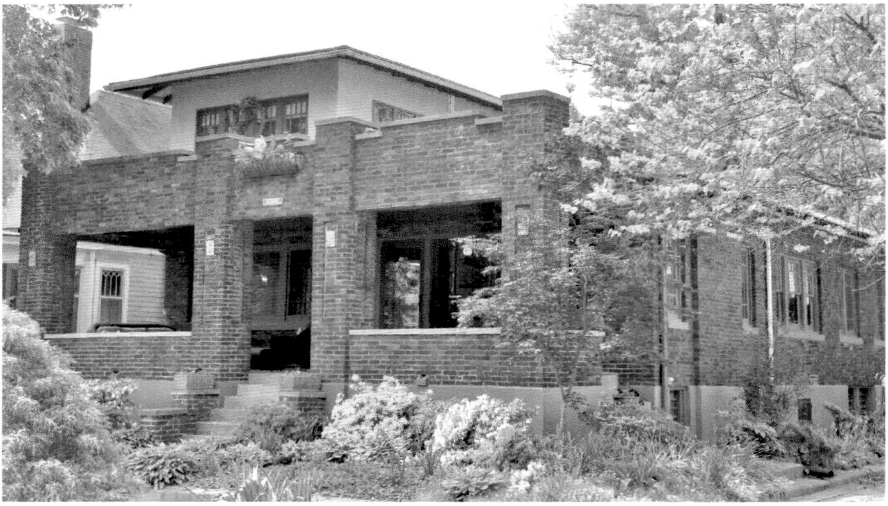

Built circa 1920, the Ferdinand T. and Mary Kahler House is a very unusual, brick Craftsman-style bungalow with extraordinary interior detailing. *Gregory Sekula.*

here include the Thornbrough, Lorch, Wunderlich, Wilcox and Hartfield families. Over the past quarter century, William and Laurie Arbaugh have painstakingly restored the house to retain its unique historic character.

The exterior of the Ferdinand T. and Mary Kahler House features a one-story main block of wire-cut brick with a parapet roofline. The parapet screens a stucco-covered second floor room lined with twelve windows and covered by a shallow-hipped roof with broad overhangs. Paneled piers that extend to the parapet level support a full-width front porch that shelters the original eleven-light entry door with matching multi-light sidelights. The interior of the house is a profusion of natural mahogany and sweet gum woodwork with paneled walls, beamed ceilings and an unusual wooden archway between the front parlor and dining room. Strip oak flooring with a variety of elaborate border treatments further enhances the interior spaces.

COLEMAN-GUTHRIE HOUSE

838 Cedar Bough Place

Built in 1910, the Coleman-Guthrie House was first occupied by Dr. Arthur N. Coleman and family. Dr. Coleman was a New Albany dentist and had his office at 319 Pearl Street. He purchased the lot on which this house stands from Martin Huncilman in the fall of 1909 and had this one-and-a-half-story frame residence built. The Coleman family first appears in the 1911–12 *New Albany City Directory* at this address. The Colemans remained here only a few years before moving to the Bull-Wright-Coleman House at 830 Cedar Bough Place.

The next owner of the property was the Thomas Guthrie family. Guthrie and his two brothers were the owners of Guthrie Brothers, wholesale dealers in paper and twine. The Guthries made their home here for over twenty years. By the mid-1930s, the house was divided into a duplex and, over the next half-century, saw numerous owners. Marvin and Melanie Riddle purchased the house in the mid-1980s and converted it back to a single-family residence. Present owner Ted Fulmore purchased the house in 2002 and embarked on an extensive exterior restoration: removing vinyl siding; repairing wood clapboards, trim and windows; and painting the exterior in a three-color paint scheme.

With its hipped roof and lower cross gables, the house is representative of a housing form and style that is prevalent in New Albany's older and historic neighborhoods. The prominent feature of the house's exterior is its full-width front porch supported by classically inspired Scamozzi Order

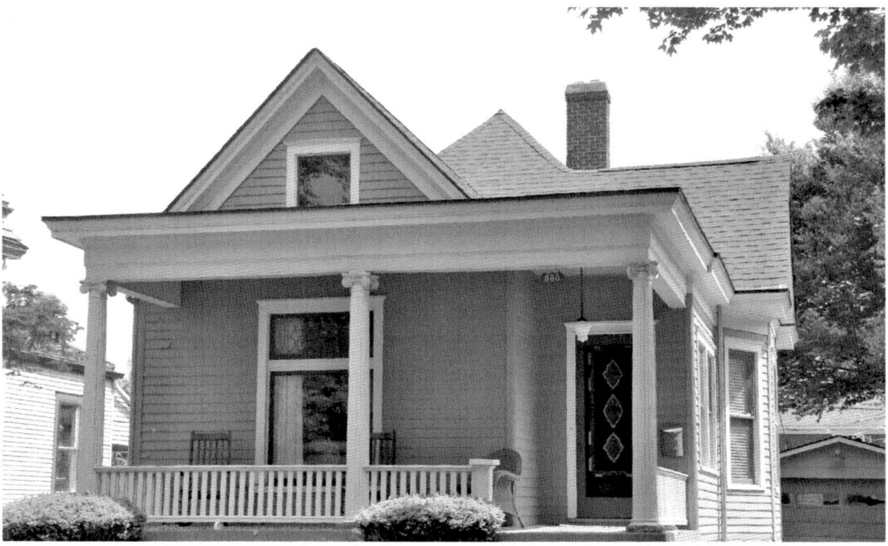

The 1910 Coleman-Guthrie House represents a housing form and style prevalent in New Albany's older neighborhoods. *Gregory Sekula.*

columns. A bay window on the house's south elevation provides further visual interest to the essentially vernacular Queen Anne form of the house. On the interior, natural oak woodwork, a pocket door between the front parlor and dining room and yellow pine flooring provide an inviting interior that speaks to the livability of New Albany's many modest historic dwellings.

BROWNING-DENNIS HOUSE

843 Cedar Bough Place

Anchoring the north end of Cedar Bough Place, this imposing Queen Anne–style dwelling was originally the home of dry goods merchant Willey Browning, who was employed with the dry goods firm of J.M. Robinson, Norton & Company in Louisville, Kentucky. The Brownings resided at the northeast corner of East Twelfth and Main Streets until this residence was completed in 1893 at a cost of $5,000. Browning died suddenly at the age of fifty-eight in September 1896, and the house was sold two years later to David Dennis. Dennis came to New Albany from Salem, Indiana, around 1892 and was engaged in a wholesale grocery business known as Fawcett, Dennis & Company, located at 317 State Street. Following his death in July 1912, the house saw several owners and eventually was subdivided into four apartments. Suzanne Sidebottom and her late husband, Robert, purchased the house in the mid-1970s and have worked to return the house to single-family use and restore its original features.

The two-and-a-half-story Queen Anne house is notable for its shingle-clad, cylinder-shaped turret with conical roof that rises above the house's complex hipped and cross-gabled roofline. Alternating patterns of decorative slate adorn the tower roof and gable ends. An unusual, metal-clad, conical roof hood with decorative wooden spandrels shelters an angled corner of the house's first floor and may be the remnants of a now lost side porch. A partial-width front porch with turned posts and arched bracket supports shelters the main entrance. Decorative wood shingle panels adorn the house's clapboard exterior on the front elevation. The interior retains much of its original woodwork, four fireplaces with original mantels and an oak staircase with turned balusters and machine-carved, square newel posts. A ghost signature of a wallpaper hanger's signature remains in the front parlor.

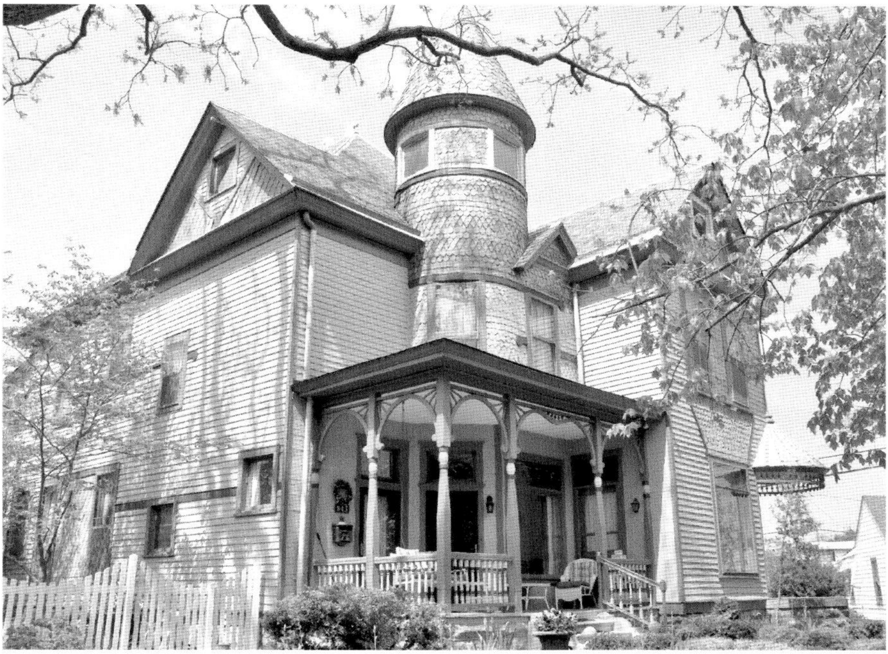

The 1893 Browning-Dennis House anchors the north end of Cedar Bough Place, historically and presently, a private street. *Gregory Sekula.*

Stylistically, the Browning-Dennis House is very similar in design to the Professor Ira. G. Strunk House located at 1310 Ridgeway Avenue in the Silver Hills section of New Albany. The Silver Hills house is a documented work of architect Milton C. Pritchett, who maintained an architectural practice in New Albany and Bedford, Indiana, and Louisville, Kentucky. He also resided on Ridgeway Avenue, where he was responsible for several of the first houses built on Ridgeway Avenue in the hilltop enclave.

7

Uptown

Like neighboring Midtown, Uptown is a contemporary identification for a residential section of the city bounded by Vincennes Street on the west, Silver Street on the east, Shelby Street on the north and East Spring Street on the south. Residential development began in the neighborhood in the last quarter of the nineteenth century and was likely jump-started, in part, by the establishment of the New Albany National Cemetery in 1862 on Poplar Street, later renamed Ekin Avenue in honor of Union army general James A. Ekin. One of the original fourteen national cemeteries created by Congress under President Abraham Lincoln, the five-and-a-half-acre cemetery was the brainchild of Dr. Thomas Fry, a former brigade surgeon at New Albany hospitals during the Civil War who advocated for a respectable resting place for Union war fatalities treated in the town.

The area's proximity to nearby factories—including the New Albany Hosiery Mill that once operated on Ekin Avenue and the vast New Albany Woolen Mills that stood on the site of present-day New Albany High School on Vincennes Street—also likely fueled working-class residential growth in this section of the town. In 1865–66, the New Albany Street Railway Company introduced streetcar service to New Albany. Ekin Avenue became one of the city's main lines by the early 1890s, thus further serving as a magnet for residential growth in the area and establishing Ekin Avenue as a prestigious middle-class residential address. The following properties are some of Uptown's more notable residences.

IDEAL CREST (HERMAN AND JOHANNA ROCKENBACH HOUSE)

1811 Ekin Avenue

Situated on a spacious hilltop lot nearly an acre in size, Ideal Crest stands as one of the oldest surviving houses in New Albany's Uptown neighborhood. The one-and-a-half-story brick house was built in 1883 for Herman Rockenbach; his wife, Johanna; and their three children. Herman Rockenbach was the owner of the Eagle Tannery, which stood on the north side of Oak Street between State and Pearl Streets. He was an avid gardener and used his expansive lot as a canvas for elaborate planting beds, including ones for tropical banana plants. His daughter, Etelka, was a well-known local educator, having taught Latin at New Albany High School for many years and, later, German at Indiana University Southeast and Latin at Providence High School in her retirement. She also served as assistant principal at New Albany High School during her tenure there.[62] A 1905 postcard of the house attributes the name "Ideal Crest" to the property.

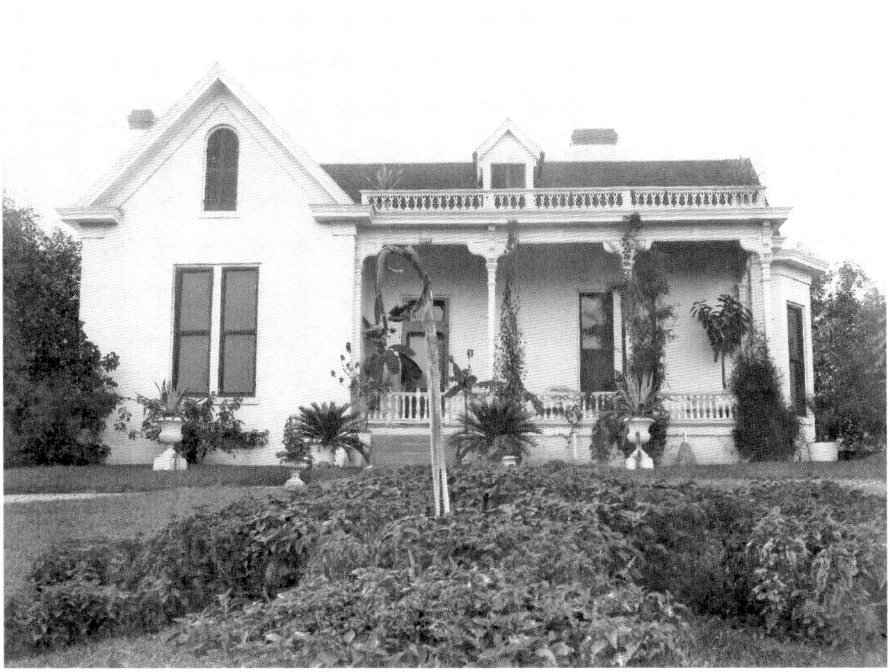

A circa-1905 view of the Herman and Johanna Rockenbach House, "Ideal Crest." *Sekula Collection.*

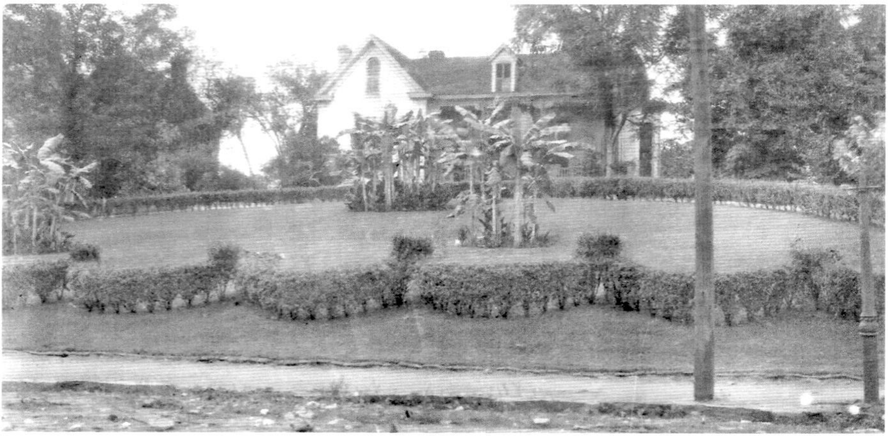

"Ideal Crest," shown in this circa-1915 image, boasted elaborate planting beds in its elevated front lawn. *Sekula Collection.*

The Herman and Johanna Rockenbach House exhibits the classic gable-and-wing form that is the hallmark of architects and master builders William and James Banes, who designed, among many New Albany residences, the William S. Culbertson Mansion and the Culbertson Widows' Home (both on East Main Street), as well as the Cornelia Memorial Orphan's Home, which originally stood to the west of this property, was demolished in the 1960s and replaced by the Whitehall Manor apartment complex.

William S. Culbertson had hired the Banes brothers to design and build his mansion and, later as an outgrowth of his philanthropic concerns, the widows' home and orphanage. Minutes from the board of the orphanage reference correspondence with Herman Rockenbach over interest in acquiring his then vacant lot for the purpose of adding to the grounds of the planned orphanage. The minutes reflect that he declined, indicating his intent to erect a residence on the site.[63] By November 1883, local newspaper accounts reported that Rockenbach had erected a fine residence on Ekin Avenue.[64] It is plausible that Rockenbach utilized the services of the Banes brothers to design and build his residence given their commission to build the orphanage next door, which was erected around the same time period.

In form, the Herman and Johanna Rockenbach House is a diminutive version of the Banes-designed Culbertson Widows' Home at 704 East Main Street. The gable-and-wing form, use of steeply pitched front gable and paired windows, the placement of the wing side one-story bay window and the unusual modified gambrel roofline strongly relate these two buildings architecturally. While the widows' home exhibits more costly exterior embellishments, such as the paired bracketed cornice and elaborate cast-iron porch, the Herman and Johanna Rockenbach House replaces the bracketing with a simple corbelled brick cornice line and cast-iron porch components give way to a wooden porch with bracketed chamfered posts in a restrained Italianate style. A sawnwork rooftop porch balustrade provides further embellishment to the exterior. The porch, likely removed in the 1960s, was reconstructed in 2003 by present owners, Greg and Robyn Sekula, based on the historic photograph depicted in this book.

The house's interior features twelve-foot ceilings, original two-part molded woodwork, louvered window shutters, paneled pocket doors and cast-iron mantels, three of which are faux painted to resemble marble. Gilded drapery cornices in the bay windows survive from the Rockenbach ownership period, as do charcoal portraits of the original owners, Herman and Johanna, dated 1877 by artist Gus Lehr, that still hang in their original gilded frames in the house's front parlor.

CHARLES AND ELIZABETH SCHAN HOUSE

1817 Ekin Avenue

One of several prominent hilltop houses on Ekin Avenue, this towered Queen Anne–style dwelling was constructed in October 1895 for $2,500 for the Schan family.[65] Charles Schan operated the Schan Shoe Store on Pearl Street in downtown New Albany for more than fifty years, succeeding his father, who founded the company. His wife, Elizabeth, died in May 1939 at the age of seventy-five. Charles Schan remained in the house until his death at age eighty-seven in August 1949. Robert and Mary Rose Hornung were the next long-term residents of the property, occupying it first as tenants and later purchasing the home and raising their family there. The house remained in the Hornung family until 2005, when Heather Wilson purchased it. She introduced a multicolor paint scheme to the exterior to celebrate the house's rich Victorian detailing.

The exterior of the Charles and Elizabeth Schan House features a notable corner tower ornamented with a sawnwork shingle frieze above the second floor and a conical roof terminating in a metal finial. A partial wraparound porch with bracketed chamfered posts, spindled fretwork spandrels, and latticework gable ornamentation further enlivens the asymmetrical massing of the house. The house's front gable features an oval window surrounded

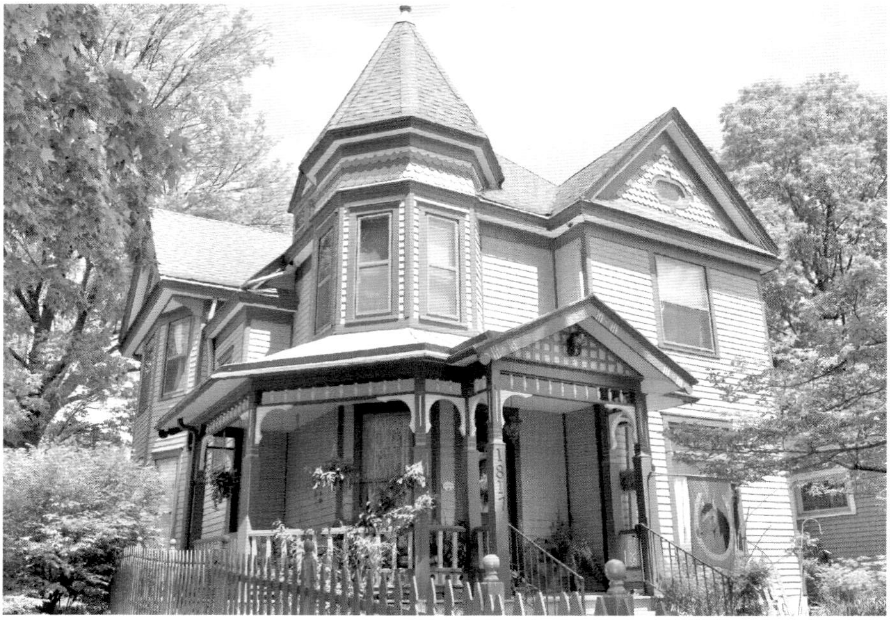

The 1895 Charles and Elizabeth Schan House, with its second-floor corner tower with conical roof, demonstrates superb Queen Anne–style detailing. *Gregory Sekula.*

by patterned sawnwork shingles. Of note on the interior is the paneled oak staircase with Eastlake-style incised carvings on the newel post. A stained-glass window with a fleur-de-lis motif illuminates the stair at the landing level. A second beveled-and stained-glass cottage window is found in the front parlor. Natural oak and pine woodwork is found throughout the house. Oak mantels with original machine carvings and tile work are found on the first and second floors. Strip oak flooring with a modified Greek Key pattern of walnut and maple embellishes the entrance hall.

AUGUST AND ELIZABETH RUTER HOUSE

1824 Ekin Avenue

Elizabeth Kraft, fiancée of August Ruter, purchased the lot on which this modest frame cottage was built in January 1892 for $600. By the spring of that year, a building permit had been procured to erect a house on the lot

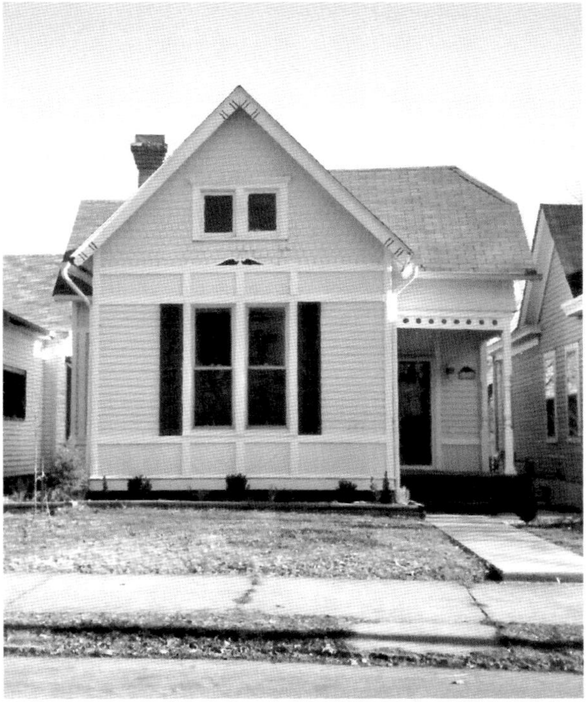

Right: Knoxville, Tennessee architect George F. Barber was responsible for this Uptown Queen Anne–style cottage. *Barksdale collection.*

Below: Design No. 10 in George F. Barber's catalogue *Cottage Souvenir No. 2* was the inspiration for the August and Elizabeth Ruter House. *Dover Publications, 2004.*

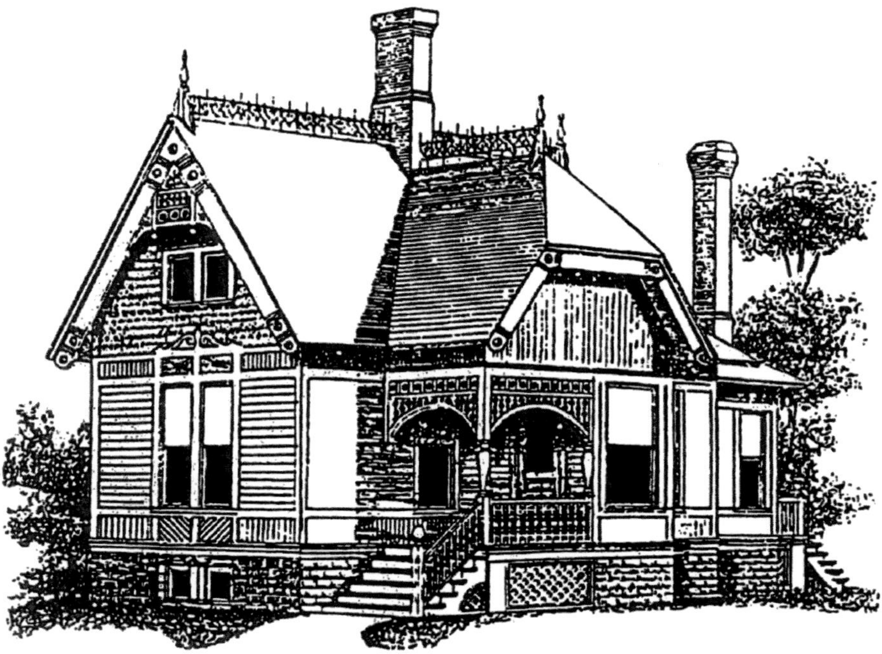

with a value of $865. August Ruter was a foreman and cigar maker for A. Schlosser, located at 211 Pearl Street. The Ruters, who were married in July 1892, had purchased their building plans from Knoxville, Tennessee architect George F. Barber, who offered a multitude of house plans by mail through a series of pattern books distributed nationally. Barber was especially known for his elaborate Queen Anne–style residences, many of which boasted towers, elaborate porches and a profusion of sawnwork ornamentation. For those of more modest means, he also offered small house designs that still were adorned with patterned shingles and fancy porches.

The Ruters chose Design No. 10 from his widely circulated catalogue *Cottage Souvenir No. 2*, which contained designs and floor plans for fifty-nine houses. A description of the Design No. 10 in Barber's catalogue reads as follows:

> *This is another example of a one story cottage. The attic is provided with windows for ventilation and light, in case that part is to be utilized for storing purposes. The kitchen is of good size and has a nice, large pantry. A cellar way can be arranged between pantry and closet if desired. The other rooms are conveniently arranged and of ample size for a house of this character…The design is tasty, as all cottages should be. It costs nothing to get good proportions, and a few dollars expended in ornamental work adds to the value of the building many times the extra expense.*

Despite the application of vinyl siding, the August and Elizabeth Ruter House retains the basic form of the original pattern book house with its cross-gabled roof and small entry porch with turned posts and decorative sawnwork spandrels. Pinwheel fretwork brackets—a modern embellishment—invoke the spirit and intent of Barber's design. Sawnwork shingles and wall panels above and below the front façade's paired windows have been maintained in the application of the synthetic siding to preserve the original design intent of this dignified Queen Anne cottage.

Charles E. Moser House

1843 Ekin Avenue

Constructed in 1912, this notable dwelling was the home of the Charles Moser family. Moser was the secretary and later president of the George

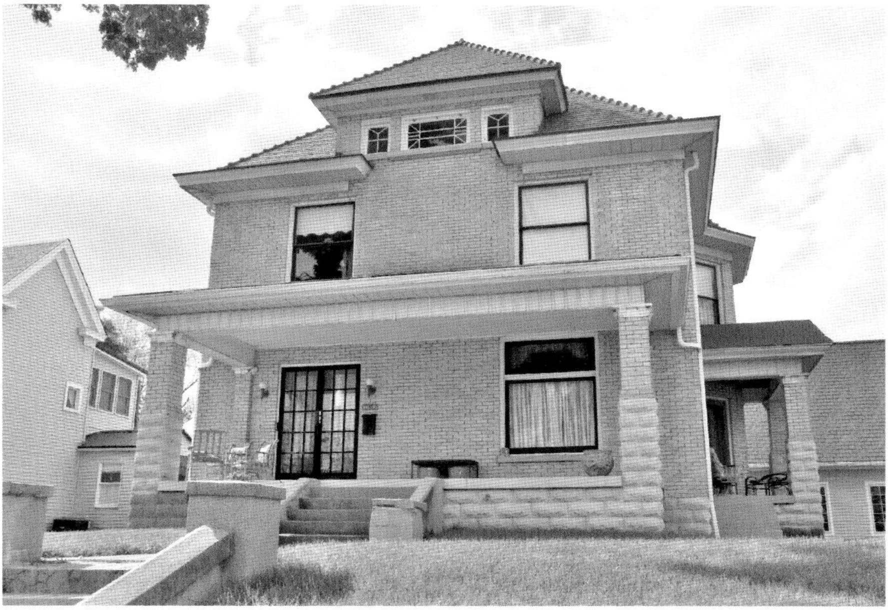

A red clay tile roof is a distinctive feature of the Charles E. Moser House on Ekin Avenue. *Gregory Sekula.*

Moser Leather Company. Founded in 1878 as the Moser Leather Company, the business was an entrepreneurial outgrowth of the industrious George Moser, a German immigrant who came to New Albany in 1867. George Moser worked initially for August Barth, who owned Barth's Tannery on East Tenth Street, which was established in 1864. After ten years at Barth's Tannery, Moser started his own business, purchasing Benjamin Lockwood's tannery on East Eighth Street in 1878. Upon upgrading that facility, he expanded his business and produced quality leather for harnesses and collar manufacturers. In 1891, George Moser's nephew, John Moser, became a partner in the company, and the name was changed to George Moser & Company. Charles Moser assumed his brother John's interest in the company in 1900. Fire destroyed the tannery on East Eighth Street in 1914, and that same year, George Moser died. His heirs renamed the business the George Moser Leather Company, with Charles Moser assuming the presidency. The company, known more recently as the Caldwell/Moser Leather Company, ceased operations in New Albany in 2002.[66]

The Charles E. Moser House is an American Foursquare plan dwelling with a dignified presence along Ekin Avenue. The two-and-a-half-story buff brick residence, believed to be the work of New Albany contractors Stephen Day & Sons, features a distinctive red clay tile pyramidal roof with a broad central hipped roof dormer with three-part decorative window sash grouping that dominates the house's front façade. A full-width hipped roof front porch is supported by buff brick piers with a contrasting stone cap set on rusticated concrete block piers. Paired French doors mark the house's entrance and a beveled- and leaded-glass transom window is located above the front parlor plate glass window. A one-story gabled side porch and two-story bay window define the house's east elevation and paired, diamond-paned, stained-glass windows are found on the house's west side, illuminating the stairwell within.

GEYER-HARTLEY HOUSE

1903 Ekin Avenue

Mr. and Mrs. John Geyer purchased this lot in February 1902 and completed construction of their new residence around 1903–04. At the time of the house's completion, John Geyer was the foreman of the New Albany Hosiery Mill, located two blocks west of their home on Ekin Avenue. The Geyers remained in the house for six years, selling it to Elizabeth and Edward Hartley in April 1910. This began the Hartley family's occupancy of the house, which lasted almost sixty years and spanned two generations. Edward Hartley was one of the proprietors of Hartley Brothers Grocery, located at 114 West Market Street. After retirement from the grocery business, Hartley was engaged in the real estate and insurance business. He died suddenly in the home in April 1932 at the age of seventy-one, and his wife remained in the house until her death in August 1936. The couple's daughter, Hannah, would continue residency here for the next thirty-one years until her death in March 1967. It was after Elizabeth Hartley's death that Hannah subdivided the house into two apartments. Ron and Deb Riall purchased the home in October 1990 and have returned the house back to single-family use and embarked upon a multi-year rehabilitation.

The two-and-a-half-story asymmetrical frame house features a two-story bay window on the west side and a large wraparound front porch with dentil work cornice and fluted columns. A broad, broken pediment, gable dormer with modified Palladian window dominates the house's roofline. An original single light oak door with sidelights defines the entrance. The interior

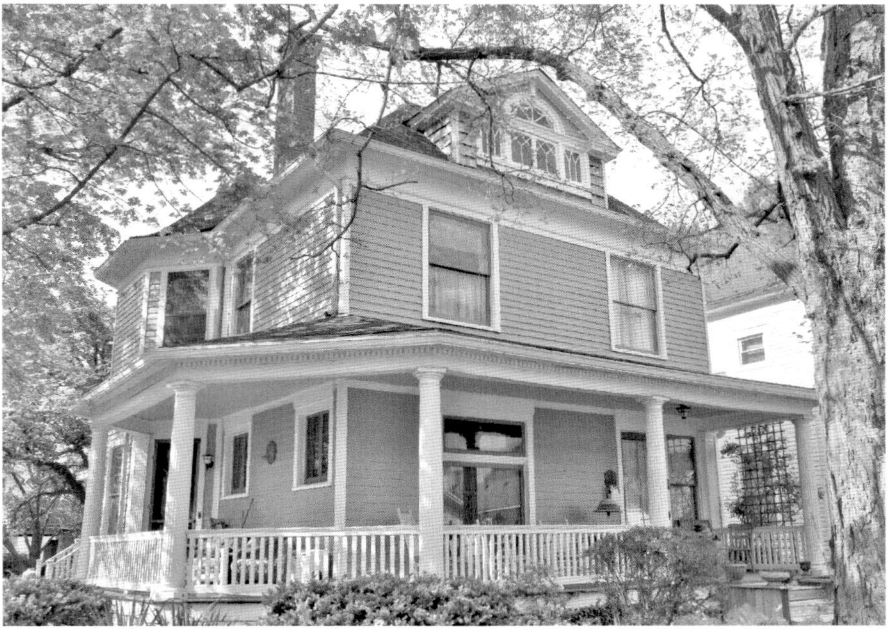

Occupying a corner lot, the Geyer-Hartley House features a wraparound front porch with dental work cornice and fluted columns. *Gregory Sekula.*

features a partially open oak staircase with a stained-glass window at the landing decorated with a stylized Art Nouveau floral design. Oak flooring is found in the principal first-floor rooms, along with a columned oak fireplace with a beveled mirror in the front parlor. A second fireplace with original mantelpiece and tile work graces a second-floor sitting room.

MOSER-CORCORAN HOUSE

1915 Ekin Avenue

This rambling frame bungalow was likely built by New Albany contractors Stephen Day & Sons in 1912 for George Moser Jr. and his wife, Emma. They resided in the house as newlyweds shortly after their wedding in June 1912.[67] George Moser Jr. was the son of George Moser Sr., who founded the George Moser Leather Company. George and Emma Moser eventually built a documented Day-built

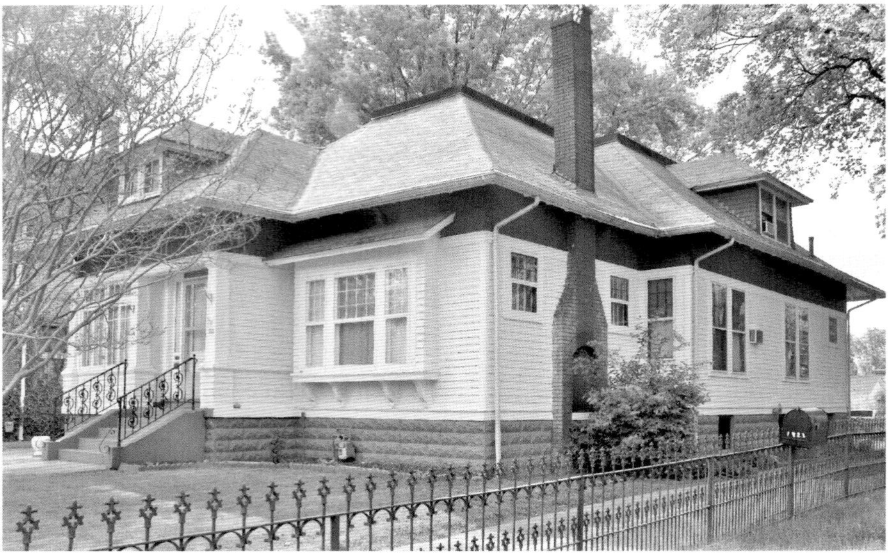

New Albany contractors Stephen Day & Sons built this rambling bungalow in 1912 for George and Emma Moser Jr. *Gregory Sekula.*

home in the Silver Hills section of New Albany and sold the Ekin Avenue home to George Moser Jr.'s uncle and aunt, Charles and Lorena Moser, in May 1923. According to Corcoran family oral history, Charles and Lorena Moser, who resided nearby at 1843 Ekin Avenue, presented the house to their daughter and son-in-law, Iola and Thomas Alvin Corcoran, upon their marriage later that year. T. Alvin, as he was known, was the director of purchasing for the *Courier Journal* and *Louisville Times* newspapers. Iola Corcoran died at age seventy-two in March 1973 and T. Alvin Corcoran in September 1975 at age seventy-seven. The Corcoran family sold the house in December 1977 to Herman and Axie Castle, ending over sixty-five years of ownership by the Moser and Corcoran families.

With its truncated hipped roof, dormers and wide overhanging eaves, the Moser-Corcoran House rests on an elevated rusticated concrete block foundation. Bands of casement windows set between tapered posts define an expansive sun porch at the house's southwest corner. A recessed half-light door with sidelights marks the main entrance. Square oriel windows supported by simple brackets are found on the house's south and west elevations. An exposed brick end chimney on the house's east elevation incorporates an arched niche.

KEYES-HARRIS HOUSE

1923 Ekin Avenue

Washington DePauw Keyes purchased the tract of land along Ekin Avenue (originally Poplar Street) west to Thomas Street from the New Albany National Cemetery in October 1887 for $11,590. He re-platted the property, along with several other parcels on Ekin Avenue, and had this large Queen Anne–style residence built by 1889.

Washington DePauw Keyes was secretary, treasurer and superintendent of Washington C. DePauw's American Plate Glass Works located in New Albany, at one time the largest plate glass manufacturing company in the country. Prior to Keyes involvement in DePauw's company, he had assumed an interest in another New Albany company, the Star Glass Works, owned by Captain John B. Ford, known as the father of plate glass manufacturing in the United States.[68]

In 1892, DePauw Glass Works was established in Alexandria, Indiana. The following year, a financial panic occurred, and by 1894, court-ordered foreclosures impacted both of DePauw's glass companies. Keyes was also adversely impacted by the financial crisis. In May 1895, he left New Albany for Alexandria, Indiana, after he lost his house to the bank.[69]

It wasn't until February 1901 that the bank sold the Ekin Avenue property. It was purchased by Dr. Robert and Anna (Mosemiller) Harris for $4,250. This began a residency of over sixty years by the Harris family. Dr. Harris was a very well-respected physician. He also was president of the Floyd County Bank and a member of the board of school trustees. Dr. Harris passed away in June 1939 at age seventy-eight.[70] His widow, who remained in the home until her death at age eighty-four in June 1955, taught Latin at New Albany High School. She also served as the national secretary for Kappa Kappa Gamma Sorority and was a founding member of the Fortnightly Club.[71] Shortly after the death of Anna Harris, her grandson Dr. Robert Harris III and his wife, LaVada, came to live in the home. By the mid-1960s, the Harris family had moved from the area.

Architecturally, the Keyes-Harris House bears striking similarity to the Merker-Klerner-Fix House at 1821 East Elm Street. Both houses share similar massing and gable detailing, the latter of which is also shared by several other houses along East Elm Street in the Uptown neighborhood. The Ekin Avenue house retains its original patterned slate roof, decorative

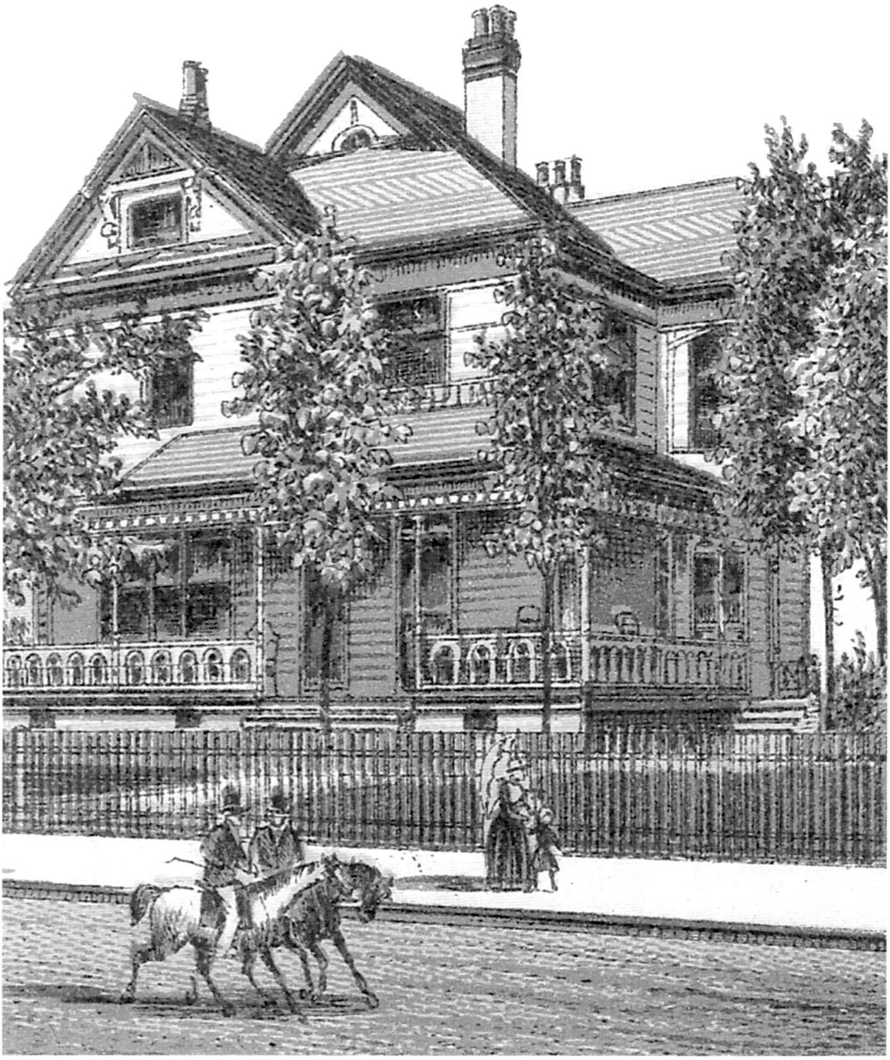

An early rendering of the Queen Anne–style Keyes-Harris House. *From* Album of New Albany, Indiana, *circa 1890.*

shingle banding, Eastlake-style front door and bay window brackets. The house's large wraparound porch has lost its original wooden porch posts and trim work, these features having been replaced with ornamental metal posts and railing.

JAMES AND EUSTASIA KINTNER HOUSE

1946 Ekin Avenue

Between 1908 and 1940, Sears, Roebuck and Company manufactured and sold thousands of homes to Americans through its mail-order catalogue service. From modest cottages to mansions, Sears offered over four hundred different designs to fit a variety of household budgets.[72] Among those who purchased their home through Sears were James and Eustasia Kintner, who chose the Glen Falls model and erected this modern residence on the site of an earlier Victorian home around 1926. James Kintner was a purchasing agent for the Indiana Veneer & Panel Company located at the south end of Silver Street. The home remained in the Kintner family until 1943, at which time it was sold to John and Olive Marquart. The Marquarts' daughter and son-in-law, Theo and William Hays, also resided in the house with the elder Marquarts. John and Olive Marquart died in February 1971 and August 1975, respectively. Theo Hays continued her residency here until her death in December 1985.

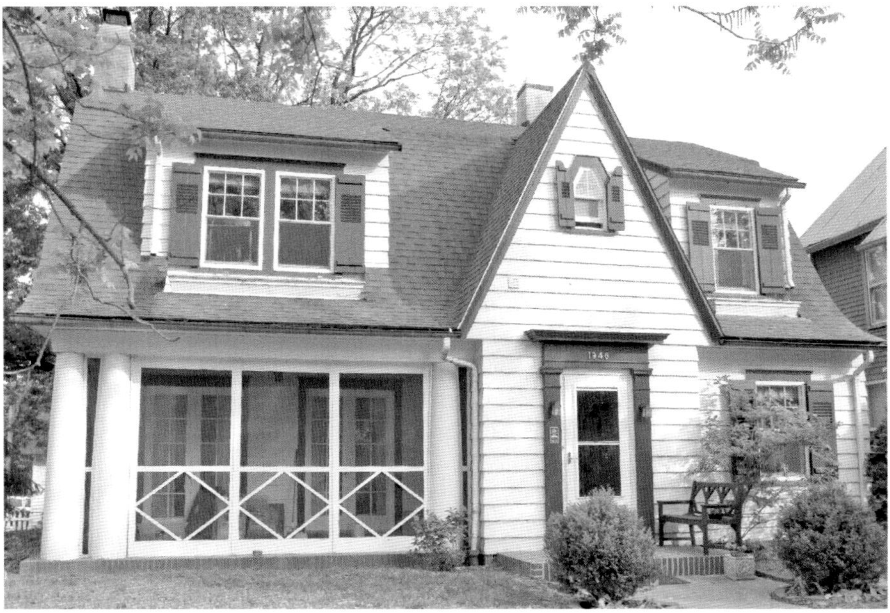

James and Eustasia Kintner purchased the Glen Falls model home from Sears, Roebuck and Company around 1926. *Gregory Sekula.*

Subsequent owners have managed to preserve this remarkable home with few changes on either the exterior or the interior. An examination of the original sketch of the house in the mail-order catalogue reveals the structure seen today, complete with the original siding, shed roof dormers, paired columned porch and window flower boxes. The interior of the house retains its original woodwork, stone fireplace in the living room, paired French doors leading to the front porch, oak floors, open staircase and kitchen complete with dining alcove and some remaining original cabinetry.

Albert Trinler House

1835 East Oak Street

Albert Trinler, his brother Adolph and father Martin, purchased block 15 in plat 47 prior to 1878 in what is known today as New Albany's Uptown neighborhood. The Trinlers replatted block 15 as plat 331 in August 1885. Adolph Trinler subsequently built his house at 1751 East Oak Street, Albert at 1835 East Oak Street and Martin at 1847 East Oak Street. There would be two other Trinler-related houses constructed on East Oak Street during this same time period, the Schmitt-Sheridan House at 1843 and the John Trinler House at 1846.

Albert Trinler was connected with the New Albany Rail Mill Company as its secretary and cashier and, later, its manager. He was also business partners with Fritz Goebel in the F. Goebel & Company, dealers in leather and shoe findings. Albert Trinler and his wife, Minnie, purchased the plans for their home from an architectural pattern book produced by George Palliser, whose Bridgeport, Connecticut, and New York City architectural firm—Palliser, Palliser & Company—was one of the leading mail-order house plan providers in the late nineteenth century.[73]

The Trinlers chose a two-and-a-half-story cross-gabled Queen Anne/Stick–style dwelling with a square tower that was later featured in Palliser's *Model Homes*, published in 1878.[74] The plan included one-story bay windows on the front and side elevations. The Trinlers would remain in their mail-order Victorian house until 1893.

In July 1897, John S. McDonald purchased the house at a sheriff's sale; it appears he used it as rental property. Noble and Anna Morris bought the house in May 1902. Noble Morris, a prominent insurance and real estate

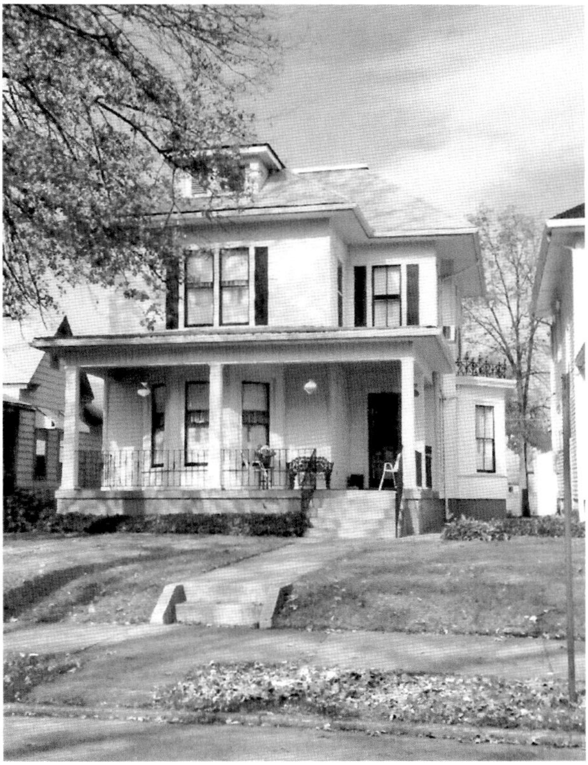

Right: A 1995 image of the Albert Trinler House showing the dwelling in its remodeled form following an April 1915 fire. *Barksdale collection.*

Below: The Albert Trinler House was originally a towered, pattern book Victorian residence designed by Palliser, Palliser & Company of Bridgeport, Connecticut. *From* Album of New Albany, Indiana, circa 1890.

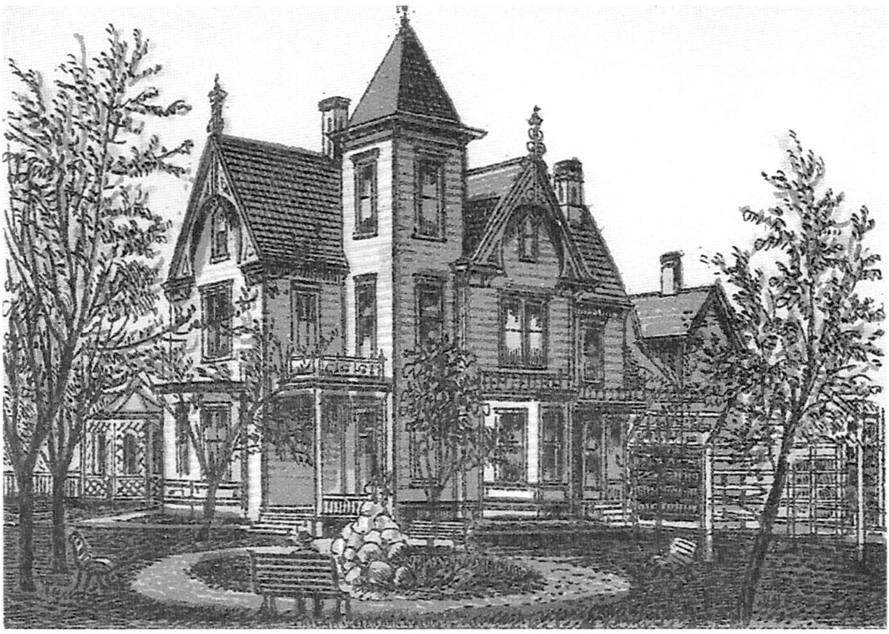

agent, died suddenly in April 1911 while assisting his neighbor Richard Hinton at 1846 East Oak Street by helping cover the Hinton's furnishings with tarps during a house fire. Anna Morris continued the insurance business. Three months after the death of Noble Morris, his widow sold a portion of the estate to Oscar Ellis for the construction of his home at 1839 East Oak Street, built around 1912. In April 1915, a devastating fire erupted from a spark in the chimney at the Morris residence that damaged the upper floor and tower of the home.[75] Anna Morris had the house next door at 1837 East Oak Street built as her family residence but salvaged the fire-damaged structure and remodeled it as a rental property. The subsequent remodeling transformed the house by adding a hipped roof with front-facing hipped dormer and a wraparound porch supported by square posts in the style favored of the day. The house's original bay windows remain, providing clues to the origins of one of the oldest documented houses in the Uptown neighborhood.

SCHMITT-SHERIDAN HOUSE

1843 East Oak Street

This house was constructed in 1892 for Carl and Albertine Louise Schmitt, daughter of Martin and Marion Barbara Trinler, who resided next door at 1847 East Oak Street. The Schmitts were married in November 1890 and received the lot as a gift from her parents in January 1891. The building permit, dated October 1891, shows the signature of Carl Schmitt with a completion date of sixty days. He was a shipping clerk at the New Albany Rail Mill Company, where A. Louise Schmitt's brother, Albert Trinler, was manager. The Albert Trinler family lived at 1835 East Oak Street. Carl and A. Louise Schmitt, along with Martin and Barbara Trinler, sold their properties in 1893 and relocated to Middleborough, Kentucky, where Martin Trinler died in January 1894 and Carl Trinler in August 1895.

The John Sheridan family was the next owner of the home. John Sheridan was the superintendent of the St. Louis/Louisville divisions of the Southern Railway system. He and his wife, Anna—along with their daughter and son-in-law, Lelia and Homer Hawes—moved from this house in the mid-1920s and relocated to the Paul E. Moosmiller–designed DePauw Apartments at 818 East Main Street.

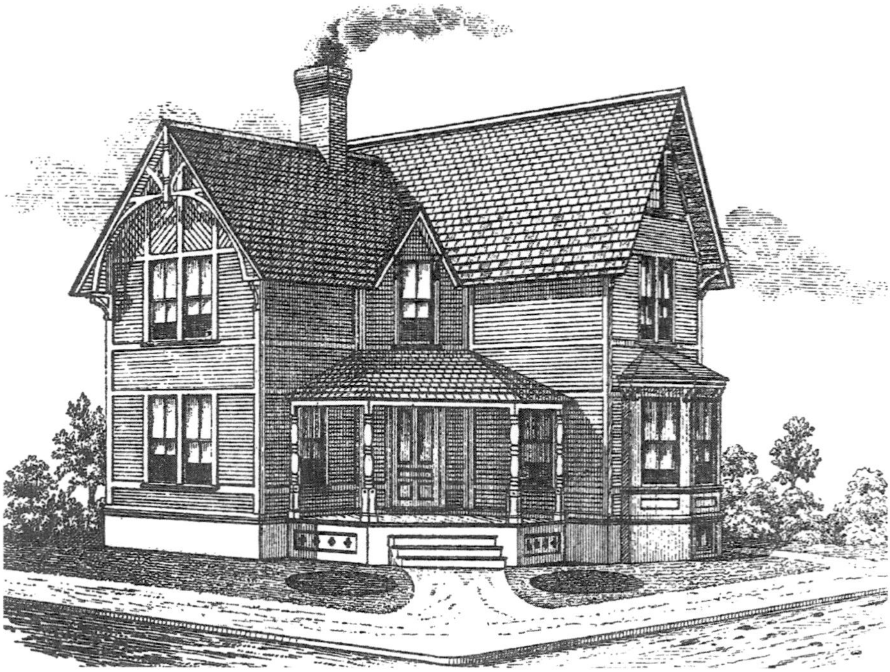

The 1892 Schmitt-Sheridan House is believed to be Design No. 42, plate 32 in Palliser, Palliser & Company's *American Victorian Cottage Homes. Dover Publications, 1990.*

The two-story gable-and-wing frame house bears a striking resemblance to Palliser, Palliser & Company's Design No. 42, which was illustrated as plate 32 in the Company's *American Cottage Homes*, published in 1878. The signature feature of this design is the unusual rounded entry porch placed between the house's front and side gable extensions. The illustrated design includes a one-story projecting bay window with bracketed cornice at the front gable section and Stick-style decoration in the gable ends.[76] The Schmitt-Sheridan House places the bay window at the end of the side gable wing, and its front gable is decorated with decorative sawnwork shingles. The front parlor window in this area has a beveled- and leaded-glass transom window with a fleur-de-lis motif. The partial rounded entry porch is supported by fluted Scamozzi Order cast-concrete columns set on paneled chamfered piers. This treatment is likely an early-twentieth-century modification and may have replaced wooden turned posts as depicted in the Palliser design. Given the Trinler family connection and the documented utilization of a Palliser pattern book home at 1835 Oak Street, it seems probable that the design inspiration for this house was also derived from Palliser's pattern book.

TRINLER-TRUNK HOUSE

1847 East Oak Street

Martin and Marion Barbara Trinler were first listed at this corner lot address in the 1880–81 *New Albany City Directory*. Their son, Albert, had already built his home at 1835 East Oak Street in 1878. It appears that this house, which has a substantially different footprint from the house depicted in an 1880s *New Albany Sanborn Map*, was constructed between late 1888 and early 1890, replacing the earlier 1880s structure.

In June 1893, the Trinlers sold the property to George and Minnie Trunk for $1,200. George Trunk was a druggist and had his drugstore at the corner of Vincennes and Oak Streets, just two blocks from his home. In 1896, the Trunks moved to Denver, Colorado, where George and his brother, Edward Trunk, opened a drugstore. George Trunk's nephew Frank E. Miller took over the Vincennes and Oak Streets location, where he ran his own drug business.

The Oetken family was the next owner of the property, buying it in August 1899 for $3,350. August Oetken Sr. had previously been a merchant

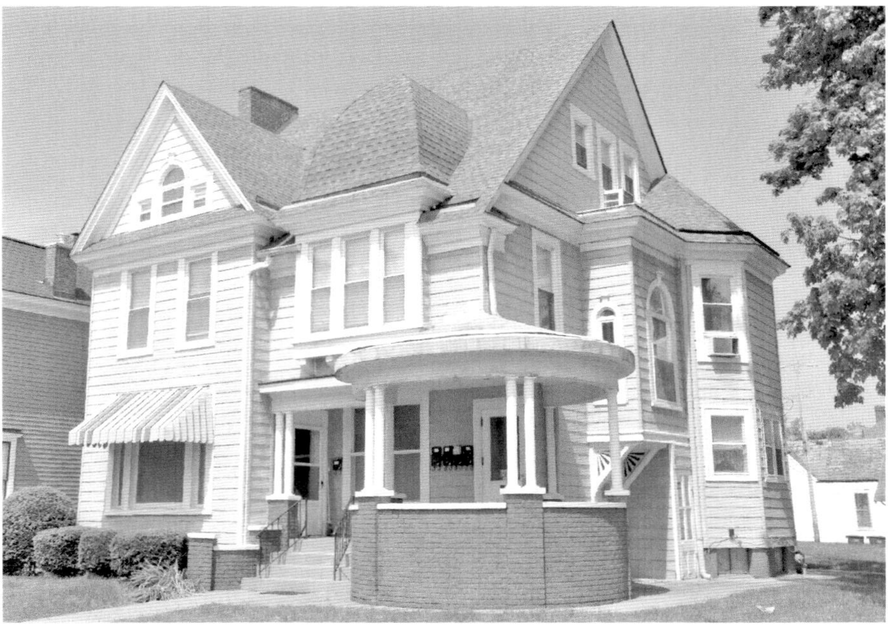

A substantial Queen Anne residence, the Trinler-Trunk House occupies a prominent corner lot on East Oak and Thomas Streets in the Uptown neighborhood. *Gregory Sekula.*

tailor while a resident of Louisville, Kentucky. After moving to New Albany around 1885, he became involved in the grocery business and had his store at 213 East Market Street, where he and his wife, Elise, would eventually relocate in 1905. Grocery salesman William Hougland—along with his wife, Alice—purchased the property from the Oetkens in April 1905 for $4,500. At the time of William Hougland's death in October 1912 at age fifty-three, he was working for the old Louisville Grocery Company in Louisville, Kentucky. His widow moved from the residence shortly after the death of her husband.

The house was then sold for $4,500 to the Judge John Paris family in October 1915. In May 1920, Grover Fleming, soon to be the husband of Emma Neat, purchased the home. Grover Fleming was the secretary and treasurer of the New Albany wholesale grocery concern of P.N. Curl. Fleming's first wife, Mayme, was the daughter of P.N. Curl. She had died at the young age of twenty-six of influenza in March 1919. The Flemings made their home here for the next thirteen years before losing it to the bank in January 1933. By the mid-1930s, the house was subdivided into rental units and remains so today.

Despite the application of aluminum siding and other modern exterior details, the Trinler-Trunk House is a substantial residence of the Queen Anne style with classical details. The two-and-a-half-story dwelling with complex gable roof features a partial wraparound porch with a rounded projection. The porch's conical roof is supported by modern fluted paired columns set on brick piers that rise slightly above a solid brick porch rail. A unique feature of the house is a projecting second-floor tripartite window supported by simple brackets. The projection is further highlighted by an unusual onion-shaped roof that ties into the slope of the house's main roof. A two-story bay window is situated on the Thomas Street elevation of the house and is located directly to the north of a projecting square stairwell bay supported by triangular brackets with a sunburst motif. A Palladian window in the house's front gable and an arched stairwell window with keystone decoration suggest the emerging interest in the Colonial Revival style in America. The overall sophistication of the Trinler-Trunk House suggests the hand of a skilled architect, such as Milton C. Pritchett, who designed several classically detailed Queen Anne houses in New Albany and other communities in southern Indiana.

LOUIS AND LILLIAN IRION HOUSE

1923 East Oak Street

This well-preserved buff brick bungalow was built for Louis Irion and his wife, Lillian, sometime after the printing of the 1925–26 *New Albany City Directory*. Mrs. Irion's parents, John and Emma Egle, also made their home here with the Irions until their deaths in February 1935 and December 1950, respectively.

Louis Irion was a business partner with Louis Wolf in the New Albany business concern of Irion & Wolf Jewelers. The jewelry establishment began in 1919 in the opera house at the northeast corner of East Spring and Pearl Streets in downtown New Albany. The business would eventually move to the 300 block of Pearl Street, where it remained until closing in 2001. Louis Irion was also a director of the Union Federal Savings and Loan Association of New Albany. He passed away in September 1965, and his widow remained in the home until shortly before her death in June 1984, ending almost sixty years of occupancy by the Irion and Egle families.

The Louise and Lillian Irion House is a rare southern Indiana example of the Chicago bungalow style known for its masonry construction and front-facing sunroom with bands of windows. In the example of the Louise and

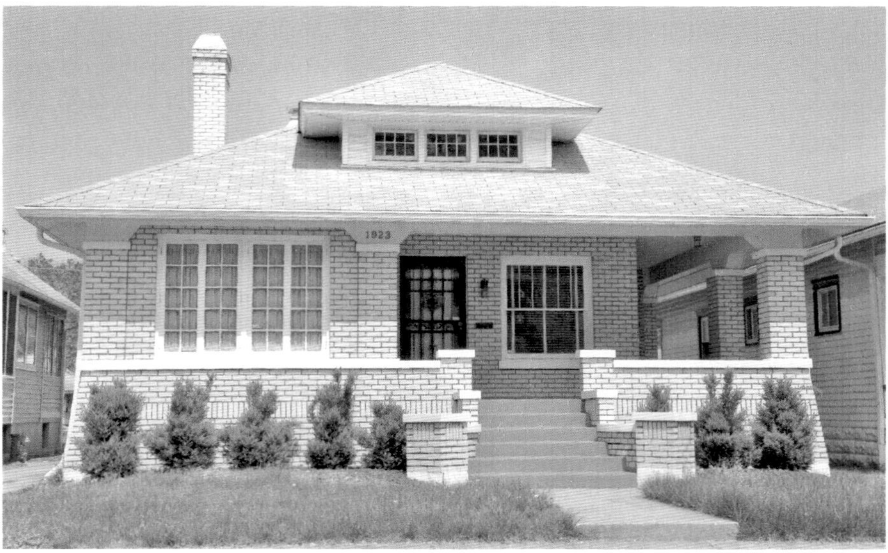

The Louis and Lillian Irion House is a rare southern Indiana example of the Chicago Bungalow style. *Gregory Sekula.*

Lillian Irion House, a low-pitched hipped roof with overhanging eaves and hipped roof front dormer give the house its horizontal emphasis. Ten light wooden casement windows in the sunroom evoke an airy feel to the front façade, which is further reinforced by a partial open porch supported by buff brick piers.

McFall-Ruoff House

1911 East Elm Street

Located in the city's Uptown neighborhood, the McFall-Ruoff House is one of New Albany's boldest examples of the residential Queen Anne style executed in brick. The imposing two-and-a-half-story pressed red brick house was built in 1893 for $3,500 for New Albany physician Dr. Hettie McFall and her husband, Charles, a carrier for the U.S. Post Office.[77] In his later years, Charles McFall had a grocery at 1422 East Elm Street. In November 1904, Dr. Hettie McFall sold the family home. There were several owners before William Ruoff, a lawyer, purchased the house in August 1913 and lived here for over thirty years. William Ruoff died in December 1944, and his widow, Lee, remained in the home until May 1965.

The McFall-Ruoff House possesses a wealth of architectural detailing on both the exterior and interior. The exterior façade is dominated by a steeply pitched cross-gable roof plan. The side gables are sheathed in slate shingles, while the front gable is highlighted by a Palladian-style window surrounded by pressed metal scrollwork in a foliated design. A two-and-a-half-story corner bay window terminates in a conical roof above the eave, providing further visual interest to the house's roofline. A second-story square oriel window provides further embellishment to the front façade and features a centrally positioned square window, originally containing stained glass, and a pressed metal griffin's head in the panel below. A rounded porch, supported by original turned porch posts, provides further elegance to this stunning piece of Victorian architectural design. A surviving 1909 photograph of the house shows the original lower railing and upper roof balustrade, now lost.

The interior of the house, now subdivided into apartments, retains many original features. The house's dramatic entry hall is dominated by an open maple staircase with paneled apron wall and fluted square newel post with medallion carvings at the top and a molded handrail with heavily turned

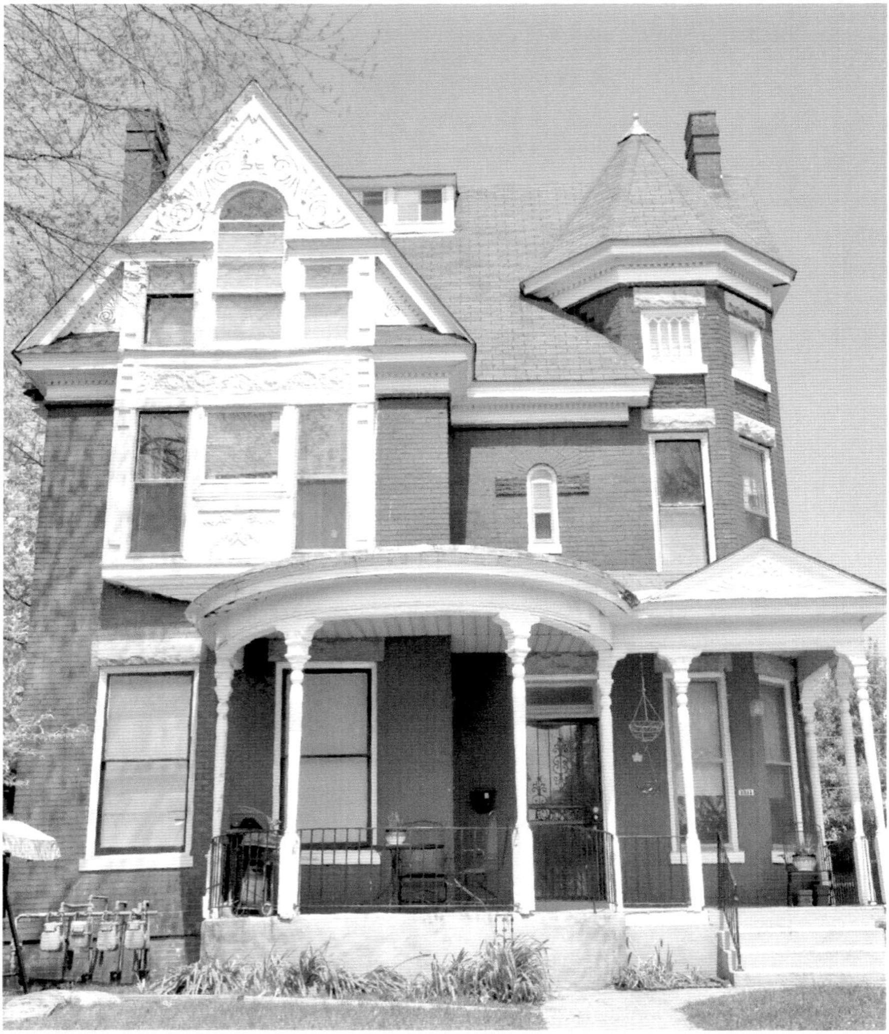

Located in the Uptown neighborhood, the McFall-Ruoff House is one of New Albany's boldest examples of the brick Queen Anne style. *Gregory Sekula.*

balusters. An arched colored-glass window illuminates the stairway at the landing level and a smaller stained-glass transom window is located above the front entry door. The room's focal point is a corner fireplace of unusual design as it is executed solely out of tile with no wooden mantelpiece. Three blue-hued tiles are of special note, with the two flanking smaller tiles containing images of the Shakespearean characters Hamlet and Ophelia. A central rectangular fireplace panel depicts charioteers with horses.

Carved oak mantels with original tile work and ornamental metal flue covers are found in the front parlor and dining room. Paneled pocket doors divide the front room from the dining room. Oak parquet flooring is found in the entrance hall, parlor and dining room. Original wood trim survives throughout most of the house. The third-floor attic space, now a separate apartment, contains a spiral stair to a mezzanine level that affords views of the downtown Louisville, Kentucky skyline.

LONG-GRAF HOUSE

1945 East Elm Street

One of Uptown's most picturesque Queen Anne–style dwellings, the Long-Graf House was constructed in 1892 on this elevated East Elm Street corner lot. Clara Long purchased the building site in November 1891 and procured a building permit the following month. The value of the building was listed at $2,200.

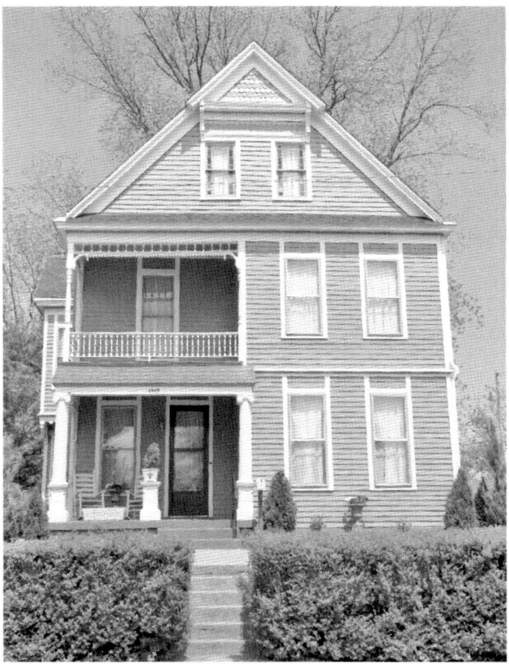

The 1892 Long-Graf House was sensitively rehabilitated in 2009 and is one of the gems of the Uptown neighborhood. *Gregory Sekula.*

Clara and her husband, James, sold the home in February 1900 to Sarah and John Vaughn and Allie Jones. The Graf family purchased the property from them in September 1904. It would remain in the Graf family until October 1976. Owner Jacob Graf, a native of Switzerland, operated the Jacob Graf Crupper Company at the rear of the property in a two-story frame structure on the alley. A crupper is a part on a horse harness that loops around the tail of the horse. Graf's business was once the largest manufacturer of cruppers in the nation, with products being distributed worldwide. As the market for cruppers waned, the major product manufactured here was grip handles. The Jacob Graf Crupper Company closed its doors in 1964, following the death of son Oscar Graf in December 1963, who had worked alongside his father in the business.[78] The factory building was demolished in 2009 due to severe deterioration; this was the same year the house was extensively rehabilitated and returned to its former glory.

The two-and-a-half-story frame residence is dominated by a gabled façade highlighted by a pair of Queen Anne–style double-hung widows with squares of colored glass in the attic story. Decorative shingles adorn the peaks of the front and side gables of the house above the windows—a treatment similar to other Queen Anne houses found in the Uptown neighborhood, perhaps suggesting a common builder and architect. A partial two-story front porch features bracketed turned posts with spindled fretwork spandrels at the second floor level and, later, cast-concrete fluted Scamozzi Order columns set on chamfered paneled piers on the first floor. Two-story bay windows with decorative eave brackets with a sunburst motif are found on the east and west sides of the house. An oculus window with colored glass in a pinwheel design located on the house's west side provides illumination to the stair hall. The interior retains its original woodwork with traditional bull's-eye corner block detailing. A handsome open staircase with square newel post with urn-shaped finial and spindles highlights the front hall, while a marbleized slate mantel with Eastlake detailing and handsome tile work is the focal point of the house's front parlor.

Gustav Kiel Jr. House

2001 East Elm Street

Situated on an elevated corner lot surrounded on two sides by a rusticated concrete block retaining wall, this well-detailed dormer-front bungalow was built for wholesale cigar and tobacco broker Gustav Kiel Jr. and his family in 1915. The lot had been purchased by the Kiels in March 1912. The house remained in the Kiel family through the late 1970s. On June 6, 1952, a fire badly damaged the house's roof structure with estimated damages of at least $10,000.[79]

The spacious one-and-a-half-story frame house features a well-preserved exterior with wood siding on the first floor and wood shingles in the gable

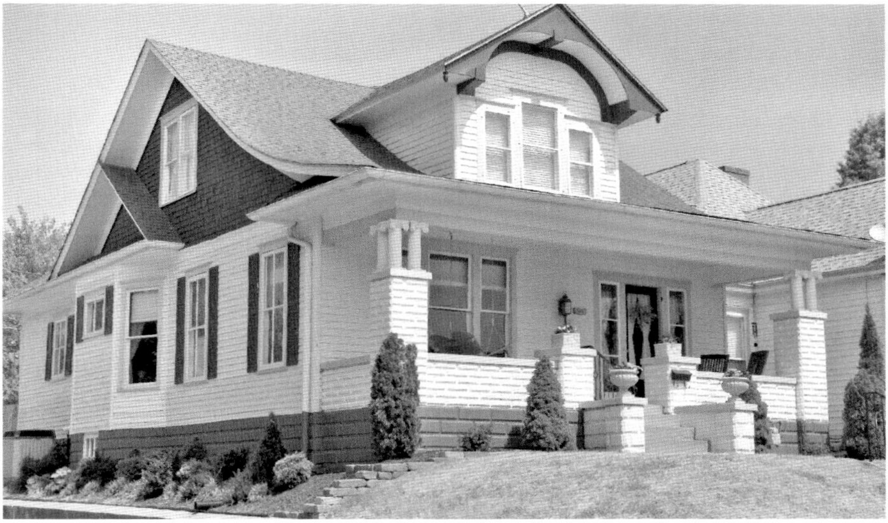

This well detailed dormer-front bungalow was built for wholesale cigar and tobacco broker Gustav Kiel Jr. and his family in 1915. *Gregory Sekula.*

ends and on the front gable dormer, which features a tripartite window. A full-width front porch dominates the front façade and features grouped Scamozzi Order columns set on elevated piers constructed of formed cast-concrete blocks with a beveled edge. Bay windows are found on each of the side elevations.

One enters the house through its original oak entrance door with beveled-glass sidelights and egg-and-dart molding. The original quartersawn oak screen door is still in place. The entry contains a beautiful paneled oak Arts and Crafts staircase. A rectangular window with opaque Florentine patterned glass provides illumination to the stairs. Oak columns set on paneled oak knee walls define the cased opening between the entry and the spacious living room. Both the living room and dining room have natural oak trim, and hardwood floors are found throughout. A set of French doors leads from the living room to the dining room. The dining room features a bay window and an original brass five-light pan light fixture with original globes. A door from the dining room leads to the kitchen, which features some original built-in cabinetry and an arched inglenook that may have originally served as a location for a table and chairs. A period Tiffany-style pendant light fixture illuminates the archway. Claw-foot bathtubs are found in the house's two bathrooms. Original five panel doors remain, many of which have their original hardware with operable skeleton keys.

William D. and Josie Sowle House

1819 East Spring Street

William D. Sowle and his wife, Josie, purchased this property in September 1902 for $1,600 and removed an earlier one-story house that stood on the lot. Construction began on the present house that same year. The Sowles had lived at 1910 East Elm Street prior to moving into their new Queen Anne–style home, a twin of which is located on nearby DePauw Avenue. William D. Sowle was the proprietor of the William D. Sowle Tool & Die Company, established in 1902 and located at the rear of the property. According to local newspaper accounts, he was a "pioneer" tool and die manufacturer in New Albany. In the 1880s, Sowle was an apprentice with the New Albany foundry of the Charles Hegewald Company.[80] Josie Sowle died at an early age in October 1918, survived by her husband and her son, William C. By the late 1940s, William C. Sowle and his wife, Katherine, had come to live in the home with his father. The son was also employed in his father's business. The elder William Sowle died at the age of ninety-one in May 1954,and the family business continued under the leadership of William C. He and his wife remained in the home until their deaths. Katherine Sowle passed away in June 1978 and William C. Sowle in September 1980, ending almost eighty years of the family's residency at this address.

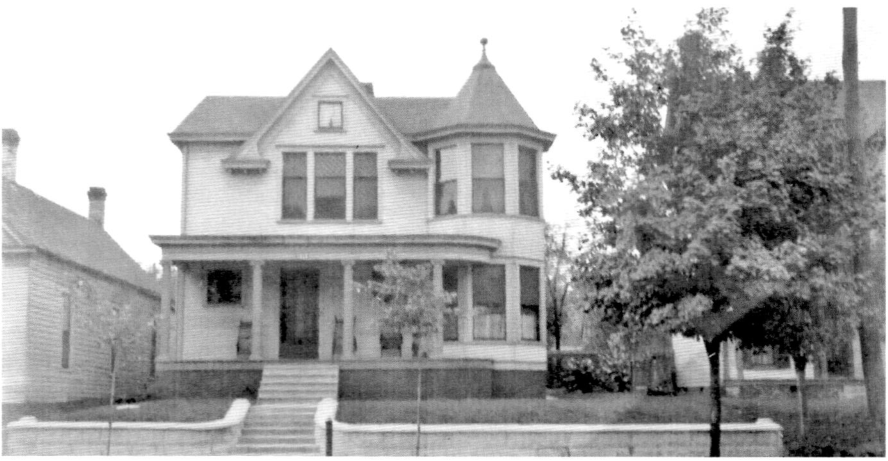

A 1908 postcard image of the William D. and Josie Sowle House. *Barksdale collection.*

The William D. and Josie Sowle House sits on an elevated lot above busy East Spring Street, with a concrete retaining wall that curves gently toward the front steps. Its exterior is dominated by a central gable with a triple window ornamented with decorative diamond-paned upper sashes. The east end of the front façade is marked by a hexagonal tower, originally covered in decorative shingles, now obscured by vinyl siding. The roof of the tower bay is topped by a metal ball finial. Centered on the façade is a front porch supported by fluted Scamozzi Order columns set on chamfered paneled piers. Tapered and fluted square balusters form the porch railing.

Highlights of the interior include a paneled oak staircase with built-in bench, a stained-glass window with floral Art Nouveau design illuminating the staircase and the front parlor with a corner tiled fireplace and built-in window seat in the bay. Parquet flooring and built-in cabinetry in the dining room provide additional beauty and interest to this well-preserved home.

KOPP-WILLIAMS HOUSE

1931 East Spring Street

This notable two-and-a-half-story dwelling was built in 1906 for Andreas Kopp, a sales agent dealing in flour and other goods. The residence became home to the Fred Williams family in April 1919. Fred Williams was the associate general agent for the Pacific Mutual Life Insurance Company and had his office here as well as his residence. He was also a Boy Scout enthusiast and the leader of Troop 2 as early as 1920, making him one of the first scoutmaster in the New Albany area.[81] After his death, his daughter, Elizabeth, continued residency here until her death in July 1972.

The house blends Queen Anne and Classical Revival features, suggesting the emerging interest in the Colonial Revival that followed the World's Columbian Exhibition in Chicago in 1893. The "Great White City" celebrated classical design, and architects and builders alike began to utilize such architectural details in domestic architecture beginning in earnest in the late 1890s. The Kopp-Williams House borrows from the Queen Anne in the use of a distinctive two-story corner turret. The feature is capped with a conical roof topped by a decorative metal finial. A partial front porch, supported by fluted wooden columns with egg-and-dart motif on their capitals, anchors the southeast corner of the house at the turret and utilizes a rounded projection to mirror the form of the turret. A Palladian window in the house's front gable, as well as a broken pediment surround framing the front façade parlor window introduce the classical vocabulary marking this residence as transitional in design.

The interior of the house boasts an abundance of natural woodwork and other period details. The entrance hall features a partially open oak staircase with paneled newel post with egg-and-dart detailing and an urn-shaped finial. An oak window seat is built into the curved bay window/turret wall at the base of the staircase. Paneled pocket doors lead from the front hall to the parlor and from the parlor to the formal dining room. The dining room features a bay window and quartersawn oak mantel with scrolled supports. A vibrant blue ceramic tiled hearth and an original cast-iron fireplace flue cover featuring a winged deity holding a cherub further embellishes the fireplace. An early electric light fixture hangs from a ceiling medallion in the center of the dining room. Strip oak parquet flooring is found in the front hall and the principal rooms on the first floor. An original built-in pantry cupboard with glass doors is found in the rear hall off the kitchen.

GEORGE AND JESSIE SCHECHTER HOUSE

702 Vincennes Street

This brick-veneered bungalow, built around 1918, was first occupied by salesman George Schechter and his wife, Jessie. Jessie Schechter, daughter of John and Fannie Baylor, was a charter member and regent for the Piankeshaw Chapter Daughters of the American Revolution (DAR). The DAR—which acquired the Joel Scribner House, home of New Albany founding father Joel Scribner, in 1917—continues to maintain the house today. The Schechters remained in this house until the late 1940s, when they moved to 714 Vincennes Street. They later purchased that house from Fannie Baylor in July 1951. The Baylors were owners of numerous investment properties in the city. Over the next twenty-five years, this home saw several owners.

The George and Jessie Schechter House is an interesting blend of Craftsman and Colonial Revival styles. The house's side-gabled roof is punctuated on the façade by an off-center gabled dormer with Palladian window with keystone trim in the Classical taste. Colonial Revival detailing is again introduced in the house's front entrance, featuring a pediment door

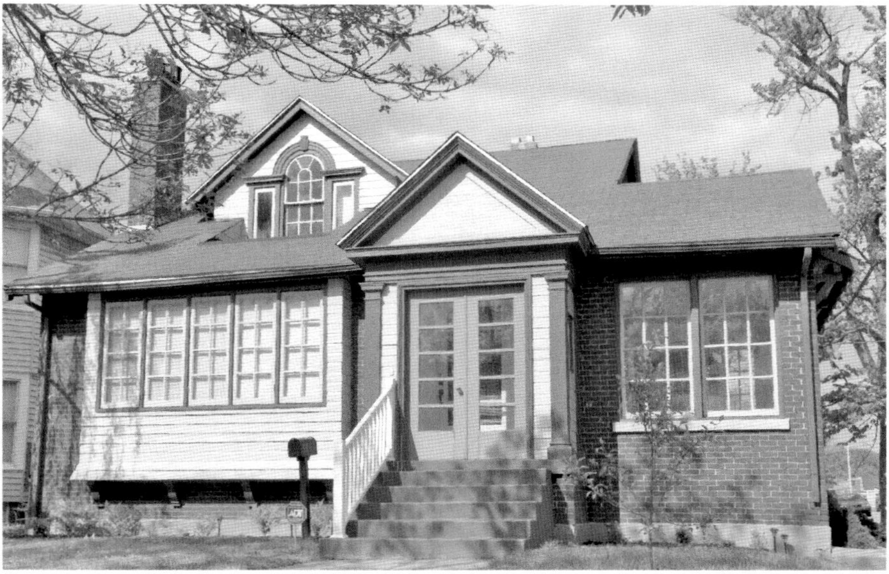

The 1918 George and Jessie Schechter House is an interesting blend of the Craftsman and Colonial Revival styles. *Gregory Sekula.*

surround with fluted pilasters framing double-leaf wooden doors. A shallow, square frame bay window containing five casement-style windows dominates the front façade of the house and is supported by simple scrolled bracket supports. Wide eaves with exposed rafter ends and triangular knee braces are typical Craftsman embellishments that are found on the home and are especially pronounced on the sheltered hood of the sunroom windows on the house's south side elevation facing Culbertson Avenue.

The interior features a large living room with a Colonial Revival wooden fireplace mantel and trim work on the walls creating panels. Strip oak flooring and simple trim are found throughout the house. A large bank of built-in cabinets is found in the second-floor hallway at the top of the enclosed stair.

BRISCOE-WELLS-SCHECHTER HOUSE

714 Vincennes Street

New Albany attorney John H. Weathers and his wife, Nattie, purchased three lots on the east side of Vincennes Street in May 1902 and are

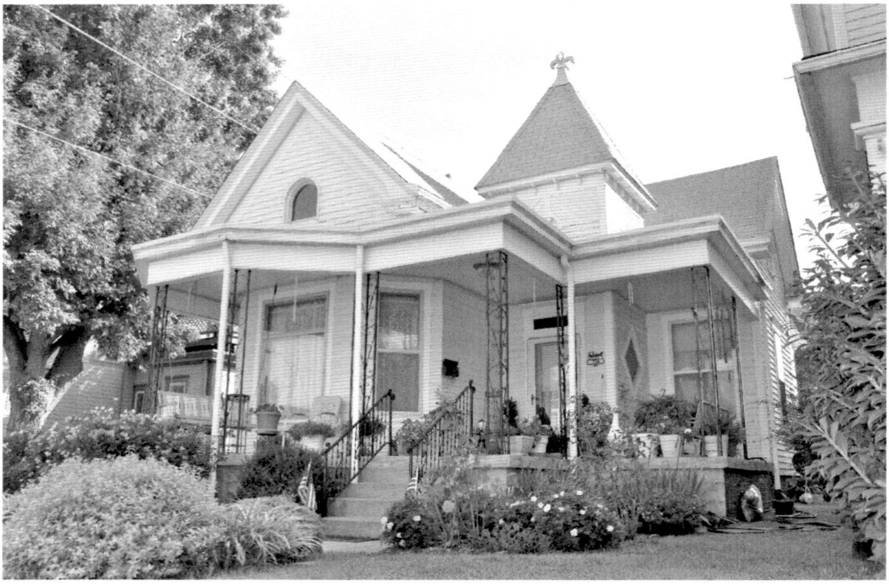

A square tower with pyramidal roof distinguishes the Queen Anne–style Briscoe-Wells-Schechter House, 714 Vincennes Street. *Gregory Sekula.*

believed to have constructed this one-story frame cottage for speculative resale purposes shortly thereafter. Joseph O. Briscoe and his wife, Bertie, purchased the new home in April 1904 for $1,200, but only lived here three years before selling it to Holmes and Anna Wells for $1,500. Holmes Wells was an agent with the Baltimore & Ohio freight office in New Albany. He died in April 1923, and his widow sold the property in August 1927. After numerous owners over the next twenty-plus years, George and Jessie Schechter bought the property in July 1951 from her mother, Fannie Baylor, and made their home here. The Schechters previously lived at 702 Vincennes Street. He was a salesman, and she was a charter member of the Piankeshaw Chapter Daughters of the American Revolution (DAR), where she also served as its regent.[82] Jessie Schechter passed away in January 1960 at the age of seventy-eight. George Schechter died just over a year later at age eighty-two in February 1961.

The Briscoe-Wells-Schechter House is Queen Anne in style and features a cross-gable roofline with a prominent square tower with bracketed cornice, specialty siding with a pinwheel medallion and a pyramidal roof capped by a decorative metal finial. The house's front gable features an arched window and a bay window sheltered by a large wraparound porch supported by iron replacement columns. An outstanding feature of the house's interior is an elaborate fretwork spandrel decorating the cased opening between the front parlor and dining room. The house retains its original wood trim throughout.

Notes

Introduction

1. Thayer and Charron, *City of New Albany Interim Report*, 11.

Chapter 1

2. *Plat of New Albany, Indiana*, 161–64.
3. Caudill, Dick, Peters and Price, *Scribner House of New Albany*, 35.
4. National Parks Service, National Register of Historic Places registration form for the William Young House.
5. Ibid.
6. Devol family files, Stuart B. Wrege Indiana History Room, New Albany–Floyd County Public Library.
7. *Louisville (KY) Courier Journal*, "Famous Pilot Capt. J. Wesley Conner Dies in New Albany. Guided *Robert E. Lee* in Race with *Natchez*. Eighty-one Years of Age," July 28, 1906.
8. Crutchfield, Barksdale and Hood, *Historic New Albany, Indiana: By the River's Edge*, 51.
9. Hamilton, "Joseph Waddell Clokey."

Chapter 2

10. *New Albany (IN) Daily Tribune*, January 30, 1855.
11. Marquis, *Who Was Who in America*.
12. Haffner, *Glass Industry of New Albany*, 77.
13. *Washington C. DePauw, 1822–1887*.
14. Stein, "Sudden Death Ends a Big-time Career," *New Albany (IN) Tribune*, January 5, 1966.
15. Samuel Culbertson Mansion, "Samuel Culbertson and Family Timeline."
16. *New Albany (IN) Tribune*, "Heart Attack Proves Fatal to S.A. Culbertson," December 11, 1948.
17. *Culbertson Mansion State Historic Site*.
18. *New Albany (IN) Tribune*, "Woman Heads School Board. Miss Mary E. Clark Is Elected President. First Time in Local History," August 1924.
19. Lillian Emery, "School Principal Writes of Miss Annetta Clark's Work in World War One," *New Albany (IN) Tribune*, October 21, 1947.
20. *New Albany (IN) Daily Ledger*, "Death of Capt. Van Dusen," May 13, 1858.
21. Byrd, "Indiana's First Cookbook: Sumptuous Beginnings."
22. Sloan, *Model Architect*, design 31, plate 18, 26–27.
23. Ibid., design 46, plate 55, 63.
24. Aiken, *Roots Grow Deep*, 7.
25. Ibid., 13.
26. Ibid., 19.
27. New Albany–Floyd County Public Library, "General James Adams Ekin."
28. *New Albany (IN) Tribune*, "Miss Green, of Oldtime Foundry Family, Is Dead," June 24, 1947.
29. *New Albany (IN) Daily Ledger*, "New Home. Mr. and Mrs. C.D. Knoefel Very Proud in Its Occupancy. It Is One of the Most Beautiful Residences in the City," November 10, 1896.
30. U.S. Congress, *Biographical Directory of the American Congress*, 1,160.
31. *New Albany (IN) Daily Ledger*, "Consolidation of the McCord & Bradley and New Albany Woolen Mills," September 11, 1869.
32. Martin, Koerner, Sekula, Beardsley and Barksdale, *Walking Tour No. 2*.
33. Dr. Morrill, personal recollections, November 3, 1889, Stuart B. Wrege Indiana History Room, New Albany–Floyd County Public Library.
34. *New Albany (IN) Ledger Tribune*, "Last Rites Held for Stotsenburg; Tribute Is Paid," August 6, 1937.

35. "The Town of Providence, Indiana." February 1821 broadside, 1626 Dewey Street vertical file, Stuart B. Wrege Indiana History Room, New Albany–Floyd County Public Library.
36. Floyd County Historical Society, *This Is Our Community*, 6–7.
37. *New Albany (IN) Tribune*, "Reminders of Days of Old Town Providence Are Found in Hedden Homestead on Dewey Street Property Changes Owners," circa 1921.

Chapter 3

38. Hilton, *Monon Route*, 14.
39. *New Albany (IN) Tribune*, "Jouett Meekin, 77, Former Diamond Star Died Today," December 14, 1944.
40. *New Albany (IN) Weekly Ledger*, "Mrs. Borgerding's Death Result of Auto Road Fiends," February 1, 1922.
41. *New Albany (IN) Daily Ledger*, "New Albany's Prosperity, the Real Estate Market Active and New Buildings Going Up in All Parts of the City," August 23, 1889.

Chapter 4

42. *New Albany (IN) Daily Ledger*, July 23, 1870.
43. *New Albany (IN) Evening Tribune*, "Judge Simeon K. Wolfe, Death of One of New Albany's Distinguished Lawyers Yesterday Morning," November 19, 1888.
44. Russell, *Greater New Albany*, 23.
45. Matt Thacker, "Flames Engulf Home. Heat Gun Was Being Used to Strip Paint during Restoration," *New Albany (IN) Tribune*, August 19, 2008.
46. *New Albany (IN) Daily Ledger*, "Former Mayor of This City Dies Suddenly," March 22, 1917.
47. Ibid., "Frank Zinsmeister, Prominent New Albany Business Man, Passes Away; Death Brings Loss to Community," February 14, 1918.
48. New Albany Bicentennial Church History Committee, *200 Years of Church Histories*, 95.
49. Chris Morris, "Longtime New Albany Physician Dies," *New Albany (IN) Tribune*, December 24, 2013.

50. *New Albany (IN) Tribune*, "Marilynn E. Cannon, 84, of New Albany," March 27, 2011.

Chapter 5

51. Mary Stein, "Intriguing Story of an Old House," *New Albany (IN) Tribune*, August 9, 1962.
52. *New Albany (IN) Daily Ledger*, "Dead," April 7, 1865.
53. Alexander Martin, partial diary, written during the Civil War, 1861–65, Stuart B. Wrege Indiana History Room, New Albany–Floyd County Public Library.
54. Schneider, *Joseph Elmer Cardinal Ritter*.
55. Day and Barksdale, *These Are the Good Old Days*, 137.
56. Ibid., 119–20.

Chapter 6

57. *New Albany (IN) Tribune*, "Frank E. Stemm," June 29, 1981.
58. Ibid., "Bernard F. Hock," August 19, 1999.
59. *New Albany (IN) Weekly Ledger*, "Company Organized," September 4, 1907.
60. Ibid., "Auto Bodies for Ford Made by Kahler Co," January 3, 1917.
61. *New Albany (IN) Daily Ledger*, "Ferdinand Kahler Turns Down Handsome Offer of Foreign Aid to Remain in New Albany," March 31, 1917.

Chapter 7

62. Lucille Reisz, "Etelka Rockenbach Will Be Remembered by Many," *New Albany (IN) Tribune*, March 11, 1977.
63. Cornelia Memorial Orphan's Home, board minute books, Stuart B. Wrege Indiana History Room, New Albany–Floyd County Public Library.
64. *New Albany (IN) Daily Ledger*, November 22, 1883.
65. City of New Albany building permit records, June 1890–May 1896, Stuart B. Wrege Indiana History Room, New Albany–Floyd County Public Library.

66. Wastelandwild, "Abandoned Tannery of the Historic Moser Leather Company."
67. *New Albany (IN) Weekly Ledger*, "Moser-Kannapel. Beautiful Wedding at St. Mary's Church this Morning," June 12, 1912.
68. Aiken, *Roots Grow Deep*, 87.
69. Floyd County Deed Book 43, 466, Stuart B. Wrege Indiana History Room, New Albany–Floyd County Public Library.
70. *New Albany (IN) Tribune*, "Dr. R.W. Harris, Bank Head Dies," June 8, 1939.
71. Ibid., "Rites Tuesday for Mrs. Harris," June 6, 1955.
72. Stevenson and Jandl, *Houses by Mail*, 19.
73. Richards and Richards, "Victorian Pattern Book Homes."
74. Palliser, Palliser & Company, *Palliser's Model Homes*, 36–37.
75. *New Albany (IN) Weekly Ledger*, "Fire Damages Handsome Residence of Mrs. Morris," April 7, 1915.
76. Palliser, Palliser & Company, *American Cottage Homes*, plate 32.
77. City of New Albany building permit records, June 1890–May 1896, Stuart B. Wrege Indiana History Room, New Albany–Floyd County Public Library.
78. *New Albany (IN) Ledger-Tribune*, "Ex-Crupper Monopolist Dies in Clark Residence," September 27, 1940.
79. *New Albany (IN) Tribune*, "Firemen Have Hard Fight in Elm Street Fire; Loss $10,000.00," June 6, 1952.
80. *New Albany (IN) Ledger-Tribune*, "William Sowle Services Today," May 30, 1954.
81. *New Albany (IN) Tribune*, "F.J. Williams, 77, Business Man, Civic Leader, Dies," November 27, 1945.
82. Ibid., "Ex-Regent of DAR Is Stricken," January 11, 1960.

Bibliography

Books

Aiken, William Earl. *The Roots Grow Deep*. Cleveland, OH: Lezius-Hiles Company, 1957.

Album of New Albany, Ind. New Albany, IN, 1890.

Amster, Betty Lou. *New Albany on the Ohio: Historical Review, 1813–1963*. New Albany, IN: Sesquicentennial Committee, 1963.

Bailey, John C.W., & Co. *Floyd County Gazetteer Containing a Directory of the City of New Albany*. Chicago, IL: John C.W. Bailey & Co., 1868.

Barksdale, David C., and Robyn Davis Sekula. *New Albany in Vintage Postcards*. Charleston, SC: Arcadia Publishing, 2005.

Bogle, Victor M. "Nineteenth Century River Town: A Socio-Economic Study of New Albany, Indiana." Dissertation, Boston University, 1951.

Caron, C.K. *Caron's Directory of the City of New Albany for 1877–1878*. Louisville, KY: C.K. Caron, 1877.

———. *Caron's Directory of the Cities of New Albany and Jeffersonville for 1880–1881 Thru 1943–1944*. Louisville, KY: C.K. Caron, 1880–1943.

Caudill, Anne, Amanda Dick, Pamela Peters and Carlene Price. *The Scribner House of New Albany*. Charleston, SC: The History Press, 2012.

Collins, Gabriel. *Louisville and New Albany Directory and Annual Advertiser for 1848*. Louisville, KY: G.H. Monsarrat & Co., 1848.

Commercial Club. *New Albany*. New Albany, IN: Commercial Club, 1909.

Cotton, C.W. *New Albany, Indiana*. New Albany, IN: C.W. Cotton, 1873.

Coy, E., & Co. *New Albany Directory, City Guide and Business Mirror for the Year 1860*. New Albany, IN: E. Coy & Co., 1860.

Crutchfield, James A., David C. Barksdale and Robin Hood. *Historic New Albany, Indiana: By the River's Edge*. Franklin, TN: Grandin Hood Publishers, 2012.

Day, Raymond P., and David C. Barksdale. *These Are the Good Old Days*. New Albany, IN: Daylily Creations, 2013.

Edwards. *Edward's Annual Directory: To Inhabitants, Institutions, Incorporated Companies, Manufacturing Establishments, Business Firms, etc. in the Cities of New Albany and Jeffersonville for 1865–1866*. Chicago: Edwards, Greenough and Deved, 1865.

Floyd County Historical Society. *This Is Our Community*. New Albany, IN: Floyd County Historical Society, 1998.

Grooms and Smith. *New Albany City Directory and Business Mirror for 1856–1857*. Indianapolis: A.C. Grooms & W.T. Smith, 1856.

Haffner, Gerald O. *The Glass Industry of New Albany*. New Albany: Indiana University Southeast Bookstore, 1982.

Hamilton, Janet. "Joseph Waddell Clokey." Fact sheet. Floyd County Historical Society program. February 24, 2009.

Harris, Cyril M. *Historic Architecture Sourcebook*. New York: McGraw-Hill Book Company, 1977.

Hawes, G.W. *New Albany Directory and Business Mirror for 1859*. New Albany, IN: James Sutherland, 1859.

Hilton, George W. *Monon Route*. La Jolla, CA: Howell-North Books, 1978.

Jegli, John B. *Louisville, New Albany, Jeffersonville & Shippingport and Portland Directory for 1845–1846*. Louisville, KY: John B. Jegli, 1845.

Kleber, John. *The Encyclopedia of Louisville*. Lexington: University Press of Kentucky, 2001.

Marquis, Albert Nelson. *Who Was Who in America: Volume I, 1897–1942*. Chicago, IL: A.N. Marquis Company, 1943.

McAlester, Virginia, and Lee McAlester. *A Field Guide to American Houses*. New York: Alfred A. Knopf, 1990.

New Albany Bicentennial Church History Committee. *200 Years of Church Histories of New Albany and Floyd County, Indiana*. Kearney, NE: Morris Publishing, 2013.

Palliser, Palliser & Company, Architects. *American Cottage Homes*. Bridgeport, CT: Pallister, Palliser & Company, 1878.

———. *Palliser's Model Homes*. Bridgeport, CT: Pallister, Palliser & Company, 1878.

Parish, W.H. *Art Work of New Albany Illustrated.* Chicago: W.H. Parish Publishing Company, 1893.

Poppeliers, John C., S. Allen Chambers Jr. and Nancy B. Schwartz. *What Style Is It?* Washington, D.C.: National Trust for Historic Preservation/ Preservation Press, 1983.

Robbins, D.P. *New Albany, Ind.: Its Advantages and Surroundings.* New Albany, IN: Ledger Company, 1892.

Russell, George L. *Greater New Albany, Indiana Centennial Celebration.* New Albany, IN: self-published, 1913.

Schneider, Nicholas. *Joseph Elmer Cardinal Ritter: His Life and Times.* Liguori, MO: Liguori Publications, 2008.

Sholes, A.E. *Sholes' Directory of the City of New Albany for 1873–1874.* New Albany, IN: A.E. Sholes, 1873.

Sloan, Samuel. *The Model Architect: A Series of Original Designs for Cottages, Villas, Suburban Residences, Etc.* Vol. 2. Philadelphia: E.S. Jones & Company, 1852.

Stevenson, Katherine Cole, and H. Ward Jandl. *Houses by Mail.* New York: John Wiley & Sons, 1986.

Thayer, Laura, and Craig Charron. *City of New Albany Interim Report: Indiana Historic Sites and Structures Inventory.* Indianapolis: Indiana Department of National Resources, 1994.

Williams, L.A., & Co. *History of the Ohio Falls Cities and Their Counties, with Illustrations and Biographical Sketches.* Vol. 2. Cleveland, OH: L.A. Williams & Co., 1882.

———. *New Albany Directory, City Guide and Business Mirror for 1863–1864.* New Albany, IN: Williams & Co., 1863.

———. *New Albany Directory for 1871–1871.* New Albany, IN: Williams & Co., 1871.

Wood, S. Holmes. *Picturesque New Albany.* New Albany, IN: Rev. S. Holmes Wood, 1923.

Maps

Sanborn Insurance Maps of New Albany, Indiana. 1886, 1891, 1898 and 1905.

Other Sources

Byrd, Cecil K. "Indiana's First Cookbook: Sumptuous Beginnings." *Indiana Alumni*, November/December 1984.

Culbertson Mansion State Historic Site: Grandest of All on Mansion Row. Indianapolis: Indiana State Museum and Historic Sites, Department of Natural Resources, n.d.

Houghlin, Abbey, Michael Koerner, Greg Sekula and David Barksdale. *Walking Tour No. 3: East Spring Street Historic District-Midtown New Albany, Indiana*. New Albany, IN: Develop New Albany, Inc.

Marr, Anthony, Jeff Gillenwater, Greg Sekula, Eli Beardsley and David Barksdale. *Walking Tour No. 1: Historic Architecture in Downtown New Albany, Indiana*. New Albany, IN: Develop New Albany, Inc.

Martin, Pako, Michael Koerner, Greg Sekula, Eli Beardsley and David Barksdale. *Walking Tour No. 2: Historic Mansion Row New Albany, Indiana*. New Albany, IN: Develop New Albany, Inc. and Main Street Preservation Association, n.d.

New Albany–Floyd County Public Library. "General James Adams Ekin." http://nafclibrary.org/wp-content/uploads/2013/08/Ekin-James-Adams.pdf.

New Albany newspapers, 1836–2015. Stuart B. Wrege Indiana History Room, New Albany–Floyd County Public Library, New Albany, IN.

Plat of New Albany, Indiana. Clark Grant Record A, 1813.

Richards, Jeffery A., and Alma L.W. Richards. "Victorian Pattern Book Homes." *Victorian Homes*, Winter 1989, 45–46.

Samuel Culbertson Mansion. "Samuel Culbertson and Family Timeline." http://www.culbertsonmansion.us/History/timeline.html.

Stuart B. Wrege Indiana History Room, New Albany–Floyd County Public Library, New Albany, IN.

U.S. Congress. *Biographical Directory of the American Congress, 1774–1961*. Washington, D.C.: U.S. Government Office, 1961.

U.S. Department of the Interior. National Parks Service. National Register of Historic Places registration form for the Cedar Bough Place Historic District. 2008.

———. National Register of Historic Places registration form for the East Spring Street Historic District. 2002.

———. National Register of Historic Places registration form for the Mansion Row Historic District. 1983.

———. National Register of Historic Places registration form for the New Albany Downtown Historic District. 1999.

———. National Register of Historic Places registration form for the William Young House, 2010.

Washington C. DePauw, 1822–1887. New Albany, IN: DePauw United Charities, n.d.

Wastlandwild. "The Abandoned Tannery of the Historic Moser Leather Company." http://www.wastelandwild.com/the-abandoned-tannery-of-the-historic-moser-leather-company.

Index

Y

Z

About the Authors

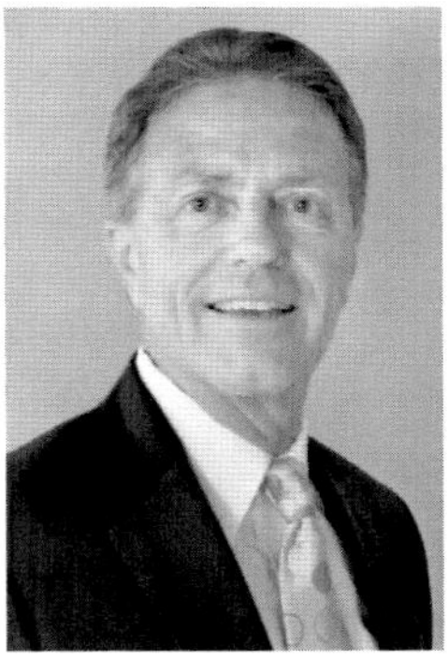

David C. Barksdale is the state-appointed Floyd County historian and president of the Floyd County Historical Society. He has written and coauthored several hundred house and building histories, along with several books, including *New Albany in Vintage Postcards* and *These Are the Good Old Days: History of the Stephan Day Family and Its Architectural Impact on New Albany, Indiana*. David was a public school educator for thirty-six years and helped initiate the Annual New Albany Historic Home Tour.

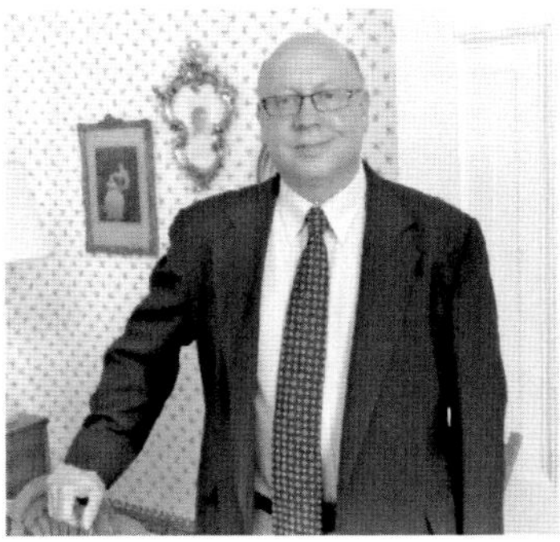

Gregory A. Sekula is director of the Southern Regional Office of Indiana Landmarks. He holds a degree in historic preservation from Roger Williams University and is a past fellow of the National Trust for Historic Preservation. A member of the American Institute of Certified Planners, Gregory previously served as preservation planner for St. Joseph, Missouri, and city planner for New Bern, North Carolina. Gregory and his family reside in the 1883 Herman and Johanna Rockenbach House in New Albany.